Opus Posthumous

OPUS POSTHUMOUS

WALLACE STEVENS

Edited, with an Introduction, by

Samuel French Morse

FABER AND FABER LTD
24 Russell Square
London

First published in mcmlix
by Faber and Faber Limited
24 Russell Square London WC1
Printed in Great Britain by
Bradford and Dickens London WC1

Preface

OF THE POEMS AND ESSAYS in this book, about one third appear for
the first time anywhere. Six of the poems have been printed before in books by Wallace Stevens; all six were omitted from the
Collected Poems. The rest—poems, plays, and prose—were found
scattered through the magazines, anthologies, and miscellanies to
which Stevens contributed generously and often. A good many of
the magazines had very short lives, and some have been dead for
almost forty years. A few still survive. One would like to thank
the editors of all the magazines that have furnished material for
this book, if only for the record. These are the living and the dead:
*Accent, Alcestis, The Atlantic Monthly, Briarcliff Quarterly, The
Chapbook, Contact, Contempo, Direction, The Hudson Review,
Imagi, Life and Letters Today, The Little Review, The Measure,
The Modern School, New World Writing, Others, Perspective,
Poetry: a Magazine of Verse, Poetry Quarterly, Quarterly Review
of Literature, The Rocking Horse, Saturday Review, Seven Arts,
Sewanee Review, Shenandoah, Smoke, Soil, Times Literary Sup-*

plement, Trend, View, Vogue, Wake, Westminster Magazine, Yale Review, and *Zero.* Thanks are also due to the following: Pierre Beres, Inc., Louis Carré et Cie, College English Association, Creative Age Press, Cummington Press, Galleon Press, Harcourt, Brace & Company, The Macmillan Company, Objectivist Press, Oxford University Press, Prairie Press, and the Saint Nicholas Society of New York. For kindly permitting me to reprint the "Two Prefaces," I am indebted to the Bollingen Foundation and Pantheon Books, sponsors and publishers of Paul Valéry's *Dialogues* (Volume Four of *The Collected Works of Paul Valéry*), copyright 1956 by Bollingen Foundation, Inc.

My greatest debt is naturally to Mrs. Wallace Stevens and to Holly Stevens, who generously turned over to me the papers that did most to make this volume a reality, and whose confidence in my editing has been all anyone could ask.

Next, I must thank Trinity College, and in particular President Albert C. Jacobs, Albert E. Holland, and Donald B. Engley, who did most to make sure that I had the time I needed to do the job. I owe much to many people for additional help: to Norman Holmes Pearson of Yale University, John L. Sweeney of Harvard, and Mrs. Judith Bond of the University of Chicago, as well as to the editors and staffs of the magazines to which Wallace Stevens contributed work. It is through the kindness of the University of Chicago and Harvard University libraries that I have been able to include some important material. Finally, I must record my thanks to the friends of Wallace Stevens who have been helpful in many ways indeed. Assistance has come, quite literally, from all over the world.

The text in every case follows manuscript, typescript, or print. In one or two instances obvious typographical errors have been corrected. I am also responsible for making a choice when alternative readings existed, and for one or two titles. Insofar as it has been possible to do so, I have arranged the poems in chronological sequence. The "Adagia" I have used as a bridge between the poetry and the prose, although I have included "A Ceremony" with the poems and plays as belonging there rather than with the essays.

The time for printing such material as remains in manuscript will undoubtedly come. The present volume, however, serves a different purpose: it adds to the total body of the published work whatever is intrinsically interesting, from the real beginning to the end.

S. F. M.

Contents

Introduction   xiii

POEMS

Poems from "Phases," I–VI   3
The Silver Plough-Boy   6
Bowl   6
Poems from "Primordia," 1–7   7
Blanche McCarthy   10
Poems from "Lettres d'un Soldat," I–IX   10
Architecture   16
Stanzas for "Le Monocle de Mon Oncle"   19
Peter Parasol   20
Exposition of the Contents of a Cab   20
Piano Practice at the Academy of the Holy Angels   21
The Indigo Glass in the Grass   22
Romance for a Demoiselle Lying in the Grass   23
Anecdote of the Abnormal   23
Infernale   24
This Vast Inelegance   25
Lulu Gay   26

Lulu Morose   27
Saturday Night at the Chiropodist's   27
Mandolin and Liqueurs   28
The Shape of the Coroner   29
Red Loves Kit   30
Metropolitan Melancholy   32
Annual Gaiety   32
Good Man, Bad Woman   33
The Woman Who Blamed Life on a Spaniard   34
Secret Man   35
The Drum-Majors in the Labor Day Parade   36
Polo Ponies Practicing   37
Lytton Strachey, Also, Enters into Heaven   38
Table Talk   40
A Room on a Garden   40
Agenda   41
Owl's Clover   43
    The Old Woman and the Statue   43
    Mr. Burnshaw and the Statue   46
    The Greenest Continent   52
    A Duck for Dinner   60
    Sombre Figuration   66
Stanzas for "The Man with the Blue Guitar"   72
Five Grotesque Pieces   74
Life on a Battleship   77
The Woman That Had More Babies than That   81
Stanzas for "Examination of the Hero in a Time of War"   83
Desire & the Object   85
Recitation after Dinner   86
This as Including That   88
Memorandum   89
First Warmth   89

x

The Sick Man	90
As at a Theatre	91
The Desire to Make Love in a Pagoda	91
Nuns Painting Water-Lilies	92
The Role of the Idea in Poetry	93
Americana	93
The Souls of Women at Night	94
A Discovery of Thought	95
The Course of a Particular	96
How Now, O, Brightener . . .	97
The Dove in Spring	97
Farewell without a Guitar	98
The Sail of Ulysses	99
Presence of an External Master of Knowledge	105
A Child Asleep in Its Own Life	106
Two Letters	107
Conversation with Three Women of New England	108
Dinner Bell in the Woods	109
Reality Is an Activity of the Most August Imagination	110
Solitaire under the Oaks	111
Local Objects	111
Artificial Populations	112
A Clear Day and No Memories	113
Banjo Boomer	114
July Mountain	114
The Region November	115
On the Way to the Bus	116
As You Leave the Room	116
Of Mere Being	117
A Mythology Reflects Its Region	118
Moment of Light	119
Three Paraphrases from Léon-Paul Fargue	121

PLAYS

Three Travelers Watch a Sunrise   127
Carlos among the Candles   144

A Ceremony   151

ADAGIA

Adagia   157

PROSE

A Collect of Philosophy   183
Two or Three Ideas   202
The Irrational Element in Poetry   216
The Whole Man: Perspectives, Horizons   229
On Poetic Truth   235
Honors and Acts   238
A Poet That Matters   247
Williams   254
Rubbings of Reality   257
John Crowe Ransom: Tennessean   259
The Shaper   262
A Note on Martha Champion   264
A Note on Samuel French Morse   266
Two Prefaces   268
Raoul Dufy   286
Marcel Gromaire   290
Notes on Jean Labasque   292
A Note on "Les Plus Belles Pages"   293
Connecticut   294

A NOTE ON THE DATES   297

Introduction

WALLACE STEVENS resisted the publication of his *Collected Poems* for a long time. His publishers and some of his friends had asked him to think about such a book even before the appearance of *Transport to Summer* in 1947. His answer was generally that a collected volume seemed final, and he was not quite ready to call things to a halt. Actually, his interest in poetry had never been greater. He sometimes complained, with characteristic restraint and humor, that he had grown to resent the way in which business took time that he might otherwise devote to poetry. With equal detachment and considerably more seriousness, he opposed any patronage system for the arts or for artists. He believed strongly in the profession of letters, but he was no sentimentalist about the plight of the artist in a materialistic society. Himself a man of real energy and great discipline, he assumed that other writers ought to be able to solve the problems of making a living and carrying on their real work at the same time. He thought that poets ought to be paid for their work, but he was always willing to send a poem to a magazine even though the magazine could not pay. He believed in and competed for prizes, and felt that public recognition and honors ought to be part of any award, although he fought shy of public appearances. He was generous in recommending younger poets for fellowships, but his name seldom appeared on a publisher's blurb or at the end of an introduction to another writer's work. He contributed to only a few of the literary symposia and answers to questionnaires that have been common in the literary magazines during the last twenty years.

Stevens's interest in poetry was intensely that of a man for whom the writing of a poem and the poem itself were more important than the glamour of the literary atmosphere. He was "an extremist in an exercise" which sustained and renewed his energy to speculate upon what he called "the theory of poetry in relation to what poetry has been and in relation to what it ought to be." From the very beginning his poems were "about" poetry; it is the one real subject of *Harmonium* and all the later work. His original title, incidentally, for the *Collected Poems* was *The Whole of Harmonium*.

"The theory of poetry," however, takes more or less formal shape for the first time in a "Memorandum" which he prepared for Henry Church in 1940, when Mr. Church was considering the establishment of a Chair of Poetry at Princeton. As a statement prefiguring the essays in *The Necessary Angel* and in this book, it has its own significance. Stevens wrote:

For this purpose, poetry means not the language of poetry but the thing itself, wherever it may be found. It does not mean verse any more than philosophy means prose. The subject-matter of poetry is the thing to be ascertained. Offhand, the subject-matter is what comes to mind when one says of the month of August . . .

"Thou art not August, unless I make thee so."

. . .

It is the aspects of the world and of men and women that have been added to them by poetry. These aspects are difficult to recognize and to measure.

While aesthetic ideas are commonplaces in this field, its import is not the import of the superficial. The major poetic idea in the world is and always has been the idea of God. One of the visible movements of the modern imagination is the movement away from the idea of God. The poetry that created the idea of God will either adapt it to our different intelligence, or create a substitute for it, or make it unnecessary. These alternatives probably mean the same thing, but the intention is not to foster a cult. The knowledge of poetry is a part of philosophy, and a part of science; the import of poetry is the import of the spirit. The figures of the essential poets should be spiritual figures. The comedy of life or the tragedy of life as the material of an art, and the mold of life as the object of its creation are contemplated.

The ambitiousness of such a Chair of Poetry is reflected in the poems that Stevens was writing at about the same time that he wrote the "Memorandum," the more or less "theoretic poems," as he called some of them, that appeared in *Parts of a World*. The writing of the "Memorandum" led directly to the invitation to speak at the *Mesures* Lectures sponsored by Mr. Church at Princeton in 1941, for which he composed "The Noble Rider and the Sound of Words." This was the first and almost the richest of the essays that eventually appeared in *The Necessary Angel*. It led ultimately to the extraordinary poems gathered together under the title "The Rock" in the *Collected Poems*, and to a handful of the poems in this book. Indirectly it must have led to the invitation from Harvard University in 1954, when Stevens was asked to be the Charles Eliot Norton professor for 1955–6. Stevens declined with great regret because he did not wish to hasten his retirement from the Hartford Accident and Indemnity Company. He was then five years beyond the mandatory retirement age of seventy, and although he believed he

XV

could stay on with the company as long as he wished, he felt that a year away from his office would make retirement inevitable. In his letter to Archibald MacLeish, he said:

There are several things that are of the utmost interest to me from which I have had to turn away and if I have been able to reconcile myself to the necessity of doing this, it is all the easier to reconcile myself to the necessity of passing up the present opportunity. One of these things is to try to find out whether it is possible to formulate a theory of poetry that would make poetry a significant humanity of such a nature and scope that it could be established as a normal, vital field of study for all comers.

Although the study of the theory of poetry never developed fully, everything Stevens wrote can be related to it. The subject creeps into even the briefest of the prose pieces, including the purely occasional bits he wrote when he received the National Book Award. It is the very substance of the "Adagia" and his few notebooks. In the poems it persists like "the prismatic formations that occur about us in nature in the case of reflections and refractions," sometimes touched with a depth of personal feeling that is surprising in a poet as detached as Stevens:

> Ariel was glad he had written his poems.
> They were of a remembered time
> Or of something seen that he had liked.
>
> Other makings of the sun
> Were waste and welter
> And the ripe shrub writhed.
>
> His self and the sun were one
> And his poems, although makings of his self
> Were no less makings of the sun.
>
> It was not important that they survive.
> What mattered was that they should bear
> Some lineament or character,

Some affluence, if only half-perceived,
In the poverty of their words,
Of the planet of which they were part.

This quality, so apparent here in "The Planet on the Table," recurs again and again in the poems written after the *Collected Poems* had gone to press. It comes through most intensely and warmly in what must be one of the very last poems he wrote, "As You Leave the Room." A much earlier version survives in the copy of *Transport to Summer* which Stevens inscribed for Mr. Herbert Weinstock in 1947, under the title "First Warmth." "As You Leave the Room" simply frames the question asked in "First Warmth," but the frame makes an astonishing difference; it transforms an improvised sketch into a finished work of art, and makes a fitting farewell.

II

The poems in this book cover the whole span of Stevens's career except for the undergraduate exercises written while he was a student at Harvard and a group of pastel lyrics written in 1913 and 1914 that survive in manuscript. Some of the undergraduate verse, which appeared originally in the *Harvard Advocate*, was reprinted in *Verses from the Harvard Advocate, Third Series, 1886–1906*, and more recently in the *Harvard Advocate Anthology*. The undergraduate prose—student editorials and *fin de siècle* sketches—survives only in the files of the *Advocate*; as editor of the magazine, Stevens wrote a good deal of the material needed to keep it going, much of which appeared under pseudonyms. Of the poems reprinted in the *Harvard Advocate Anthology*, Stevens noted: "Some of one's early things give one the creeps." They are not remarkable, but they faintly foreshadow some interests that emerge later: an interest in the comic irony of the quotidian and a glance at the grotesque.

Only one poem appeared in print after Stevens left Harvard,

between 1901 and 1914. Of the poems surviving in manuscript, the earliest belongs to 1913. The lyrics that follow divide into two groups: fifteen or twenty "Intermezzi," exercises in texture and coloring in which there is an obvious influence of Verlaine; and a handful of somewhat sturdier and more characteristic pieces in the mode in which he made his first appearances in *Poetry* and *Others*. Some of the "Intermezzi" he arranged in a sequence, and then abandoned the sequence. Some of the others fell into the group to which he gave the title "Phases." These he sent off to Harriet Monroe under the pseudonym Peter Parasol, in competition for a prize offered in September 1914 for a "war poem."

"Phases" did not win the prize, but did fire the enthusiasm of Miss Monroe, who scrawled across the top of the manuscript: "Jewel." Of the eleven poems he sent her, Miss Monroe printed four in the November 1914 issue of *Poetry*. The rest she kept but never published, and of these one survives incomplete. The four that were printed, and two others, together with the epigraph from Pascal (restored from Stevens's manuscript, along with the original title for V), properly stand at the beginning of this book. Some of the others might have been added, but the difficulty of determining the original order of the sequence would have resulted in an obvious patchwork. It seemed better, therefore, to follow Miss Monroe's order and to give a sample of the rest.

"Blanche McCarthy," "Bowl," and the poems from "Primordia" are also very early. "Blanche McCarthy" has not, so far as I know, ever been published. "Bowl" appeared in *Others*, in a group that contained "Domination of Black," "Tattoo," and "Six Significant Landscapes" (which were originally eight). Stevens allowed Miss Monroe to include "Bowl" in *The New Poetry*, but he never reprinted it in any of his own volumes. "Primordia" appeared in *Soil*. The five pieces under the general title "In the Northwest" have never been reprinted; of the four "In the South" poems, the original No. 7 appeared in *Harmonium* as "In the Carolinas," and the original No. 9 appeared in the revised edition of *Harmonium* as "Indian River." The tailpiece to the group, "To the Roaring Wind," stands at the end of *Harmonium*.

None of the "Lettres d'un Soldat" appeared in the first edition of *Harmonium*, but for the revised edition Stevens selected the original Nos. V ("The Surprises of the Superhuman"), VII ("Negation"), and IX ("The Death of a Soldier"). The manuscript version found among Stevens's own papers reveals that the sequence was to have contained at least seventeen sections, but I have been unable to discover copies of some of them. Stevens sent Miss Monroe thirteen poems, of which she used all but Nos. I ("Common Soldier"), VII ("Lunar Paraphrase," which was salvaged for the revised edition of *Harmonium*), XII, and XIII. I have restored the original epigraphs from the book which suggested the sequence, but have omitted the poems reprinted in *Harmonium*. The epigraphs, after all, helped to tie the poems together as a group, although the individual pieces stand on their own feet. Oblique as the treatment of war is in the poems, Stevens evidently regarded most of them as too topical to survive, but one or two are the real thing and almost the equal of "The Death of a Soldier."

Whether "Le Monocle de Mon Oncle" was originally to have been called "The Naked Eye of the Aunt" is a little uncertain. The title at least survives, as do the stanzas to which I have somewhat arbitrarily given the title "Stanzas for 'Le Monocle de Mon Oncle.'" As an improviser, Stevens very much enjoyed making variations on a theme; and one poem often suggested another, as he himself said, and as the "Two Letters" in the present volume indicate. At any rate, the "Stanzas for 'Le Monocle de Mon Oncle'" have a special interest in a volume of this kind, although the finished poem as we have it is far better without them. The stanzas are preliminary studies by comparison.

"Peter Parasol," "Exposition of the Contents of a Cab," and "The Indigo Glass in the Grass" originally appeared in *Poetry* in the group called "Pecksniffiana," which won for Stevens the Levinson Prize in 1920. "Exposition of the Contents of a Cab" appeared in the first edition of *Harmonium*, but was dropped in 1931, along with two others, "Architecture" and the much earlier poem "The Silver Plough-Boy." Stevens's objections to "Peter Parasol" persisted for years. In a letter to Miss Monroe in the summer of 1919, he suggested some last-minute changes in "Pecksniffiana." He wanted to omit "Peter Parasol" because "the element of pastiche present . . . will not be apparent and the poem will go off on its substance and not on its style. . . ." As for "Exposition of the Contents of a Cab," he felt that he had "not yet learned how to do things" of the kind. "The Indigo Glass . . ." he considered to be a mere trifle. Finally, he was uncertain about "Piano Practice at the Academy of the Holy Angels," and would not permit Miss Monroe to use it. Miss Monroe, for her part, would have printed almost anything Stevens sent, and she did persuade him to allow publication of "Peter Parasol" and "Exposition of the Contents of a Cab," as well as the substitutes Stevens had sent: "The Weeping Burgher," "Banal Sojourn," and "Anecdote of the Jar."

By 1921, Stevens had written enough to make a book. Even before that, some of his friends had tried to persuade him to publish a volume; but he had put them off by saying that he had a distaste for miscellany. Even so, arrangements for the publication of *Harmonium* were completed in the summer of 1922. When he wrote the news to Miss Monroe—she was the first to know—he said: "The book will naturally be a collection of things that have already appeared, for since the manuscript is to be ready by November 1 this year it will not be possible for me to do anything new in the interim." He spent the summer revising "The Comedian as the Letter C," and in reply to a request from Miss Monroe that *Poetry* be allowed to print the poem, wrote that he had promised it to Pitts Sanborn for an issue of *The Measure.* He added:

When I get back from the South I expect to do some short poems and then to start again on a rather longish one; so that sooner or later I shall have something for *Poetry,* to which I send what I like most. But it takes time and, besides, I have no desire to write a great deal. I know that people judge one by volume. However, having elected to regard poetry as a form of retreat, the judgment of people is neither here nor there. The desire to write a long poem or two is not obsequiousness to the judgment of people. On the contrary, I find that this prolonged attention to a single subject has the same result that prolonged attention to a senora has, according to the authorities. All manner of favors drop from it. Only it requires a skill in the varying of the serenade that occasionally makes me feel like a Guatemalan when one particularly wants to feel like an Italian. I expect that after a while Crispin . . . will become rudimentary and abhorrent.

Putting together the manuscript of *Harmonium* occupied Stevens for some little time and led to further comments. At the end of October he wrote to Miss Monroe: "Gathering together the things for my book has been so depressing that I wonder at *Poetry's* friendliness. All my earlier things seem like horrid cocoons from which later abortive insides have sprung. The book will amount to nothing, except that it may teach me something." He had more to say on the subject of long poems, especially his desire to "do long stretches at a time," which he believed was essential to get "anywhere in writing or thinking or observing." He concluded by adding: "the reading of these outmoded and debilitated poems does make me wish rather desperately to keep on dabbling and to be as obscure as possible until I have perfected an authentic and fluent speech for myself."

He excluded from the manuscript of *Harmonium* a good many poems that had appeared in magazines and a few that had never been published at all. Among the latter are some now printed for the first time, which are more interesting than a few that appeared in *Others* in 1916 and 1917. The short poems contemplated in the letter to Miss Monroe amounted to a handful of pieces that eventually appeared in *The Measure* (as a gesture of kindness to his friend Pitts Sanborn), *The Dial*, and *Broom*. Some found their way into *Harmonium*, either in the original or the later edition. "Academic Discourse at Havana," published again in *Hound and Horn* in 1929, was reprinted in *Ideas of Order*. The rest dropped out of sight. I have included most of the rejected poems written between 1920 and 1922 and all of the uncollected or unpublished poems I have found which were written after the manuscript of *Harmonium* was completed.

Many of these pieces have a strong satirical edge. Some have the earmarks of being preliminary studies for poems that ultimately took different shape. The stanzas omitted from the published version of "The Man with the Blue Guitar" are certainly the equal of several that Stevens included; on the other hand, those from "Examination of the Hero in a Time of War" are less good. Still others of the later poems simply got overlooked when Stevens put together the manuscript of a book, as, for example, six poems originally printed in *Wake*, or the fine poem, "The Course of a Particular," which should have appeared in the final section of the *Collected Poems*. Finally, there are the poems written after the *Collected Poems* went to press, beginning, more or less roughly, with "The Dove in Spring."

The satirical poems Stevens regarded as occasional verse, exercises fit for fugitive publication only. Or they belonged to a genre he had not mastered. In the same way, he omitted "Owl's Clover," "Life on a Battleship," and "The Woman That Had More Babies than That" from the *Collected Poems* on the grounds that they were "rhetorical." Their rhetoric is, however, characteristic; and "Owl's Clover" is far too ambitious a poem to be omitted from a book such as this. I have, incidentally, used the original version published by the Alcestis Press rather than the later one, which is still in print. Of the nearly two hundred lines Stevens cut, a great many are worth keeping. The same may be said of "Recitation after Dinner," written especially for the Saint Nicholas Society of New York and printed in the yearbook of the Society under the title "Tradition." As for its prose companion-piece, "A Ceremony," which I have placed after the plays, it has never been published before.

"The Sail of Ulysses," written for the Phi Beta Kappa exercises at Columbia in 1954, is pre-eminently an occasional poem. The real difficulty with it, for Stevens, seems to have been his uncertainty about being able to write a poem that would accommodate the theme of the Columbia University Bientennial without lapsing into banality or mere artificiality. Although the poem shows the hand, at least, of a master, it moves with a rigidity and deliberateness unusual in his later work. Although he would not allow it to be printed, he salvaged from it the poem "Presence of an External Master of Knowledge" and the title of the charming lyric "A Child Asleep in Its Own Life."

The poems that follow are the last. Some of them are certainly the equal of those in "The Rock," the final section of the *Collected Poems*. They speak for themselves without comment. The untitled piece ("A Mythology Reflects Its Region") may very well be the last poem Stevens wrote; it has something in common with the prose statement, "Connecticut," which he prepared for the Voice of America in 1955. It may also be no more than a fragment, despite its apparent completeness. With this manuscript was the skeleton plan for what might have been a companion piece to "Examination of the Hero in a Time of War" or "Esthetique du Mal." It was to be called "Abecedarium of Finesoldier." The opening lines for the first ten sections had been jotted down; what was to have been the beginning of the eleventh section was not filled in:

I

I am bound by the will of other men.

II

Only one purpose exists but it is not mine

III

I must impale myself on reality

IV

Invisible fate becomes visible

V

Cry out against the commander so that I obey

VI

In the uproar of cymbals I stand still

VII

They are equally hapless in the contagion innate
in their numbers

VIII

The narrative stops. . . . Good-bye to the narration.

IX

As great as a javelin, as futile, as old

X

But did he have any value as a person

This outline, apparently, completes the record.

It remains only to make note of the translations from Jean Le Roy and Léon-Paul Fargue. The translation of Le Roy's "Moment of Light" appeared in *The Modern School* in 1918, and is mentioned by Walter Pach in his autobiography, *Queer Thing, Painting*. In response to a request for further information about the translation—almost unique in Stevens's career—Mr. Pach wrote that it was made specifically for *The Modern School*, edited by Carl Zigrosser. Stevens and Pach had met originally at the home of Walter Arensberg, and their association had been strengthened by their mutual interest in the magazine, to which Stevens had contributed poems with drawings by Pach to accompany them.

The "paraphrases" as Stevens called them, from Fargue belong to a much later period. They were read originally at the Poetry Center in New York in 1951, with the following brief preface:

I should like to close this program by turning, now, for a very few minutes, to the work of someone else, a Frenchman, Léon-Paul Fargue, who lived as a poet all his life in Paris and died there two or three years ago. As a boy of eight or nine he was a member of Mallarmé's class in English at the College Rollin and ten years or more thereafter became one of those that were accustomed to gather in Mallarmé's apartment. He was a friend of Paul Valéry for fifty years. I suppose it could be said that during the greater part of the last half-century he knew everyone in Paris having to do with poetry. It is not possible to comment on his work beyond saying that most of his poems were prose poems. Claudine Chonez in a study she made of him for the series *Poètes d'Aujourd'hui*, Poets of To-Day, speaks (p. 66) of the solemnity of his strophe, of its somewhat ritual, not to say theatrical character. I shall read paraphrases of two of the poems contained in *Poèmes* (1912), his first book of importance, and the one best liked, and also of a page of his prose from *Portraits de Famille* (1947). I call these translations paraphrases because, in order to carry over the sense of cadence, paraphrase seemed more useful than literal translation.

It is easy to see the attraction of a writer like Fargue for Stevens. A poet thoroughly at home in his time and place, a friend of Mallarmé and Valéry, and of most of the great painters of the age, Fargue was a romantic figure for the imagination. Incidentally, when Stevens bought an illustrated edition of Fargue's poems, he wrote to his Paris bookseller:

I read the poems in the original edition. Then, when I knew them pretty well, I went over some of them again in the edition illustrated by Alexieff. I was very much pleased with this big Alexieff book because I love large pages for poetry. On the other hand, I cannot say that I think that Alexieff's designs are truthful illustrations of the text; they are too individual. The eccentricity of Fargue should be delineated in its own right and not doubled by an additional eccentricity on the part of an illustrator.

What Stevens demanded of illustrations for a poetic text—and he was always intensely interested in the appearance of his own books—was nothing less than illumination in its fundamental sense. Poetry was for him revelation, and his poems were illustrations of that single text. The severity of the standard he imposed upon his own work whenever he came to put together a new volume is apparent always in the cumulative impression of power that the individual volumes reveal. Although the illustrations in this book are sometimes only sketches, they reveal much that we want to know. At their best, they show us "the thing that is incessantly overlooked: the artist, the presence of the determining personality. Without that reality no amount of other things matters much." Writing about the integrity of Cézanne, Stevens was writing about his own integrity.

III

"Three Travelers Watch a Sunrise," the earliest of the three plays, is also the best. It appeared in *Poetry* for July 1916 as the prize-winning one-act verse play in a contest sponsored by the Players' Producing Company; it was later performed at the Provincetown Playhouse in New York and elsewhere. "Carlos among the Candles" and "Bowl, Cat and Broomstick" were written at the request of Laura Sherry for the 1917–18 season of the Wisconsin Players. "Carlos" appeared on the opening-night bill of the group's brief New York season; "Bowl, Cat and Broomstick" had a performance a few nights later. Neither piece survived what was at best a mixed reception, although "Carlos among the Candles" appeared in the December 1917 issue of *Poetry*, to which Stevens generally sent what he considered to be his best work. "Bowl, Cat and Broomstick" remained in manuscript.

Stevens took great pains with "Three Travelers Watch a Sunrise." He wanted, he wrote Miss Monroe, "to have the play a play and not merely a poem, if possible." At the same time, he deliberately avoided any overt action because he did not wish "to become involved in the story or characters of the man and girl." The drama was to reside in the characters of the three Chinese, in their discussion of the different ways in which every individual affects and is affected by the world around him. Everything was to be done by implication:

The point of the play . . . is . . . in the last sentence of the final speech. God forbid that I should moralize. The play is simply intended to demonstrate that just as objects in nature affect us, as, for example,

> Dead trees do not resemble
> Beaten drums,

so, on the other hand, we affect objects in nature, by projecting our moods, emotions, etc:

> an old man from Pekin
> Observes sunrise,
> Through Pekin, reddening.

As a "demonstration" the play achieves considerable success. The theme is basic and characteristic, reaching its ultimate refinement in the late essays and poems. From a distance of forty years, the *chinoiserie* looks a little suspect; the discourse of the three Chinese seems somewhat fussy and overwrought. Like some of the early poems he rejected from *Harmonium*, the play was an experiment about which Stevens quickly became "uncertain." He knew that the play was a pastiche, but he felt that it was "cabbage instead of the crisp lettuce intended."

What he was trying to do in drama he made clear in a letter to Miss Monroe about "Carlos among the Candles." He had sent her the criticisms of the New York performance, one of which, by Ralph Block, had been sympathetic but not altogether kind. Block had characterized the flavor of the monologue as "not unlike a combination of Gertrude Stein's 'In a Department Store' and Henry James's story, 'The Altar of the Dead,' with a leaning toward the less successful futurist of the two, Miss Stein." He had gone on to suggest that "with real poetry behind it" such drama "would yield an entirely new crop of sensations for the miniature stage." To all this Stevens was not unresponsive:

I am not in the least interested in proving anything to the critics. They were justified—would have been in saying almost anything. One is tempted to put the blame on the performance. But the important thing is to learn something. After raving about the performance, the possibility remains that there was little or nothing to perform. A theatre without action or characters ought to be within the range of human interests. Not as a new thing—a source of new sensations, purposely, only; but naturally, normally, why not? But no, as we say: the theatre is a definite thing; a play has a form and requirements, like a sonnet—there must be passion and development and so on.

"Carlos" carries out the argument of "Three Travelers Watch a Sunrise" in terms of the most frivolous comedy; and Carlos himself is a prototype of Crispin in "The Comedian as the Letter C." The piece as a whole is almost a caricature of

Stevens's early work, but its fastidious wit and genuinely high spirits give it a measure of distinction. Like the "Study of Two Pears," the monologue is an "*opusculum pedagogum*" intended to show that the style is the man and the man is the style. It has the merit of being not an idea about the thing but the thing itself. The thing is not, as Stevens knew, a play in any conventional sense. It is an essay in the discovery of shifting relationships and resemblances, which was for Stevens always more dramatic and satisfying than any other kind of action. The play of words, although substantially an end in itself, leads to illumination. In "Carlos" the joke is somewhat over extended and a little too rare, but it is consistently interesting in its details.

"Bowl, Cat and Broomstick" was characterized by Walter Pach as "a book review." The most extravagant of Stevens's dramatic experiments, it is also the least satisfactory. It is really an examination of the idea expressed in the final section of "Peter Quince at the Clavier":

> Beauty is momentary in the mind—
> The fitful tracing of a portal;
> But in the flesh it is immortal.

The three characters who give the play its name discuss their ideas of a poetess whose work they are reading. Each one, perceiving the poetry in his own way, creates for himself an individual portrait of the poetess. Broomstick, having read the preface to the book of poems, points out to Cat and Bowl that what they imagine the poetess to be like bears no relation to the facts set forth in the preface. Bowl is so greatly disillusioned that he gives up poetry; Cat damns all prefaces that interfere with one's immediate and true apprehension of a poem. The play simply stops with Cat's collapse following his denunciation of prefaces, as Broomstick helps him off the stage.

Incidental to the discussion of the proper attitude toward poetry and poetess are the epigrams of Broomstick and the high sentence of Bowl and Cat:

A man with so firm a faith in the meaning of words should not listen to poetry.

It is only the poetess of forty-two that sits for a portrait covered.

There's no truer comedy than this hodge-podge of men and sun-light, women and moonlight, houses and clouds, and so on.

To be herself she must be free. She looks free. But she is not free in spirit, and therefore her portrait fails. . . . To be free, Claire Dupray must be as free from to-day as from yesterday.

Much in the play is amusing and pertinent to Stevens's own work. The seeds of some of the best short poems in *Harmonium* seem to have fallen here. At least one idea that takes final form as late as 1949, in "An Ordinary Evening in New Haven," shows up for the first time in "Bowl, Cat and Broomstick," when Boomstick toys with the difficulty of being oneself in one's own day. There is also some satire on Imagist poetry and on self-conscious modernism. On the whole, however, the play is more important as source material than as a finished work.

The plays bear out the judgment often made on Stevens, that his poetry is dramatically weak. Laura Sherry, in an outburst of enthusiasm, wrote to Stevens that she felt he would eventually produce something extraordinary in drama, and that his genius made him a member of the company that included "Synge, Verhaeren, Tchekov, Andreyev, some of von Hofmannstahl, Shaw's 'Androcles & the Lion,' Schnitzler, Hauptmann's natural-istic plays, Duhamel and Dunsany." This was a mixed group, certainly. Stevens, however, was a better judge of his own capaci-ties and talents than some of his friends who urged him to con-tinue writing for the theater. Except for one or two experiments nearly contemporary with the plays, his experience with the drama had little noticeable effect on his work, unless it can be said that it helped him to refine the soliloquizing technique he used in such poems as "From the Misery of Don Joost" and "The Man Whose Pharynx Was Bad." The plays may also have helped Stevens see that for him the most dramatic aspect of life arose from the interplay of imagination and reality in everyday experience that gives his poems their true shape. This sense of the dramatic, however, is apparent from the beginning. An awareness of its limitations persisted. More than twenty years after he had written the plays, Stevens wrote in his "Adagia": "Life is an affair of people not of places. But for me life is an affair of places and that is the trouble." He could, of course, turn limitations to advantage that was more than paradox. A later entry in the "Adagia" states: "Life is not people and scene but thought and feeling"; and the final entry in another notebook reads simply: "One Must Sit Still to Discover the World."

IV

What Stevens learned from his flirtation with playwriting has an analogue in his investigations into philosophy. Among the early papers are numerous jottings and quotations: Chinese proverbs (in French translation), passages from an early nineteenth-century essay on composition in painting, notes from the *Revue des Deux Mondes*, names of saints and painters—fragments for poems. The later papers are more orderly and less miscellaneous. One notebook, "From Pieces of Paper," is a collection of titles for poems. Two others, "Sur Plusieurs Beaux Sujets," consist largely of passages copied from books and reviews, and are a reflection of his reading and the ideas which interested him at the time. The "Adagia," included almost complete in the present volume, comprise his book of proverbs. There is also a miscellany book of "Poetic Exercises of 1948," adages, and notes on reading.

"Sur Plusieurs Beaux Sujets" and the "Adagia" delineate

Stevens's quarrel with the philosophers most clearly. It was a personal quarrel, a rebellion against the strictures of thought and feeling which he believed philosophers would impose upon him as poet and as human being. Much given to his own kind of abstraction and generalization, he nevertheless distrusted any system of thought which discredited the particulars of experience. Most philosophy, for him, ignored or belittled the imagination, and he found a similar weakness in much poetry. Again and again he insisted that a successful work of art achieved integration of imagination and reality "as equals"; and the essay "A Collect of Philosophy" is his ultimate statement of the nature of that integration as he conceived it. The "supreme fiction," synonymous with poetry, is life at its most satisfying, when, momentarily, everything composes itself in proportion and order, when even "change composes, too." It is the state that resolves all oppositions and contradictions—more exactly, the state in which all oppositions and contradictions are resolved: a whole greater than the sum of its parts and larger than any description of it. Everything in experience and thought relates to it, and it is therefore something far greater than the written word or the literary temperament: "the hermitage at the center." This is the "order" to which the poems, the essays, the notebooks and jottings refer.

In "Sur Plusieurs Beaux Sujets," for example, the comments on the excerpts Stevens copied into his notebook are sparse but revealing. He quotes from *The Divine Origin of Christianity Indicated by Its Historical Effects*, by R. S. Storrs: "The philosopher could not love the indefinite and impersonal principle of order pervading the universe, any more than he could love atmospheres or oceans." His comment on this is exactly what one would expect:

For myself, the indefinite, the impersonal, atmospheres and oceans and, above all, the principle of order are precisely what I love; and

I don't see why, for a philosopher, they should not be the ultimate inamorata. The premise to Storrs is that the universe is explicable only in terms of humanity.

The notebooks also suggest the range of Stevens's reading, which was at times as surprising as the seeming miscellany of certain of the poems. A good many of the excerpts in "Sur Plusieurs Beaux Sujets" come from reviews in *The New Statesman and Nation, Life and Letters Today, Apollo, Marianne, The Musical Quarterly,* and *French Studies.* Others come from Pascal, Walter Leaf, Kate O'Brien, Mario Rossi, Christina Stead, George Chapman, Jules Renard, Gounod, Henry Adams, Justice Holmes, Horace Bushnell, and James Guthrie. Various as the subjects may be, the passages reflect almost uniformly some aspect of "the principle of order." Most of the entries deal in broad terms with their general subject. It is in the poems, of course (and often in his letters), that the subject is particularized.

"From Pieces of Paper," like the "Schemata" Stevens jotted down while he was composing the poems that eventually added up to *Harmonium,* supplied him with kernels and titles of poems, "memorias antiguas" as he once called them: things seen or overheard, felt and thought about, literally picked up off the sidewalk like the chalk-scrawls ("Red Loves Kit," "Meyer is a bum") that sometimes became part of the *collage.* A good many of these jottings turn up as titles or images for poems; some were never used: "The Cow in the Clouds," "The alp at the end of the street," "Man & Catsup Bottle," "Idiom of the Hero," "This rain was meant to fall in Salamanca," "A quiet normal life," "Cats & Marigolds," "A poem like a season of the mind," "Sketch of a river," "Asides on the Oboe," "It's going to be pretty around here," "Pax, Ajax & the Crocuses," "Description of a cartwheel," "A Few Pages in C Major," "All About the Bride's Grandparents," "A Guide Through Poetic Dogma,"

c

"Still Life with Aspirin," etc. There are three hundred and fifty odd entries of this kind.

The "Adagia," however, are real *pensées* in the manner of Braque's in his *Notebook*: the aphorisms or *materia poetica* of an artist rather than the more general sayings of a Pascal. Stevens was something of a collector of sayings and proverbs; his library contained a good many volumes of folk-sayings from all over the world, and one finds in his notebooks pungent and epigrammatic bits from various writers. His own aphorisms at their best have much in common with the poems. Part of the persistent charm and character of "The Snow Man," for example, is its apparent concentration in the final line of something closely akin to the pictorial truth of an adage. So it is with the "anecdote" poems of *Harmonium*, including "The Comedian as the Letter C," which Stevens characterized as

> this anecdote
> Invented for its pith, not doctrinal
> In form though in design, as Crispin willed,
> Disguised pronunciamento, summary,
> Autumn's compendium, strident in itself
> But muted, mused, and perfectly revolved
> In those portentous accents, syllables,
> And sounds of music coming to accord
> Upon his lap . . .

From one point of view, the poetry as a whole comprises a collection of adages. From so narrow a perspective it is possible, I think, to learn much about the poetry without necessarily falling into the errors of distortion. Poetry, after all, concentrates and compresses the disorder of experience into a memorable and significant whole: it makes of "the intricate Alps" "a single nest." The right metaphor in the right place achieves a temporary illusion of wholeness, completeness that resists any analysis of it.

A good proverb has this same kind of inexhaustibility and finality; its perennial rightness and freshness is its truth. Its authority is sententious and ancient, rooted in experience rather than in the reason. It is no accident, then, that the "Adagia," like the entries in "From Pieces of Paper," turn up in the essays and the poems. The essays, organized like poems, reproduce some of the "Adagia" exactly; and the "Adagia" get into the poetry. Some turn up almost word for word: "Poetry must resist the intelligence almost successfully," in "Man Carrying Thing"; "The death of one god is the death of all," in "Notes toward a Supreme Fiction." Others undergo subtler transformation. "Description is an element, like air or water," appears to have been the springboard for "Description without Place."

This search for the pithy generalization, obvious in such poems as "Like Decorations in a Nigger Cemetery," "The Man with the Blue Guitar," "New England Verses," and most of the pieces in *Parts of a World,* is apparent everywhere; and "pure" as the poetry is, it is always "doctrinal." The search accounts in part for the Shakespearean tone noted by Marianne Moore in an essay on "Owl's Clover" and *Ideas of Order;* it also helps to account for a tone akin to that of Pope, an elegance and gusto in the exploitation of language that defines meaning in terms of style. As a habit of mind and manner, the use of adages and aphorisms helps to account, too, for the bravado of Stevens's vocabulary. His feats with nonsense syllables and animal and bird sounds are something more than demonstrations of virtuosity; at his best, he manages to make them part of "life's nonsense" that "pierces us with strange relation."

Like the poems, the "Adagia" are uneven and, taken all together at once, somewhat repetitious. It could hardly be otherwise with a poet of so firmly fixed a point of view, who very early in his career wrote:

My idea is that in order to carry a thing to the extreme [necessary] to convey it one has to stick to it. . . . Given a fixed point of view, realistic, imagistic, or what you will, everything adjusts itself to that point of view; and the process of adjustment is a world in flux, as it should be for a poet. But to fidget with points of view leads always to new beginnings and incessant new beginnings lead to sterility. A single manner or mood thoroughly matured and exploited is that fresh thing, etc. . . .

It is a short step, in any case, from the *"materia poetica"* to the poems and the essays. With the exception of his review of the *Selected Poems* of Marianne Moore and a handful of tributes to fellow poets and contemporaries, almost everything he did in prose was originally written as a lecture. "A Collect of Philosophy," in some respects the most ambitious of his essays, is the important exception. It was intended as a contribution to one of the professional philosophy journals, but was judged by the editor to be better suited for a literary review. The essay is not, of course, a technical study; but Stevens never submitted it elsewhere. "Two or Three Ideas" was read at a meeting of the New England section of the College English Association. "The Irrational Element in Poetry" served as a preface to one of the rare public readings from his own poetry that he gave during the last fifteen or twenty years of his life. The group of short statements I have gathered together under the general title "Honors and Acts" comprises the statements made on those occasions when Stevens received official recognition of his genius. They are not so important as the longer essays, nor perhaps of so much significance as some of the short pieces on his contemporaries, but they deserve printing. The brief essay "On Poetic Truth" was the only prose piece in manuscript found among his papers. Except, perhaps, for a poem or two, the "Two Prefaces" to Valéry's dialogues "Eupalinos" and "Dance and the Soul" are Stevens's last significant work. The quoted texts were translated by William McCausland Stewart, whose translation of the *Dialogues* is introduced by these essays. The analysis of the poem "Les Plus Belles Pages" was written for the Poetry Collection of the Lamont Library at Harvard. It is one of the extremely rare examples of the poet's commentary on his own work, the best of which he confined to letters.

Like the poems included in the present volume, these prose pieces indicate the range of Stevens's work rather than the best of it. On the other hand, all of the prose pieces have an intrinsic interest, and one or two must be ranked among his best. I have not included anything that seems to me merely fugitive. There will be another time and place more appropriate for these things.

v

It would be easy to overestimate the virtues of much that this book contains. It would be almost equally easy to underestimate its value and interest. Although the book is superficially a miscellany, it is clearly held together by a "fixed point of view" apparent from the beginning and by an intention that reveals itself with equal clarity in the prose and the poetry. The brief statement Stevens wrote for the editors of the *Oxford Anthology of American Literature* in 1938 sums up precisely and characteristically the whole drift of that intention. Fittingly enough, it lets Wallace Stevens, at the conclusion of these notes, speak for himself:

My intention in poetry is to write poetry: to reach and express that which, without any particular definition, everyone recognizes to be poetry, and to do this because I feel the need of doing it.

There is such a complete freedom now-a-days in respect to technique that I am rather inclined to disregard form so long as I am free and can express myself freely. I don't know of anything, respecting form, that makes much difference. The essential thing in form is to be free in whatever form is used. A free form does not assure freedom. As a form, it is just one more form. So that it comes to this, I suppose, that I believe in freedom regardless of form.

—SAMUEL FRENCH MORSE

Hancock Point, Maine
August 1956

Cézanne at the Lefèvre

"But these . . . qualities (of 'varied and inimitable' colour and his handling) . . . do not account for the look of hard and unrelenting authenticity that distinguishes his work from that of lesser men. It is Cézanne's peculiar determination to pin down his sensation, and the exactness and intensity of notation resulting from this, that made Cézanne pre-eminent. . . . In a Cézanne there can be no question of juggling with the elements of design, no possibility of glossing over difficulties, no equivocation. With Cézanne integrity was the thing, and integrity never allowed him to become fixed at any one point in his development, but sent him onward toward new discoveries of technique, new realisations of the motive."

GRAHAM BELL, The New Statesman and Nation,
June 12, 1937, p. 963.

I note the above both for itself and because it adds to subject and manner the thing that is incessantly overlooked: the artist, the presence of the determining personality. Without that reality no amount of other things matters much.

(from a notebook, "Sur Plusieurs Beaux Sujets, I")

POEMS

POEMS FROM "PHASES"

> *"La justice sans la force est con-*
> *tredite, parce qu'il y a toujours*
> *des méchants: la force sans la*
> *justice est accusée."*
>
> PASCAL

I

There's a little square in Paris,
Waiting until we pass.
They sit idly there,
They sip the glass.

There's a cab-horse at the corner,
There's rain. The season grieves.
It was silver once,
And green with leaves.

There's a parrot in a window,
Will see us on parade,
Hear the loud drums roll—
And serenade.

II

This was the salty taste of glory,
That it was not
Like Agamemnon's story.
Only, an eyeball in the mud,
And Hopkins,
Flat and pale and gory!

III

But the bugles, in the night,
Were wings that bore
To where our comfort was;

Arabesques of candle beams,
Winding
Through our heavy dreams;

Winds that blew
Where the bending iris grew;

Birds of intermitted bliss,
Singing in the night's abyss;

Vines with yellow fruit,
That fell
Along the walls
That bordered Hell.

IV

Death's nobility again
Beautified the simplest men.
Fallen Winkle felt the pride
Of Agamemnon
When he died.

What could London's
Work and waste
Give him—
To that salty, sacrificial taste?

4

What could London's
Sorrow bring—
To that short, triumphant sting?

V

Belgian Farm, October, 1914

The vaguest line of smoke (a year ago)
Wavered in evening air, above the roof,
As if some Old Man of the Chimney, sick
Of summer and that unused hearth below,

Stretched out a shadowy arm to feel the night.
The children heard him in their chilly beds,
Mumbling and musing of the silent farm.
They heard his mumble in the morning light.

Now, soldiers, hear me: mark this very breeze,
That blows about in such a hopeless way,
Mumbling and musing like the most forlorn.
It is that Old Man, lost among the trees.

VI

There was heaven,
Full of Raphael's costumes;
And earth,
A thing of shadows,
Stiff as stone,
Where Time, in fitful turns,
Resumes
His own . . .

5

A dead hand tapped the drum,
An old voice cried out, "Come!"
We were obedient and dumb.

❖❖❖❖❖❖❖❖❖❖❖❖❖❖❖❖❖❖❖❖❖❖❖❖❖❖❖❖❖

THE SILVER PLOUGH-BOY

A black figure dances in a black field.
It seizes a sheet, from the ground, from a bush, as if spread there
  by some wash-woman for the night.
It wraps the sheet around its body, until the black figure is
  silver.
It dances down a furrow, in the early light, back of a crazy
  plough, the green blades following.
How soon the silver fades in the dust! How soon the black
  figure slips from the wrinkled sheet!
How softly the sheet falls to the ground!

❖❖❖❖❖❖❖❖❖❖❖❖❖❖❖❖❖❖❖❖❖❖❖❖❖❖❖❖❖

BOWL

For what emperor
Was this bowl of Earth designed?
Here are more things
Than on any bowl of the Sungs,
Even the rarest—

6

Vines that take
The various obscurities of the moon,
Approaching rain
And leaves that would be loose upon the wind,
Pears on pointed trees,
The dresses of women,
Oxen . . .
I never tire
To think of this.

◇◇◇

POEMS FROM "PRIMORDIA"

In the Northwest

1

All over Minnesota,
Cerise sopranos,
Walking in the snow,
Answer, humming,
The male voice of the wind in the dry leaves
Of the lake-hollows.
For one,
The syllables of the gulls and of the crows
And of the blue-bird
Meet in the name
Of Jalmar Lillygreen.
There is his motion
In the flowing of black water.

2

The child's hair is of the color of the hay in the haystack,
    around which the four black horses stand.
There is the same color in the bellies of frogs, in clays,
    withered reeds, skins, wood, sunlight.

3

The blunt ice flows down the Mississippi,
At night.
In the morning, the clear river
Is full of reflections,
Beautiful alliterations of shadows and of
    things shadowed.

4

The horses gnaw the bark from the trees.
The horses are hollow,
The trunks of the trees are hollow.
Why do the horses have eyes and ears?
The trees do not.
Why can the horses move about on the ground?
The trees cannot.
The horses weary themselves hunting for green grass.
The trees stand still,
The trees drink.
The water runs away from the horses.
La, la, la, la, la, la, la, la,
Dee, dum, diddle, dee, dee, diddle, dee, da.

5

The birch trees draw up whiteness from the ground.
In the swamps, bushes draw up dark red,
Or yellow.

O, boatman,
What are you drawing from the rain-pointed water?
O, boatman,
What are you drawing from the rain-pointed water?
Are you two boatmen
Different from each other?

In the South

6

Unctuous furrows,
The ploughman portrays in you
The spring about him:
Compilation of the effects
Of magenta blooming in the Judas-tree
And of purple blooming in the eucalyptus—
Map of yesterday's earth
And of tomorrow's heaven.

7

The black mother of eleven children
Hangs her quilt under the pine-trees.
There is a connection between the colors,
The shapes of the patches,
And the eleven children . . .
Frail princes of distant Monaco,
That paragon of a parasol
Discloses
At least one baby in you.

BLANCHE McCARTHY

Look in the terrible mirror of the sky
And not in this dead glass, which can reflect
Only the surfaces—the bending arm,
The leaning shoulder and the searching eye.

Look in the terrible mirror of the sky.
Oh, bend against the invisible; and lean
To symbols of descending night; and search
The glare of revelations going by!

Look in the terrible mirror of the sky.
See how the absent moon waits in a glade
Of your dark self, and how the wings of stars,
Upward, from unimagined coverts, fly.

POEMS FROM "LETTRES D'UN SOLDAT"

*"Combattre avec ses frères, à sa place,
à son rang, avec des yeux dessillés,
sans espoir de gloire et de profit, et
simplement parce que telle est la loi,
voilà le commandement que donne le
dieu au guerrier Arjuna, quand celui-
ci doute s'il doit se détourner de l'ab-
solu pour le cauchemar humain de la
bataille. . . . Simplement, qu'Arjuna bande son arc avec les autres
Kshettryas!"*
PRÉFACE D'ANDRÉ CHEVRILLON

7 septembre
. . . *Nous sommes embarqués dans l'aventure sans aucune
sensation dominante, sauf peut-être une acceptation assez
belle de la fatalité* . . .

COMMON SOLDIER

No introspective chaos . . . I accept:
War, too, although I do not understand.
And that, then, is my final aphorism.

I have been pupil under bishops' rods
And got my learning from the orthodox.
I mark the virtue of the common-place.

I take all things as stated—so and so
Of men and earth: I quote the line and page,
I quote the very phrase my masters used.

If I should fall, as soldier, I know well
The final pulse of blood from this good heart
Would taste, precisely, as they said it would.

27 septembre
*Jamais la majesté de la nuit ne m'apporta autant de con-
solation qu'en cette accumulation d'épreuves. Vénus,
étincelante, m'est une amie.*

IN AN ANCIENT, SOLEMN MANNER

The spirit wakes in the night wind—is naked.
What is it that hides in the night wind
Near by it?

Is it, once more, the mysterious beauté,
Like a woman inhibiting passion
In solace—

The multiform beauty, sinking in night wind,
Quick to be gone, yet never
Quite going?

She will leap back from the swift constellations,
As they enter the place of their western
Seclusion.

III

22 octobre

Ce qu'il faut, c'est reconnaître l'amour et la beauté triomphante de toute violence.

ANECDOTAL REVERY

The streets contain a crowd
Of blind men tapping their way
By inches—
This man to complain to the grocer
Of yesterday's cheese,
This man to visit a woman,
This man to take the air.
Am I to pick my way
Through these crickets?—
I, that have a head
In the bag
Slung over my shoulder?
I have secrets
That prick
Like a heart full of pins.

Permit me, gentlemen,
I have killed the mayor,
And am escaping from you.
Get out of the way!
(*The blind men strike him down with their sticks.*)

IV

31 octobre

Jusqu'à présent j'ai possedé une sagesse de renoncement, mais maintenant je veux une sagesse qui accepte tout, en s'orientant vers l'action future.

MORALE

And so France feels. A menace that impends,
Too long, is like a bayonet that bends.

V

7 novembre

Si tu voyais la sécurité des petits animaux des bois, souris, mulots! L'autre jour, dans notre abri de feuillage, je suivais les évolutions de ces petites bêtes. Elles étaient jolies comme une estampe japonaise, avec l'interieur de leurs oreilles rose comme un coquillage.

COMME DIEU DISPENSE DE GRACES

Here I keep thinking of the Primitives—
The sensitive and conscientious schemes
Of mountain pallors ebbing into air;

And I remember sharp Japonica—
The driving rain, the willows in the rain,
The birds that wait out rain in willow leaves.

Although life seems a goblin mummery,
These images return and are increased,
As for a child in an oblivion:

13

Even by mice—these scamper and are still;
They cock small ears, more glistening and pale
Than fragile volutes in a rose sea-shell.

VI

*Bien chère Mère aimeé. . . . Pour ce qui est de ton cœur,
j'ai tellement confiance en ton courage, qu'à l'heure ac-
tuelle cette certitude est mon grand reconfort. Je sais que
ma mère a atteint à cette liberté d'âme qui permet de con-
templer le spectacle universel.*

There is another mother whom I love,
O chère maman, another, who, in turn,
Is mother to the two of us, and more,
In whose hard service both of us endure
Our petty portion in the sacrifice.
Not France! France, also, serves the invincible eye,
That, from her helmet, terrible and bright,
Commands the armies; the relentless arm,
Devising proud, majestic issuance.
Wait now; have no rememberings of hope,
Poor penury. There will be voluble hymns
Come swelling, when, regardless of my end,
The mightier mother raises up her cry;
And little will or wish, that day, for tears.

VII

4 février

*Hier soir, rentrant dans ma grange, ivresse, rixes, cris,
chants et hurlements. Voilà la vie!*

John Smith and his son, John Smith,
    And his son's son John, and-a-one
    And-a-two and-a-three

14

And-a-rum-tum-tum, and-a
Lean John, and his son, lean John,
    And his lean son's John, and-a-one
    And-a-two and-a-three
And-a-drum-rum-rum, and-a
Rich John, and his son, rich John,
    And his rich son's John, and-a-one
    And-a-two and-a-three
And-a-pom-pom-pom, and-a
Wise John, and his son, wise John,
    And his wise son's John, and-a-one
    And-a-two and-a-three
And-a-fee and-a-fee and-a-fee
    And-a-fee-fo-fum—
Voilà la vie, la vie, la vie,
    And-a-rummy-tummy-tum
    And-a-rummy-tummy-tum.

VIII

17 mars

*J'ai oublié de te dire que, l'autre fois, pendant la tempête,
j'ai vu dans le soir les grues revenir. Une accalmie permet-
tait d'entendre leur cri.*

In a theatre, full of tragedy,
The stage becomes an atmosphere
Of seeping rose—banal machine
In an appointed repertoire . . .

IX

26 mars

*Rien de nouveau sur notre hauteur que l'on continue d'or-
ganiser. . . . De temps à autre la pioche rencontre un
pauvre mort que la guerre tourmente jusque dans la terre.*

Death was a reaper with sickle and stone,
Or swipling flail, sun-black in the sun,
A laborer.

Or Death was a rider beating his horse,
Gesturing grandiose things in the air,
Seen by a muse. . . .

Symbols of sentiment . . . Take this phrase,
Men of the line, take this new phrase
Of the truth of Death—

Death, that will never be satisfied,
Digs up the earth when want returns . . .
You know the phrase.

◇◇◇

ARCHITECTURE

I

What manner of building shall we build?
Let us design a chastel de chasteté.
De pensée. . . .
Never cease to deploy the structure.
Keep the laborers shouldering plinths.
Pass the whole of life earing the clink of the
Chisels of the stone-cutters cutting the stones.

II

In this house, what manner of utterance shall there be?
What heavenly dithyramb

16

And cantilene?
What niggling forms of gargoyle patter?
Of what shall the speech be,
In that splay of marble
And of obedient pillars?

III

And how shall those come vested that come there?
In their ugly reminders?
Or gaudy as tulips?
As they climb the stairs
To the group of Flora Coddling Hecuba?
As they climb the flights
To the closes
Overlooking whole seasons?

IV

Let us build the building of light.
Push up the towers
To the cock-tops.
These are the pointings of our edifice,
Which, like a gorgeous palm,
Shall tuft the commonplace.
These are the window-sill
On which the quiet moonlight lies.

V

How shall we hew the sun,
Split it and make blocks,
To build a ruddy palace?
How carve the violet moon
To set in nicks?
Let us fix portals, east and west,

Abhorring green-blue north and blue-green south.
Our chiefest dome a demoiselle of gold.
Pierce the interior with pouring shafts,
In diverse chambers.
Pierce, too, with buttresses of coral air
And purple timbers,
Various argentines,
Embossings of the sky.

VI

And, finally, set guardians in the grounds,
Gray, gruesome grumblers.
For no one proud, nor stiff,
No solemn one, nor pale,
No chafferer, may come
To sully the begonias, nor vex
With holy or sublime ado
The kremlin of kermess.

VII

Only the lusty and the plenteous
Shall walk
The bronze-filled plazas
And the nut-shell esplanades.

STANZAS FOR "LE MONOCLE DE MON ONCLE"

("The Naked Eye of the Aunt")

I

I peopled the dark park with gowns
In which were yellow, rancid skeletons.
Oh! How suave a purple passed me by!
But twiddling *mon idée*, as old men will,
And knowing the monotony of thought,
I said, "She thumbs the memories of dress."
Can I take fire from so benign an ash?
It is enough she comes upon the eye.
A maid of forty is no feathery girl.
Green bosoms and black legs, beguile
These ample lustres from the new-come moon.

II

Poets of pimpernel, unlucky pimps
Of pomp, in love and good ensample, see
How I exhort her, huckstering my woe.
"Oh, hideous, horrible, horrendous hocks!"
Is there one word of sunshine in this plaint?
Do I commend myself to leafy things
Or melancholy crows as shadowing clouds?
I grieve the pinch of her long-stiffening bones.
"Oh, lissomeness turned lagging ligaments!"
Eheu! Eheu! With what a weedy face
Black fact emerges from her swishing dreams.

PETER PARASOL

Aux taureaux Dieu cornes donne
Et sabots durs aux chevaux. . .

Why are not women fair,
All, as Andromache,
Having, each one, most praisable
Ears, eyes, souls, skins, hair?

Ah, good God! That all beasts should have
The tusks of the elephant,
Or be beautiful
As large ferocious tigers are.

It is not so with women.
I wish they were all fair
And walked in fine clothes,
With parasols, in the afternoon air.

EXPOSITION OF THE CONTENTS OF A CAB

Victoria Clementina, negress,
Took seven white dogs
To ride in a cab.

Bells of the dogs chinked.
Harness of the horses shuffled
Like brazen shells.

Oh-hé-hé! Fragrant puppets
By the green lake-pallors,
She too is flesh,

And a breech-cloth might wear,
Netted of topaz and ruby
And savage blooms;

Thridding the squawkiest jungle
In a golden sedan,
White dogs at bay.

What breech-cloth might you wear—
Except linen, embroidered
By elderly women?

❀◇

PIANO PRACTICE AT THE ACADEMY
OF THE HOLY ANGELS

The time will come for these children, seated before their long
    black instruments, to strike the themes of love—
All of them, darkened by time, moved by they know not what,
    amending the airs they play to fulfill themselves;
Seated before these shining forms, like the duskiest glass, re-
    flecting the piebald of roses or what you will.

Blanche, the blonde, whose eyes are not wholly straight, in a
    room of lustres, shed by turquoise falling,
Whose heart will murmur with the music that will be a voice for
    her, speaking the dreaded change of speech;
And Rosa, the muslin dreamer of satin and cowry-kin, disdaining
    the empty keys; and the young infanta,
Jocunda, who will arrange the roses and rearrange, letting the
    leaves lie on the water-like lacquer;
And that confident one, Marie, the wearer of cheap stones, who
    will have grown still and restless;
And Crispine, the blade, reddened by some touch, demanding
    the most from the phrases
Of the well-thumbed, infinite pages of her masters, who will seem
    old to her, requiting less and less her feeling:
In the days when the mood of love will be swarming for solace
    and sink deeply into the thin stuff of being,
And these long, black instruments will be so little to them that
    will be needing so much, seeking so much in their music.

THE INDIGO GLASS IN THE GRASS

Which is real—
This bottle of indigo glass in the grass,
Or the bench with the pot of geraniums, the stained
    mattress and the washed overalls drying in
    the sun?
Which of these truly contains the world?
Neither one, nor the two together.

ROMANCE FOR A DEMOISELLE
LYING IN THE GRASS

It is grass.
It is monotonous.

The monotony
Is like your port which conceals
All your characters
And their desires.

I might make many images of this
And twang nobler notes
Of larger sentiment.

But I invoke the monotony of monotonies
Free from images and change.

Why should I savor love
With tragedy or comedy?

Clasp me,
Delicatest machine.

ANECDOTE OF THE ABNORMAL

He called hydrangeas purple. And they were.
Not fixed and deadly (like a curving line

23

That merely makes a ring).
It was a purple changeable to see.
And so hydrangeas came to be.

The common grass is green.
But there are regions where the grass
Assumes a pale, Italianate sheen—
Is almost Byzantine.
And there the common grass is never seen.

And in those regions one still feels the rose
And feels the grass
Because new colors make new things
And new things make old things again . . .
And so with men.

Crispin-valet, Crispin-saint!
The exhausted realist beholds
His tattered manikin arise,
Tuck in the straw,
And stalk the skies.

❀❀❀❀❀❀❀❀❀❀❀❀❀❀❀❀❀❀❀❀❀❀❀❀❀❀❀❀❀❀

INFERNALE

(A *boor of night in middle earth cries out.*)
Hola! Hola! What steps are those that break
This crust of air? . . (*He pauses.*) Can breath shake
The solid wax from which the warmth dies out? . .

24

I saw a waxen woman in a smock
Fly from the black toward the purple air.
(*He shouts.*) Hola! Of that strange light, beware!
(*A woman's voice is heard, replying.*) Mock

The bondage of the Stygian concubine,
Hallooing haggler; for the wax is blown,
And downward, from this purple region, thrown;
And I fly forth, the naked Proserpine.

(*Her pale smock sparkles in a light begun
To be diffused, and, as she disappears,
The silent watcher, far below her, hears:*)
Soaring Olympus glitters in the sun.

<hr />

THIS VAST INELEGANCE

This vast inelegance may seem the blankest desolation,
Beginning of a green Cockaigne to be, disliked, abandoned,

In which the bliss of clouds is mark of an intended meeting
Between the matin air and color, goldenest generating,

Soother and lustier than this vexed, autumnal exhalation,
So sullen with sighing and surrender to marauding ennui.

Which choir makes the most faultless medley in its celebration?
The choir that choirs the first fatigue in deep bell of canzoni?

Or this, whose music, sweeping irradiation of a sea-night,
Piercing the tide by which it moves, is constantly within us?

Or this, whose jingling glorias, importunate of perfection,
Are the fulfilling rhapsodies that hymn it to creation?

Is any choir the whole voice of this fretful habitation,
This parlor of farcical dames, this clowns' colonnade, this kites'
    pavilion?

See, now, the ways beleaguered by black, dropsical duennas,
Young weasels racing steep horizons in pursuit of planets . . .

LULU GAY

Lulu sang of barbarians before the eunuchs
Of gobs, who called her orchidean,
Sniffed her and slapped heavy hands
Upon her.
She made the eunuchs ululate.
She described for them
The manners of the barbarians,
What they did with their thumbs.
The eunuchs heard her
With continual ululation.
She described how the barbarians kissed her
With their wide mouths
And breaths as true
As the gum of the gum-tree.
"Olu" the eunuchs cried. "Ululalu."

LULU MOROSE

Is there a sharp edge?
Is there a sharp edge?
On which to lean
Like a belly puckered by a spear.

The cliffs are rough.
Are rough
And not all birds sing cuck
Sing coo, sing cuck, cuckoo.

Oh! Sal, the butcher's wife ate clams
And died amid uproarious damns.
And mother nature sick of silk
Shot lightning at the kind cow's milk.

And father nature, full of butter
Made the maelstrom oceans mutter.
Stabbing at his teat-like corns
From an ottoman of thorns.

SATURDAY NIGHT AT THE CHIROPODIST'S

Histoire

For simple pleasure, he beheld,
The rotting man for pleasure saw,
The new spring tumble in the sky.

27

The wry of neck and the wry of heart
Stood by him when the tumbler fell,
And the mighty, musty belly of tears.

Did they behold themselves in this
And see themselves as once they were,
O spirit of bones, O mountain of graves?

Take counsel, all hierophants
And sentimental roisterers,
They did not so. But in their throats

They pied and chuckled like a flock,
They were so glad to see the spring.
The rotting man was first to sing.

MANDOLIN AND LIQUEURS

La-la! The cat is in the violets
And the awnings are let down.
The cat should not be where she is
And the awnings are too brown,
Emphatically so.

If awnings were celeste and gay,
Iris and orange, crimson and green,
Blue and vermilion, purple and white,
And not this tinsmith's galaxy,
Things would be different.

The sun is gold, the moon is silver.
There must be a planet that is copper
And in whose light the roses
Would have a most singular appearance,
Or nearly so.

I love to sit and read the *Telegraph*,
That vast confect of telegrams,
And to find how much that really matters
Does not really matter
At all.

THE SHAPE OF THE CORONER

It was the morn
And the palms were waved
And the brass was played.
Then the coroner came
In his limpid shoes.

The palms were waved
For the beau of illusions.
The termagant fans
Of his orange days
Fell, famous and flat,
And folded him round,

Folded and fell
And the brass grew cold

29

And the coroner's hand
Dismissed the band.

It was the coroner
Poured this elixir
Into the ground,
And a shabby man,
An eye too sleek,
And a biscuit cheek.

And the coroner bent
Over the palms.
The elysium lay
In a parlor of day.

<hr />

RED LOVES KIT

I

Your yes her no, your no her yes. The words
Make little difference, for being wrong
And wronging her, if only as she thinks,
You never can be right. You are the man.
You brought the incredible calm in ecstasy,
Which, like a virgin visionary spent
In this spent world, she must possess. The gift
Came not from you. Shall the world be spent again,
Wasted in what would be an ultimate waste,
A deprivation muffled in eclipse,
The final theft? That you are innocent

And love her still, still leaves you in the wrong.
Where is that calm and where that ecstasy?
Her words accuse you of adulteries
That sack the sun, though metaphysical.

II

A beautiful thing, milord, is beautiful
Not only in itself but in the things
Around it. Thus it has a large expanse,
As the moon has in its moonlight, worlds away,
As the sea has in its coastal clamorings.
So she, when in her mystic aureole
She walks, triumphing humbly, should express
Her beauty in your love. She should reflect
Her glory in your passion and be proud.
Her music should repeat itself in you,
Impelled by a convulsive harmony.
Milord, I ask you, though you will to sing,
Does she will to be proud? True, you may love
And she have beauty of a kind, but such
Unhappy love reveals vast blemishes.

III

Rest, crows, upon the edges of the moon,
Cover the golden altar deepest black,
Fly upward thick in numbers, fly across
The blueness of the half-night, fill the air
And darken it, make an unbroken mat
Out of the whirl and denseness of your wings,
Spread over heaven shutting out the light.
Then turn your heads and let your spiral eyes
Look backward. Let your swiftly-flying flocks
Look suddenly downward with their shining eyes

And move the night by their intelligent motes.
Make a sidereal splendor as you fly.
And you, good galliard, to enchant black thoughts
Beseech them for an overpowering gloom.
It will be fecund in rapt curios.

METROPOLITAN MELANCHOLY

A purple woman with a lavender tongue
Said hic, said hac,
Said ha.

To dab things even nicely pink
Adds very little,
So I think.
Oh ha, Oh ha.

The silks they wear in all the cities
Are really much a million pities.

ANNUAL GAIETY

In the morning in the blue snow
The catholic sun, its majesty,
Pinks and pinks the ice-hard melanchole.

Wherefore those prayers to the moon?
Or is it that alligators lie
Along the edges of your eye
Basking in desert Florida?

Père Guzz, in heaven thumb your lyre
And chant the January fire
And joy of snow and snow.

◇◇◇

GOOD MAN, BAD WOMAN

You say that spite avails her nothing, that
You rest intact in conscience and intact
In self, a man of longer time than days,
Of larger company than one. Therefore,
Pure scientist, you look with nice aplomb
At this indifferent experience,
Deploring sentiment. When May came last
And equally as scientist you walked
Among the orchards in the apple-blocks
And saw the blossoms, snow-bred pink and white,
Making your heart of brass to intercept
The childish onslaughts of such innocence,
Why was it that you cast the brass away
And bared yourself, and bared yourself in vain?
She can corrode your world, if never you.

THE WOMAN WHO BLAMED LIFE ON A SPANIARD

I

You do not understand her evil mood.
You think that like the moon she is obscured
But clears and clears until an open night
Reveals her, rounded in beneficence,
Pellucid love; and for that image, like
Some merciful divination, you forgive.
And you forgive dark broachings growing great
Night after night because the hemisphere
And still the final quarter, still the rim,
And still the impassioned place of it remain.
If she is like the moon, she never clears
But spreads an evil lustre whose increase
Is evil, crisply bright, disclosing you
Stooped in a night of vast inquietude.
Observe her shining in the deadly trees.

II

That tragic prattle of the fates, astute
To bring destruction, often seems high-pitched.
The babble of generations magnifies
A mot into a dictum, communal,
Of inescapable force, itself a fate.
How, then, if nothing more than vanity
Is at the bottom of her as pique-pain
And picador? Be briny-blooded bull.
Flutter her lance with your tempestuous dust,
Make melic groans and tooter at her strokes,

Rage in the ring and shake the corridors.
Perhaps at so much mastery, the bliss
She needs will come consolingly. Alas,
It is a most spectacular role, and yet
Less than contending with fictitious doom.

III

The choice twixt dove and goose is over-close.
The fowl of Venus may consist of both
And more. It may have feathery color-frets,
A paragon of lustre; may have voice
Like the mother of all nightingales; be wise
As a seraglio-parrot; feel disdain
In concert with the eagle's valiance.
Let this be as it may. It must have tears
And memory and claws: a paragon
Well-wetted; a decoying voice that sings
Arpeggi of celestial souvenirs,
A skillful apprehension and eye proud
In venting lacerations. So composed,
This hallowed visitant, chimerical,
Sinks into likeness blessedly beknown.

❀❁❀❁❀❁❀❁❀❁❀❁❀❁❀❁❀❁❀❁❀❁❀❁❀❁❀❁❀❁❀

SECRET MAN

The sounds of rain on the roof
Are like the sound of doves.
It is long since there have been doves
On any house of mine.

35

It is better for me
In the rushes of autumn wind
To embrace autumn, without turning
To remember summer.

Besides, the world is a tower.
Its winds are blue.
The rain falls at its base,
Summers sink from it.

The doves will fly round.
When morning comes
The high clouds will move,
Nobly as autumn moves.

The man of autumn,
Behind its melancholy mask,
Will laugh in the brown grass,
Will shout from the tower's rim.

THE DRUM-MAJORS IN THE
LABOR DAY PARADE

If each of them wasn't a prig
And didn't care a fig,
They would show it.

They would throw their batons far up
To return in a glittering wheel
And make the Dagoes squeal.

But they are empty as balloons
The trombones are like baboons,
The parade's no good.

Are they really mechanical bears,
Toys of the millionaires,
Morbid and bleak?

They ought to be muscular men,
Naked and stamping the earth,
Whipping the air.

The banners should brighten the sun.
The women should sing as they march.
Let's go home.

POLO PONIES PRACTICING

The constant cry against an old order,
An order constantly old,
Is itself old and stale.

Here is the world of a moment,
Fitted by men and horses
For hymns,

In a freshness of poetry by the sea,
In galloping hedges,
In thudding air:

Beyond any order,
Beyond any rebellion,
A brilliant air

On the flanks of horses,
On the clear grass,
On the shapes of the mind.

ↀↀↀↀↀↀↀↀↀↀↀↀↀↀↀↀↀↀↀↀↀↀↀↀↀↀↀↀↀↀ

LYTTON STRACHEY, ALSO, ENTERS INTO HEAVEN

I care for neither fugues nor feathers.
What interests me most is the people
Who have always interested me most,
To see them without their passions
And to understand them.

Perhaps, without their passions, they will be
Men of memories explaining what they meant.
One man opposing a society
If properly misunderstood becomes a myth.
I fear the understanding.

Death ought to spare their passions.
Memory without passion would be better lost.
But memory and passion, and with these
The understanding of heaven, would be bliss,
If anything would be bliss.

38

How strange a thing it was to understand
And how strange it ought to be again, this time
Without the distortions of the theatre,
Without the revolutions' ruin,
In the presence of the barefoot ghosts!

Perception as an act of intelligence
And perception as an act of grace
Are two quite different things, in particular
When applied to the mythical.
As for myself, I feel a doubt:

I am uncertain whether the perception
Applied on earth to those that were myths
In every various sense, ought not to be preferred
To an untried perception applied
In heaven. But I have no choice.

In this apologetic air, one well
Might muff the mighty spirit of Lenin.
That sort of thing was always rather stiff.
Let's hope for Mademoiselle de Lespinasse,
Instead, or Horace Walpole or Mrs. Thrale.

He is nothing, I know, to me nor I to him.
I had looked forward to understanding. Yet
An understanding may be troublesome.
I'd rather not. No doubt there's a quarter here,
Dixhuitième and Georgian and serene.

TABLE TALK

Granted, we die for good.
Life, then, is largely a thing
Of happens to like, not should.

And that, too, granted, why
Do I happen to like red bush,
Gray grass and green-gray sky?

What else remains? But red,
Gray, green, why those of all?
That is not what I said:

Not those of all. But those.
One likes what one happens to like.
One likes the way red grows.

It cannot matter at all.
Happens to like is one
Of the ways things happen to fall.

A ROOM ON A GARDEN

O stagnant east-wind, palsied mare,
Giddap! The ruby roses' hair
Must blow.

Behold how order is the end
Of everything. The roses bend
As one.

Order, the law of hoes and rakes,
May be perceived in windy quakes
And squalls.

The gardener searches earth and sky
The truth in nature to espy
In vain.

He well might find that eager balm
In lilies' stately-statued calm;
But then

He well might find it in this fret
Of lilies rusted, rotting, wet
With rain.

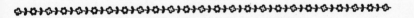

AGENDA

Whipped creams and the Blue Danube,
The lin-lan-lone of Babson,
And yet the damned thing doesn't come right.

Boston should be in the keys
Painting the saints among palms.
Charleston should be New York.

And what a good thing it would be
If Shasta roared up in Nassau,
Cooling the sugary air.

Perhaps if the orchestras stood on their heads
And dancers danced ballets on top of their beds—
We haven't tried that.

The early centuries were full
Of very haphazard people and things,
The whole of them turning black;

Yet in trees round the College of Heralds,
No doubt, the well-tuned birds are singing,
Slowly and sweetly.

OWL'S CLOVER

◇◇◇◇◇

THE OLD WOMAN AND THE STATUE

I

Another evening in another park,
A group of marble horses rose on wings
In the midst of a circle of trees, from which the leaves
Raced with the horses in bright hurricanes.

II

So much the sculptor had foreseen: autumn,
The sky above the plaza widening
Before the horses, clouds of bronze imposed
On clouds of gold, and green engulfing bronze,
The marble leaping in the storms of light.
So much he had devised: white forelegs taut
To the muscles' very tip for the vivid plunge,
The heads held high and gathered in a ring
At the center of the mass, the haunches low,
Contorted, staggering from the thrust against
The earth as the bodies rose on feathery wings,
Clumped carvings, circular, like blunted fans,
Arranged for phantasy to form an edge
Of crisping light along the statue's rim.
More than his muddy hand was in the manes,
More than his mind in the wings. The rotten leaves
Swirled round them in immense autumnal sounds.

43

But her he had not foreseen: the bitter mind
In a flapping cloak. She walked along the paths
Of the park with chalky brow scratched over black
And black by thought that could not understand
Or, if it understood, repressed itself
Without any pity in a somnolent dream.
The golden clouds that turned to bronze, the sounds
Descending, did not touch her eye and left
Her ear unmoved. She was that tortured one,
So destitute that nothing but herself
Remained and nothing of herself except
A fear too naked for her shadow's shape.
To search for clearness all an afternoon
And without knowing, and then upon the wind
To hear the stroke of one's certain solitude,
What sound could comfort away the sudden sense?
What path could lead apart from what she was
And was to be? Could it happen to be this,
This atmosphere in which the horses rose,
This atmosphere in which her musty mind
Lay black and full of black misshapen? Wings
And light lay deeper for her than her sight.

IV

The mass of stone collapsed to marble hulk,
Stood stiffly, as if the black of what she thought
Conflicting with the moving colors there
Changed them, at last, to its triumphant hue,
Triumphant as that always upward wind
Blowing among the trees its meaningless sound.
The space above the trees might still be bright
Yet the light fell falsely on the marble skulls,

44

Manes matted of marble across the air, the light
Fell falsely on the matchless skeletons,
A change so felt, a fear in her so known,
Now felt, now known as this. The clouds of bronze
Slowly submerging in flatness disappeared.
If the sky that followed, smaller than the night,
Still eked out luminous wrinklings on the leaves,
Whitened, again, forms formless in the dark,
It was as if transparence touched her mind.
The statue stood in stars like water-spheres,
Washed over by their green, their flowing blue.
A mood that had become so fixed it was
A manner of the mind, a mind in a night
That was whatever the mind might make of it,
A night that was that mind so magnified
It lost the common shape of night and came
To be the sovereign shape in a world of shapes.
A woman walking in the autumn leaves,
Thinking of heaven and earth and of herself
And looking at the place in which she walked,
As a place in which each thing was motionless
Except the thing she felt but did not know.

V

Without her, evening like a budding yew
Would soon be brilliant, as it was, before
The harridan self and ever-maladive fate
Went crying their desolate syllables, before
Their voice and the voice of the tortured wind were one,
Each voice within the other, seeming one,
Crying against a need that pressed like cold,
Deadly and deep. It would become a yew
Grown great and grave beyond imagined trees,

45

Branching through heavens heavy with the sheen
And shadowy hanging of it, thick with stars
Of a lunar light, dark-belted sorcerers
Dazzling by simplest beams and soothly still,
The space beneath it still, a smooth domain,
Untroubled by suffering, which fate assigns
To the moment. There the horses would rise again,
Yet hardly to be seen and again the legs
Would flash in air, and the muscular bodies thrust
Hoofs grinding against the stubborn earth, until
The light wings lifted through the crystal space
Of night. How clearly that would be defined!

❖❀❖

[OWL'S CLOVER]

MR. BURNSHAW AND THE STATUE

I

The thing is dead . . . Everything is dead
Except the future. Always everything
That is is dead except what ought to be.
All things destroy themselves or are destroyed.

These are not even Russian animals.
They are horses as they were in the sculptor's mind.
They might be sugar or paste or citron-skin
Made by a cook that never rode the back
Of his angel through the skies. They might be mud
Left here by moonlit muckers when they fled
At the burst of day, crepuscular images
Made to remember a life they never lived
In the witching wilderness, night's witchingness,

46

Made to affect a dream they never had,
Like a word in the mind that sticks at artichoke
And remains inarticulate, horses with cream.
The statue seems a thing from Schwarz's, a thing
Of the dank imagination, much below
Our crusted outlines hot and huge with fact,
Ugly as an idea, not beautiful
As sequels without thought. In the rudest red
Of autumn, these horses should go clattering
Along the thin horizons, nobly more
Than this jotting-down of the sculptor's foppishness
Long after the worms and the curious carvings of
Their snouts.

II

Come, all celestial paramours,
Whether in-dwelling haughty clouds, frigid
And crisply musical, or holy caverns temple-toned,
Entwine your arms and moving to and fro,
Now like a ballet infantine in awkward steps,
Chant sibilant requiems for this effigy.
Bring down from nowhere nothing's wax-like blooms,
Calling them what you will but loosely-named
In a mortal lullaby, like porcelain.
Then, while the music makes you, make, yourselves,
Long autumn sheens and pittering sounds like sounds
On pattering leaves and suddenly with lights,
Astral and Shelleyan, diffuse new day;
And on this ring of marble horses shed
The rainbow in its glistening serpentines
Made by the sun ascending seventy seas.
Agree: the apple in the orchard, round
And red, will not be redder, rounder then
Than now. No: nor the ploughman in his bed

47

Be free to sleep there sounder, for the plough
And the dew and the ploughman still will best be one.
But this gawky plaster will not be here.

III

The stones
That will replace it shall be carved, *"The Mass
Appoints These Marbles Of Itself To Be
Itself."* No more than that, no subterfuge,
No memorable muffing, bare and blunt.

IV

Mesdames, one might believe that Shelley lies
Less in the stars than in their earthy wake,
Since the radiant disclosures that you make
Are of an eternal vista, manqué and gold
And brown, an Italy of the mind, a place
Of fear before the disorder of the strange,
A time in which the poets' politics
Will rule in a poets' world. Yet that will be
A world impossible for poets, who
Complain and prophesy, in their complaints,
And are never of the world in which they live.
Disclose the rude and ruddy at their jobs
And if you weep for peacocks that are gone
Or dance the death of doves, most sallowly,
Who knows? The ploughman may not live alone
With his plough, the peacock may abandon pride,
The dove's adagio may lose its depth
And change. If ploughmen, peacocks, doves alike
In vast disorder live in the ruins, free,
The charts destroyed, even disorder may,

So seen, have an order of its own, a peace
Not now to be perceived yet order's own.

v

A solemn voice, not Mr. Burnshaw's says:
At some gigantic, solitary urn,
A trash can at the end of the world, the dead
Give up dead things and the living turn away.
There buzzards pile their sticks among the bones
Of buzzards and eat the bellies of the rich,
Fat with a thousand butters, and the crows
Sip the wild honey of the poor man's life,
The blood of his bitter brain; and there the sun
Shines without fire on columns intercrossed,
White slapped on white, majestic, marble heads,
Severed and tumbled into seedless grass,
Motionless, knowing neither dew nor frost.
There lies the head of the sculptor in which the thought
Of lizards, in its eye, is more acute
Than the thought that once was native to the skull;
And there are the white-maned horses' heads, beyond
The help of any wind or any sky:
Parts of the immense detritus of a world
That is completely waste, that moves from waste
To waste, out of the hopeless waste of the past
Into a hopeful waste to come. There even
The colorless light in which this wreckage lies
Has faint, portentous lustres, shades and shapes
Of rose, or what will once more rise to rose,
When younger bodies, because they are younger, rise
And chant the rose-points of their birth, and when
For a little time, again, rose-breasted birds

Sing rose-beliefs. Above that urn two lights
Commingle, not like the commingling of sun and moon
At dawn, nor of summer-light and winter-light
In an autumn afternoon, but two immense
Reflections, whirling apart and wide away.

VI

Mesdames, it is not enough to be reconciled
Before the strange, having wept and having thought
And having said farewell. It is not enough
That the vista retain ploughmen, peacocks, doves,
However tarnished, companions out of the past,
And that, heavily, you move with them in the dust.
It is not enough that you are indifferent,
Because time moves on columns intercrossed
And because the temple is never quite composed,
Silent and turquoised and perpetual,
Visible over the sea. It is only enough
To live incessantly in change. See how
On a day still full of summer, when the leaves
Appear to sleep within a sleeping air,
They suddenly fall and the leafless sound of the wind
Is no longer a sound of summer. So great a change
Is constant. The time you call serene descends
Through a moving chaos that never ends. Mesdames,
Leaves are not always falling and the birds
Of chaos are not always sad nor lost
In melancholy distances. You held
Each other moving in a chant and danced
Beside the statue, while you sang. Your eyes
Were solemn and your gowns were blown and grief
Was under every temple-tone. You sang
A tragic lullaby, like porcelain.

But change composes, too, and chaos comes
To momentary calm, spectacular flocks
Of crimson and hoods of Venezuelan green
And the sound of z in the grass all day, though these
Are chaos and of archaic change. Shall you,
Then, fear a drastic community evolved
From the whirling, slowly and by trial; or fear
Men gathering for a mighty flight of men,
An abysmal migration into a possible blue?

VII

Dance, now, and with sharp voices cry, but cry
Like damsels daubed and let your feet be bare
To touch the grass and, as you circle, turn
Your backs upon the vivid statue. Then,
Weaving ring in radiant ring and quickly, fling
Yourselves away and at a distance join
Your hands held high and cry again, but cry,
This time, like damsels captured by the sky,
Seized by that possible blue. Be maidens formed
Of the most evasive hue of a lesser blue,
Of the least appreciable shade of green
And despicable shades of red, just seen,
And vaguely to be seen, a matinal red,
A dewy flashing blanks away from fire,
As if your gowns were woven of the light
Yet were not bright, came shining as things come
That enter day from night, came mirror-dark,
With each fold sweeping in a sweeping play.
Let your golden hands wave fastly and be gay
And your braids bear brightening of crimson bands.
Conceive that while you dance the statue falls,
The heads are severed, topple, tumble, tip

51

In the soil and rest. Conceive that marble men
Serenely selves, transfigured by the selves
From which they came, make real the attitudes
Appointed for them and that the pediment
Bears words that are the speech of marble men.
In the glassy sound of your voices, the porcelain cries,
The alto clank of the long recitation, in these
Speak, and in these repeat: *To Be Itself*,
Until the sharply-colored glass transforms
Itself into the speech of the spirit, until
The porcelain bell-borrowings become
Implicit clarities in the way you cry
And are your feelings changed to sound, without
A change, until the waterish ditherings turn
To the tense, the maudlin, true meridian
That is yourselves, when, at last, you are yourselves,
Speaking and strutting broadly, fair and bloomed,
No longer of air but of the breathing earth,
Impassioned seducers and seduced, the pale
Pitched into swelling bodies, upward, drift
In a storm blown into glittering shapes, and flames
Wind-beaten into freshest, brightest fire.

[OWL'S CLOVER]

THE GREENEST CONTINENT

I

Large-leaved and many-footed shadowing,
What god rules over Africa, what shape,
What avuncular cloud-man beamier than spears?

The heaven of Europe is empty, like a Schloss
Abandoned because of taxes . . . It was enough:
It made up for everything, it was all selves
Become rude robes among white candle lights,
Motions of air, robes moving in torrents of air,
And through the torrents a jutting, jagged tower,
A broken wall—and it ceased to exist, became
A Schloss, and empty Schlossbibliothek, the books
For sale in Vienna and Zurich to people in Maine,
Ontario, Canton. It was the way
Things jutted up, the way the jagged stacks,
The foul immovables, came through the clouds,
Colossal blacks that leaped across the points
Of Boucher pink, the sheens of Venetian gray.
That's what did it. Everything did it at last.
The binders did it with armorial books.
And the cooks, the cooks, the bar-men and the maids,
The churches and their long parades, Seville
At Easter on a London screen, the seeds
Of Vilmorin, Verhaeren in his grave,
The flute on the gramophone, the Daimlers that
Dissolved the woods, war and the fatal farce
Of war, the rust on the steeples, these jutted up,
These streaked the mother-of-pearl, the lunar cress.
Everything did.

III

There was a heaven once,
But not that Salzburg of the skies. It was
The spirit's episcopate, hallowed and high,
To which the spirit ascended, to increase
Itself, beyond the utmost increase come

53

From youngest day or oldest night and far
Beyond thought's regulation. There each man,
Through long cloud-cloister-porches, walked alone,
Noble within perfecting solitude,
Like a solitude of the sun, in which the mind
Acquired transparence and beheld itself
And beheld the source from which transparence came;
And there he heard the voices that were once
The confusion of men's voices, intricate
Made extricate by meanings, meanings made
Into a music never touched to sound.
There, too, he saw, since he must see, the domes
Of azure round an upper dome, brightest
Because it rose above them all, stippled
By waverings of stars, the joy of day
And its immaculate fire, the middle dome,
The temple of the altar where each man
Beheld the truth and knew it to be true.

IV

That was never the heaven of Africa, which had
No heaven, had death without a heaven, death
In a heaven of death. Beneath the heavy foils,
Beneath the spangling greens, fear might placate
And the serpent might become a god, quick-eyed,
Rising from indolent coils. If the statue rose,
If once the statue were to rise, if it stood,
Thinly, among the elephantine palms,
Sleekly the serpent would draw himself across.
The horses are a part of a northern sky
Too starkly pallid for the jaguar's light,
In which he and the lion and the serpent hide
Even in sleep, deep in the grass of sleep,

Deep grass that totters under the weight of light.
There sleep and waking fill with jaguar-men
And lion-men and the flicking serpent-kin
In flowery nations, crashing and alert.
No god rules over Africa, no throne,
Single, of burly ivory, inched of gold,
Disposed upon the central of what we see,
That purges the wrack or makes the jungle shine,
As brilliant as mystic, as mystic as single, all
In one, except a throne raised up beyond
Men's bones, beyond their breaths, the black sublime,
Toward which, in the nights, the glittering serpents climb,
Dark-skinned and sinuous, winding upwardly,
Winding and waving, slowly, waving in air,
Darting envenomed eyes about, like fangs,
Hissing, across the silence, puissant sounds.
Death, only, sits upon the serpent throne:
Death, the herdsman of elephants,
To whom the jaguars cry and lions roar
Their petty dirges of fallen forest-men,
Forever hunting or hunted, rushing through
Endless pursuit or endlessly pursued,
Until each tree, each evil-blossomed vine,
Each fretful fern drops down a fear like dew
And Africa, basking in antiquest sun,
Contains for its children not a gill of sweet.

v

Forth from their tabernacles once again
The angels come, armed, gloriously to slay
The black and ruin his sepulchral throne.
Hé quoi! Angels go pricking elephants?
Wings spread and whirling over jaguar-men?

55

Angels tiptoe upon the snowy cones
Of palmy peaks sighting machine-guns? These,
Seraphim of Europe? Pouring out of dawn,
Fresh from the sacred clarities, chanters
Of the pith of mind, cuirassiers against
The milkiest bowmen. This makes a new design,
Filleted angels over flapping ears,
Combatting bushmen for a patch of gourds,
Loosing black slaves to make black infantry,
Angels returning after war with belts
And beads and bangles of gold and trumpets raised,
Racking the world with clarion puffs. This must
Be merely a masquerade or else a rare
Tractatus, of military things, with plates,
Miraculously preserved, full fickle-fine,
Of an imagination flashed with irony
And by a hand of certitude to cut
The heavenly cocks, the bowmen, and the gourds,
The oracular trumpets round and roundly hooped,
In Leonardo's way, to magnify
Concentric bosh. To their tabernacles, then,
Remoter than Athos, the effulgent hordes
Return, affecting roseate aureoles,
To contemplate time's golden paladin
And purpose, to hear the wild bee drone, to feel
The ecstasy of sense in a sensuous air.

VI

But could the statue stand in Africa?
The marble was imagined in the cold.
Its edges were taken from tumultous wind
That beat out slimmest edges in the ear,

Made of the eye an insatiable intellect.
Its surfaces came from distant fire; and it
Was meant to stand, not in a tumbling green,
Intensified and grandiose, but among
The common-places of which it formed a part
And there, by feat extenuations, to make
A visible clear cap, a visible wreath
To men, to houses, streets and the squalid whole.
There it would be of the mode of common dreams,
A ring of horses rising from memory
Or rising in the appointments of desire,
The spirit's natural images, carriers,
The drafts of gay beginnings and bright ends,
Majestic bearers or solemn haulers trapped
In endless elegies. But in Africa
The memory moves on leopards' feet, desire
Appoints its florid messengers with wings
Wildly curvetted, color-scarred, so beaked,
With tongues unclipped and throats so stuffed with thorns,
So clawed, so sopped with sun, that in these things
The message is half-borne. Could marble still
Be marble after the drenching reds, the dark
And drenching crimsons, or endure? It came
If not from winter, from a summer like
A winter's noon, in which the colors sprang
From snow, and would return again to snow,
As summer would return to weazened days.

VII

The diplomats of the cafés expound:
Fromage and coffee and cognac and no gods.
It was a mistake to paint the gods. The gold

Of constellations on the beachy air
Is difficult. It blights in the studios.
Magnificence most shiningly expressed
Is, after all, draped damask pampaluned,
Color and color brightening into one,
A majestic weavers' job, a summer's sweat.
It was a mistake to think of them. They have
No place in the sense of colonists, no place
In Africa. The serpent's throne is dust
At the unbeliever's touch. Cloud-cloisters blow
Out of the eye when the loud wind gathers up
And blows, with heaped-up shoulders loudly blows
And bares an earth that has no gods, and bares
The gods like marble figures fallen, left
In the streets. There will always be cafés and cards
And the obese proprietor, who has a son
In Capricorn. The statue has a form
That will always be and will be everywhere.
Why should it fail to stand? Victoria Platz,
To make its factories content, must have
A cavernous and a cruel past, tropic
Benitia, lapis Ville des Pins must soothe
The impoverished waste with dewy vibrancies
Of April here and May to come. Champagne
On a hot night and a long cigar and talk
About the weather and women and the way
Of things, why bother about the back of stars?
The statue belongs to the cavernous past, belongs
To April here and May to come. Why think,
Why feel the sun or, feeling, why feel more
Than purple paste of fruit, to taste, or leaves
Of purple flowers, to see? The black will still
Be free to sing, if only a sorrowful song.

VIII

Fatal Ananke is the common god.
He looks upon the statue, where it is,
And the sun and the sun-reek piled and peaked above
The jostled ferns, where it might be, having eyes
Of the shape of eyes, like blunt intaglios,
And nothing more. He sees but not by sight.
He does not hear by sound. His spirit knows
Each look and each necessitous cry, as a god
Knows, knowing that he does not care, and knows,
Knowing and meaning that he cannot care.
He sees the angel in the nigger's mind
And hears the nigger's prayer in motets, belched
From pipes that swarm clerestory walls. The voice
In the jungle is a voice in Fontainebleau.
The long recessional at parish eves wails round
The cuckoo trees and the widow of Madrid
Weeps in Segovia. The beggar in Rome
Is the beggar in Bogotá. The kraal
Chants a death that is a medieval death . . .
Fateful Ananke is the final god.
His hymn, his psalm, his cithern song of praise
Is the exile of the disinherited,
Life's foreigners, pale aliens of the mud,
Those whose Jerusalem is Glasgow-frost
Or Paris-rain. He thinks of the noble lives
Of the gods and, for him, a thousand litanies
Are like the perpetual verses in a poet's mind.
He is that obdurate ruler who ordains
For races, not for men, powerful beyond
A grace to nature, a changeless element.
His place is large and high, an ether flamed
By his presence, the seat of his ubiquitous will.

He, only, caused the statue to be made
And he shall fix the place where it will stand.
Be glory to this unmerciful pontifex,
Lord without any deviation, lord
And origin and resplendent end of law,
Sultan of African sultans, starless crown.

◇◇

[OWL'S CLOVER]

A DUCK FOR DINNER

I

The Bulgar said, "After pineapple with fresh mint
We went to walk in the park; for, after all,
The workers do not rise, as Venus rose,
Out of a violet sea. They rise a bit
On summer Sundays in the park, a duck
To a million, a duck with apples and without wine.
They rise to the muddy, metropolitan elms,
To the camellia-chateaux and an inch beyond,
Forgetting work, not caring for angels, hunting a lift,
The triumph of the arcs of heaven's blue
For themselves, and space and time and ease for the duck.
If you caricature the way they rise, yet they rise.
True, only an inch, but an inch at a time, and inch
By inch, Sunday by Sunday, many men.
At least, conceive what these hands from Sweden mean,
These English noses and edged, Italian eyes,
Massed for a head they mean to make for themselves,
From which their grizzled voice will speak and be heard."

O buckskin, O crosser of snowy divides,
For whom men were to be ends in themselves,
Are the cities to breed as mountains bred, the streets
To trundle children like the sea? For you,
Day came upon the spirit as life comes
And deep winds flooded you; for these, day comes,
A penny sun in a tinsel sky, unrhymed,
And the spirit writhes to be wakened, writhes
To see, once more, this hacked-up world of tools,
The heart in slattern pinnacles, the clouds,
Which were their thoughts, squeezed into shapes, the sun
Streamed white and stoked and engined wrick-a-wrack.
In your cadaverous Eden, they desire
The same down-dropping fruit in yellow leaves,
The same return at heavy evening, love
Without any horror of the helpless loss.
The scholar's outline that you had, the print
Of London, the paper of Paris magnified
By poets, the Italian lives preserved
For poverty are gaudy bosh to these.
Their destiny is just as much machine
As death itself, and never can be changed
By print or paper, the trivial chance foregone,
And only an agony of dreams can help,
Not the agony of a single dreamer, but
The wide night mused by tell-tale muttering,
Time's fortune near, the sleepless sleepers moved
By the torture of things that will be realized,
Will, will, but how and all of them asking how
And sighing. These lives are not your lives, O free,
O bold, that rode your horses straight away.

Again the Bulgar said, "There are more things
Than poodles in Pomerania. This man
Is all the birds he ever heard and that,
The admiral of his race and everyman,
Infected by unreality, rapt round
By dense unreason, irreproachable force,
Is cast in pandemonium, flittered, howled
By harmonies beyond known harmony.
These bands, these swarms, these motions, what of them?
They keep to the paths of the skeleton architect
Of the park. They obey the rules of every skeleton.
But of what are they thinking, of what, in spite of the duck,
In spite of the watch-chains aus Wien, in spite
Of the Balkan shoes, the bonnets from Moldau, beards
From the steppes, are they being part, feeling the strength,
Seeing the fulgent shadows upward heaped,
Spelling out pandects and haggard institutes?
Is each man thinking his separate thoughts or, for once,
Are all men thinking together as one, thinking
Each other's thoughts, thinking a single thought,
Disclosed in everything, transcended, poised
For the syllable, poised for the touch? But that
Apocalypse was not contrived for parks,
Geranium budgets, pay-roll water-falls,
The clank of the carrousel and, under the trees,
The sheep-like falling-in of distances,
Converging on the statue, white and high."

Then Basilewsky in the band-stand played
"Concerto for Airplane and Pianoforte,"
The newest Soviet reclame. Profound

Abortion, fit for the enchanting of basilisks.
They chanced to think. Suppose the future fails.
If platitude and inspiration are alike
As evils, and if reason, fatuous fire,
Is only another egoist wearing a mask,
What man of folk-lore shall rebuild the world,
What lesser man shall measure sun and moon,
What super-animal dictate our fates?
As the man the state, not as the state the man,
Perennial doctrine and most florid truth;
But man means more, means the million and the duck.
It cannot mean a sea-wide country strewn
With squalid cells, unless New York is Cocos
Or Chicago a Kaffir kraal. It means this mob.
The man in the band-stand could be orator.
It may be the future depends on an orator,
Some pebble-chewer practiced in Tyrian speech,
An apparition, twanging instruments
Within us hitherto unknown, he that
Confounds all opposites and spins a sphere
Created, like a bubble, of bright sheens,
With a tendency to bulge as it floats away.
Basilewsky's bulged before it floated, turned
Caramel and would not, could not float. And yet
In an age of concentric mobs would any sphere
Escape all deformation, much less this,
This source and patriarch of other spheres,
This base of every future, vibrant spring,
The volcano Apostrophe, the sea Behold?
Suppose, instead of failing, it never comes,
This future, although the elephants pass and the blare,
Prolonged, repeated and once more prolonged,
Goes off a little on the side and stops.

Yet to think of the future is a genius,
To think of the future is a thing and he
That thinks of it is inscribed on walls and stands
Complete in bronze on enormous pedestals.

v

The statue is white and high, white brillianter
Than the color white and high beyond any height
That rises in the air. The sprawlers on the grass
See more than marble in their eyes, see more
Than the horses quivering to be gone, flashed through
With senses chiseled on bright stone. They see
The metropolitan of mind, they feel
The central of the composition, in which
They live. They see and feel themselves, seeing
And feeling the world in which they live. The manes,
The leaping bodies, come from the truculent hand,
The stubborn eye, of the conformer who conforms
The manes to his image of the flying wind,
The leaping bodies to his strength, convulsed
By tautest pinions lifted through his thought.
The statue is the sculptor not the stone.
In this he carved himself, he carved his age,
He carved the feathery walkers standing by,
Twitching a little with crude souvenirs
Of young identities, Aprilian stubs.
Exceeding sex, he touched another race,
Above our race, yet of ourselves transformed,
Don Juan turned furious divinity,
Ethereal compounder, pater patriae,
Great mud-ancestor, oozer and Abraham,
Progenitor wearing the diamond crown of crowns,
He from whose beard the future springs, elect.

64

More of ourselves in a world that is more our own,
For the million, perhaps, two ducks instead of one;
More of ourselves, the mood of life made strong
As by a juicier season; and more our own
As against each other, the dead, the phantomesque.

VI

If these were theoretical people, like
Small bees of spring, sniffing the coldest buds
Of a time to come—A shade of horror turns
The bees to scorpions blackly-barbed, a shade
Of fear changes the scorpions to skins
Concealed in glittering grass, dank reptile skins.
The civil fiction, the calico idea,
The Johnsonian composition, abstract man,
All are evasions like a repeated phrase,
Which, by its repetition, comes to bear
A meaning without a meaning. These people have
A meaning within the meaning they convey,
Walking the paths, watching the gilding sun,
To be swept across them when they are revealed,
For a moment, once each century or two.
The future for them is always the deepest dome,
The darkest blue of the dome and the wings around
The giant Phosphor of their earliest prayers.
Once each century or two. But then so great,
So epical a twist, catastrophe
For Isaac Watts: the diverting of the dream
Of heaven from heaven to the future, as a god,
Takes time and tinkering, melodious
And practical. The envoi to the past
Is largely another winding of the clock.
The tempo, in short, of this complicated shift,

65

With interruptions by vast hymns, blood odes,
Parades of whole races with attendant bands,
And the bees, the scorpions, the men that think,
The summer Sundays in the park, must be
A leaden ticking circular in width.
How shall we face the edge of time? We walk
In the park. We regret we have no nightingale.
We must have the throstle on the gramophone.
Where shall we find more than derisive words?
When shall lush chorals spiral through our fire
And daunt that old assassin, heart's desire?

❖◈❖

[OWL'S CLOVER]

SOMBRE FIGURATION

I

There is a man whom rhapsodies of change,
Of which he is the cause, have never changed
And never will, a subman under all
The rest, to whom in the end the rest return,
The man below the man below the man,
Steeped in night's opium, evading day.

II

We have grown weary of the man that thinks.
He thinks and it is not true. The man below
Imagines and it is true, as if he thought
By imagining, anti-logician, quick
With a logic of transforming certitudes.
It is not that he was born in another land,
Powdered with primitive lights, and lives with us

66

In glimpses, on the edge or at the tip,
Playing a crackled reed, wind-stopped, in bleats.
He was born within us as a second self,
A self of parents who have never died,
Whose lives return, simply, upon our lips,
Their words and ours; in what we see, their hues
Without a season, unstinted in livery,
And ours, of rigid measure, a miser's paint;
And most in what we hear, sound brushed away,
A mumbling at the elbow, turgid tunes,
As of insects or cloud-stricken birds, away
And away, dialogues between incognitos.
He dwells below, the man below, in less
Than body and in less than mind, ogre,
Inhabitant, in less than shape, of shapes
That are dissembled in vague memory
Yet still retain resemblances, remain
Remembrances, a place of a field of lights,
As a church is a bell and people are an eye,
A cry, the pallor of a dress, a touch.
He turns us into scholars, studying
The masks of music. We perceive each mask
To be the musician's own and, thence, become
An audience to mimics glistening
With meanings, doubled by the closest sound,
Mimics that play on instruments discerned
In the beat of the blood.
                              Green is the path we take
Between chimeras and garlanded the way,
The down-descent into November's void.
The spontaneities of rain or snow
Surprise the sterile rationalist who sees
Maidens in bloom, bulls under sea, the lark

On urns and oak-leaves twisted into rhyme.
The man, but not the man below, for whom
The pheasant in a field was pheasant, field,
Until they changed to eagle in white air,
Lives in a fluid, not on solid rock.
The solid was an age, a period
With appropriate, largely English, furniture,
Barbers with charts of the only possible modes,
Cities that would not wash away in the mist,
Each man in his asylum maundering,
Policed by the hope of Christmas. Summer night,
Night gold, and winter night, night silver, these
Were the fluid, the cat-eyed atmosphere, in which
The man and the man below were reconciled,
The east wind in the west, order destroyed,
The cycle of the solid having turned.

III

High up in heaven a sprawling portent moves,
As if it bears all darkness in its bulk.
But this we cannot see. The shaggy top
Broods in tense meditation, constantly,
On the city, on which it leans, the people there,
Its shadow on their houses, on their walls,
Their beds, their faces drawn in distant sleep.
This is invisible. The supporting arms
Reach from the horizons, rim to rim,
While the shaggy top collects itself to do
And the shoulders turn, breathing immense intent.
All this is hidden from sight.

                                    It is the form
Of a generation that does not know itself,
Still questioning if to crush the soaring stacks,

The churches, like dalmatics stooped in prayer,
And the people suddenly evil, waked, accused,
Destroyed by a vengeful movement of the arms,
A mass overtaken by the blackest sky,
Each one as part of the total wrath, obscure
In slaughter; or if to match its furious wit
Against the sleepers to re-create for them,
Out of their wilderness, a special fane,
Midmost in its design, the arms grown swift,
The body bent, like Hercules, to build.
If the fane were clear, if the city shone in mind,
If more than the wished-for ruin racked the night,
If more than pity and despair were sure,
If the flashy extravaganzas of the lean
Could ever make them fat, these are delays
For ponderous revolving, without help.
And, while revolving, ancient hyacinths
And fragrant fomentations of the spring
Come, baffling discontent. These, too, must be
Revolved.
       Which counts for most, the anger borne
In anger; or the fear that from the death
Of evil, evil springs; or catholic hope,
Young catechumen answering the worms?
The man below beholds the portent poised,
An image of his making, beyond the eye,
Poised, but poised as the mind through which a storm
Of other images blows, images of time
Like the time of the portent, images like leaves,
Except that this is an image of black spring
And those the leaves of autumn-afterwards,
Leaves of the autumns in which the man below
Lived as the man lives now, and hated, loved,

As the man hates now, loves now, the self-same things.
The year's dim elongations stretch below
To rumbled rock, its bright projections lie
The shallowest iris on the emptiest eye.
The future must bear within it every past,
Not least the pasts destroyed, magniloquent
Syllables, pewter on ebony, yet still
A board for bishops' grapes, the happy form
That revolution takes for connoisseurs:
The portent may itself be memory;
And memory may itself be time to come
And must be, when the portent, changed, takes on
A mask up-gathered brilliantly from the dirt,
And memory's lord is the lord of prophecy
And steps forth, priestly in severity,
Yet lord, a mask of flame, the sprawling form
A wandering orb upon a path grown clear.

IV

High up in heaven the sprawling portent moves.
The statue in a crow's perspective of trees
Stands brimming white, chiaroscuro scaled
To space. To space? The statue scaled to space
Would be a ring of heads and haunches, torn
From size, backs larger than the eye, not flesh
In marble, but marble massive as the thrust
Of that which is not seen and cannot be.
The portent would become man-haggard to
A race of dwarfs, the meditative arms
And head a shadow trampled under hoofs,
Man-misty to a race star-humped, astride
In a clamor thudding up from central earth.
Not the space in camera of the man below,
Immeasurable, the space in which he knows

The locust's titter and the turtle's sob.
The statue stands in true perspective. Crows
Give only their color to the leaves. The trees
Are full of fanfares of farewell, as night
And the portent end in night, composed, before
Its wheel begins to turn.

                      The statue stands
In hum-drum space, farewell, farewell, by day
The green, white, blue of the ballad-eye, by night
The mirror of other nights combined in one.
The spring is hum-drum like an instrument,
That a man without passion plays in an aimless way.
Even imagination has an end,
When the statue is not a thing imagined, a stone
That changed in sleep. It is, it is, let be
The way it came, let be what it may become.
Even the man below, the subverter, stops
The flight of emblemata through his mind,
Thoughts by descent. To flourish the great cloak we wear
At night, to turn away from the abominable
Farewells and, in the darkness, to feel again
The reconciliation, the rapture of a time
Without imagination, without past
And without future, a present time, is that
The passion, indifferent to the poet's hum,
That we conceal? A passion to fling the cloak,
Adorned for a multitude, in a gesture spent
In the gesture's whim, a passion merely to be
For the gaudium of being, Jocundus instead
Of the black-blooded scholar, the man of the cloud, to be
The medium man among other medium men,
The cloak to be clipped, the night to be re-designed,
Its land-breath to be stifled, its color changed,
Night and the imagination being one.

71

STANZAS FOR
"THE MAN WITH THE BLUE GUITAR"

I

The day is green and the wind is young.
The world is young and I play my guitar.

The skeletons sit on the wall. They drop
Red mango peels and I play my guitar.

The gate is not jasper. It is not bone.
It is mud and mud long baked in the sun,

An eighteenth century fern or two
And the dewiest beads of insipid fruit

And honey from thorns and I play my guitar.
The negro with laundry passes me by.

The boatman goes humming. He smokes a cigar
And I play my guitar. The vines have grown wild.

The oranges glitter as part of the sky,
A tiara from Cohen's, this summer sea.

II

I play them on a blue guitar
And then things are not as they are.

The shapings of the instrument
Distort the shape of what I meant,

72

Which takes a shape by accident.
Yet what I mean I always say.

The accident is how I play.
I still intend things as they are.

The greenish quaverings of day
Quiver upon the blue guitar.

III

To ride an old mule round the keys—
Mature emotional gesture, that—

Blond weather. One is born a saint,
Complete in wind-sucked poverty.

In such an air, poor as one's mule.
Here, if there was a peak to climb,

One could watch the blue sea's blueness flow
And blacken into indigo.

But squint and squeak, where no people are:
On such a peak, the blue guitar—

Blond weather. Give the mule his hay.
True, things are people as they are.

FIVE GROTESQUE PIECES

I

One of Those Hibiscuses of Damozels

She was all of her airs and, for all of her airs,
She was all of her airs and ears and hairs,
Her pearly ears, her jeweler's ears
And the painted hairs that composed her hair.

In spite of her airs, that's what she was. She was all
Of her airs, as surely cologne as that she was bone
Was what she was and flesh, sure enough, but airs;
Rather rings than fingers, rather fingers than hands.

How could you ever, how could think that you saw her,
Knew her, how could you see the woman that wore the beads,
The ball-like beads, the bazzling and the bangling beads
Or hear her step in the way she walked?

This was not how she walked for she walked in a way
And the way was more than the walk and was hard to see.
You saw the eye-blue, sky-blue, eye-blue, and the powdered ears
And the cheeks like flower-pots under her hair.

II

Hieroglyphica

People that live in the biggest houses
Often have the worst breaths.
Hey-di-ho.

The humming-bird is the national bird
Of the humming-bird.
Hey-di-ho.

X understands Aristotle
Instinctively, not otherwise.
Hey-di-ho.

Let wise men piece the world together with wisdom
Or poets with holy magic.
Hey-di-ho.

III

Communications of Meaning

The parrot in its palmy boughs
Repeats the farmer's almanac.

A duckling of the wildest blood
Convinces Athens with its quack.

Much too much thought, too little thought,
No thought at all: a guttural growl,

A snort across the silverware,
The petals flying through the air.

IV

What They Call Red Cherry Pie

Meyer is a bum. He eats his pie.
He eats red cherry pie and never says—
He makes no choice of words—

75

Cherries are ri . . . He would never say that.
He could not. Neither of us could ever say that.
But Meyer is a bum.

He says "That's what I call red cherry pie."
And that's his way. And that's my way as well.
We two share that at least.

What is it that we share? Red cherry pie
When cherries are in season, or, at least
The way we speak of it.

Meyer has my five senses. I have his.
This matters most in things that matter least.
And that's red cherry pie.

v

Outside of Wedlock

The strong music of hard times,
In a world forever without a plan
For itself as a world,
Must be played on the concertina.

The poor piano forte
Whimpers when the moon above East Hartford
Wakes us to the emotion, grand fortissimo,
Of our sense of evil,

Of our sense that time has been
Like water running in a gutter
Through an alley to nowhere,
Without beginning or the concept of an end.

The old woman that knocks at the door
Is not our grandiose destiny.
It is an old bitch, an old drunk,
That has been yelling in the dark.

Sing for her the seventy-fold Amen,
White February wind,
Through banks and banks of voices,
In the cathedral-shanty,

To the sound of the concertina,
Like the voice of all our ancestors,
The *père* Benjamin, the *mère* Blandenah,
Saying we have forgot them, they never lived.

❖◈❖

LIFE ON A BATTLESHIP

I

The rape of the bourgeoisie accomplished, the men
Returned on board *The Masculine*. That night,
The captain said,

   "The war between classes is
A preliminary, provincial phase,
Of the war between individuals. In time,
When earth has become a paradise, it will be
A paradise full of assassins. Suppose I seize
The ship, make it my own and, bit by bit,
Seize yards and docks, machinery and men,
As others have, and then, unlike the others,

77

Instead of building ships, in numbers, build
A single ship, a cloud on the sea, the largest
Possible machine, a divinity of steel,
Of which I am the captain. Given what I intend,
The ship would become the center of the world.
My cabin as the center of the ship and I
As the center of the cabin, the center of
The divinity, the divinity's mind, the mind
Of the world would have only to ring and ft!
It would be done. If, only to please myself,
I said that men should wear stone masks and, to make
The word respected, fired ten thousand guns
In mid-Atlantic, bellowing, to command,
It would be done. And once the thing was done,
Once the assassins wore stone masks and did
As I wished, once they fell backward when my breath
Blew against them or bowed from the hips, when I turned
My head, the sorrow of the world, except
As man is natural, would be at an end."

II

So posed, the captain drafted rules of the world,
Regulæ mundi, as apprentice of
Descartes:

      First. The grand simplifications reduce
Themselves to one.

          Of this the captain said,
"It is a lesser law than the one itself,
Unless it is the one itself, or unless
The Masculine, much magnified, that cloud
On the sea, is both law and evidence in one,
As the final simplification is meant to be.
It is clear that it is not a moral law.

It appears to be what there is of life compressed
Into its own illustration, a divinity
Like any other, rex by right of the crown,
The jewels in his beard, the mystic wand,
And imperator because of death to oppose
The illustrious arms, the symbolic horns, the red
For battle, the purple for victory. But if
It is the absolute why must it be
This immemorial grandiose, why not
A cockle-shell, a trivial emblem great
With its final force, a thing invincible
In more than phrase? There's the true masculine,
The spirit's ring and seal, the naked heart.
It was a rabbi's question. Let the rabbis reply.
It implies a flaw in the battleship, a defeat
As of a make-believe.

III

Second. The part

Is the equal of the whole.

The captain said,

"The ephebi say that there is only the whole,
The race, the nation, the state. But society
Is a phase. We approach a society
Without a society, the politicians
Gone, as in Calypso's isle or in Citare,
Where I or one or the part is the equal of
The whole. The sound of a dozen orchestras
May rush to extinguish the theme, the basses thump
And the fiddles smack, the horns yahoo, the flutes
Strike fire, but the part is the equal of the whole,
Unless society is a mystical mass.
This is a thing to twang a philosopher's sleep,

79

A vacuum for the dozen orchestras
To fill, the grindstone of antiquest time,
Breakfast in Paris, music and madness and mud,
The perspective squirming as it tries to take
A shape, the vista twisted and burning, a thing
Kicked through the roof, caressed by the river-side.
On *The Masculine* one asserts and fires the guns.
But one lives to think of this growing, this pushing life,
The vine, at the roots, this vine of Key West, splurging,
Covered one morning with blue, one morning with white,
Coming from the East, forcing itself to the West,
The jungle of tropical part and tropical whole."

IV

The first and second rules are reconciled
In a Third: The whole cannot exist without
The parts. Thus: Out of the number of his thoughts
The thinker knows. The gunman of the commune
Kills the commune.

               Captain, high captain, how is it, now,
With our affair, our destiny, our hash?
Your guns are not rhapsodic strophes, red
And true. The good, the strength, the sceptre moves
From constable to god, from earth to air,
The circle of the sceptre growing large
And larger as it moves, moving toward
A hand that fails to seize it. High captain, the grand
Simplifications approach but do not touch
The ultimate one, though they are parts of it.
Without them it could not exist. That's our affair,
That's this grandiose battleship of yours and your
Regulæ mundi . . . That much is out of the way.
If the sceptre returns to earth, still moving, still

Precious from the region of the hand, still bright
With saintly imagination and the stains
Of martyrs, to be arrogant in our need,
It will be all we have. Our fate is our own:
Our good, from this the rhapsodic strophes flow,
Through prophets and succeeding prophets, whose prophecies
Grow large and larger. Our fate is our own. The hand,
It must be the hand of one, it must be the hand
Of a man, that seizes our strength, will seize it to be
Merely the center of a circle, spread
To the final full, an end without rhetoric.

⊙⊦

THE WOMAN THAT HAD MORE BABIES
THAN THAT

I

An acrobat on the border of the sea
Observed the waves, the rising and the swell
And the first line spreading up the beach; again,
The rising and the swell, the preparation
And the first line foaming over the sand; again,
The rising and the swell, the first line's glitter,
Like a dancer's skirt, flung round and settling down.
This was repeated day by day. The waves
Were mechanical, muscular. They never changed,
They never stopped, a repetition repeated
Continually—There is a woman has had
More babies than that. The merely revolving wheel
Returns and returns, along the dry, salt shore.

81

There is a mother whose children need more than that.
She is not the mother of landscapes but of those
That question the repetition on the shore,
Listening to the whole sea for a sound
Of more or less, ascetically sated
By amical tones.

     The acrobat observed
The universal machine. There he perceived
The need for a thesis, a music constant to move.

II

Berceuse, transatlantic. The children are men, old men,
Who, when they think and speak of the central man,
Of the humming of the central man, the whole sound
Of the sea, the central humming of the sea,
Are old men breathed on by a maternal voice,
Children and old men and philosophers,
Bald heads with their mother's voice still in their ears.
The self is a cloister full of remembered sounds
And of sounds so far forgotten, like her voice,
That they return unrecognized. The self
Detects the sound of a voice that doubles its own,
In the images of desire, the forms that speak,
The ideas that come to it with a sense of speech.
The old men, the philosophers, are haunted by that
Maternal voice, the explanation at night.
They are more than parts of the universal machine.
Their need in solitude: that is the need,
The desire, for the fiery lullaby.

III

      If her head
Stood on a plain of marble, high and cold;

82

If her eyes were chinks in which the sparrows built;
If she was deaf with falling grass in her ears—
But there is more than a marble, massive head.
They find her in the crackling summer night,
In the *Duft* of towns, beside a window, beside
A lamp, in a day of the week, the time before spring,
A manner of walking, yellow fruit, a house,
A street. She has a supernatural head.
On her lips familiar words become the words
Of an elevation, an elixir of the whole.

<hr/>

STANZAS FOR "EXAMINATION OF THE HERO IN A TIME OF WAR"

I

An immense drum rolls through a clamor of people.
The women with eyes like opals vanish
And men look inwardly, for the emblem:
The star-yplaited, visible sanction,
The strength of death or triumph. Oheu!
That the choice should come on them so early.
They had hardly grown to know the sunshine,
Before the sun brought them that destruction
And with it, the antiquest wishing
To bear virile grace before their fellows,
Regardless of gods that were praised in goldness
And triple chime . . . The self-same rhythm
Moves in lamenting and the fatal,
The bold, obedience to Ananke.

83

The words are in the way and thoughts are.
Forgetful of death in war, there rises
From the middens of life, rotten and acrid,
A race that is a hero, entirely
Without heroic words, heroic
Hybrids impossible to the wardens
Within us. False hybrids and false heroes,
Half men and half new, modern monsters . . .
The hero is the man who is himself, who
As a man among other men, divested
Of attributes, naked of myth, true,
Not true to this or that, but true, knows
The frame of the hero. Yet, willingly, he
Becomes the hero without heroics.

It is the common man against evil,
Now. War as a punishment. The hero
As hangman, a little sick of blood, of
The deep sigh with which the hanging ends, close
To his gorge, hangman, once helmet-maker
And headsman and trumpeteer and feather
In casque and scaffold orator, fortified
By gestures of a mortal perfection.
What misanthrope, impugning heroica,
Maligning his costumes and disputing
His roles, would leave to the clouds the righting,
The immediate and intolerable need
Of the very body instinctively crying
A challenge to a final solution.

DESIRE & THE OBJECT

It is curious that I should have spoken of Raël,
When it never existed, the order
That I desired. It could be—

Curious that I should have spoken of Jaffa
By her sexual name, saying that that high marriage
Could be, it could be.

I had not invented my own thoughts,
When I was sleeping, nor by day,
So that thinking was a madness, and is:

It was to be as mad as everyone was,
And is. Perhaps I had been moved
By feeling the like of thought in sleep,

So that feeling was a madness, and is.
Consider that I had asked
Was it desire that created Raël

Or was it Jaffa that created desire?
The origin could have its origin.
It could be, could be.

It could be that the sun shines
Because I desire it to shine or else
That I desire it to shine because it shines.

RECITATION AFTER DINNER

A poem about tradition could easily be
A windy thing . . . However, since we are here,
Cousins of the calendar if not of kin,
To be a part of tradition, to identify
Its actual appearance, suppose we begin
By giving it a form. But the character
Of tradition does not easily take form.

It is not a set of laws. Therefore, its form
Is not lean marble, trenchant-eyed. There is
No book of the past in which time's senators
Have inscribed life's do and don't. The commanding codes
Are not tradition. To identify it
Is to define its form, to say: this image
Is its body visible to the important eye.

The bronze of the wise man seated in repose
Is not its form. Tradition is wise but not
The figure of the wise man fixed in sense.
The scholar is always distant in the space
Around him and in that distance meditates
Things still more distant. And tradition is near.
It joins and does not separate. What, then,

Is its true form? Is it the memory
That hears a pin fall in New Amsterdam
Or sees the new North River heaping up
Dutch ice on English boats? The memory

Is part of the classic imagination, posed
Too often to be more than secondhand.
Tradition is much more than the memory.

Is it experience, say, the final form
To which all other forms, at last, return,
The frame of a repeated effect, is it that?
Are we characters in an arithmetic
Or letters of a curious alphabet;
And is tradition an unfamiliar sum,
A legend scrawled in script we cannot read?

It has a clear, a single, a solid form,
That of the son who bears upon his back
The father that he loves, and bears him from
The ruins of the past, out of nothing left,
Made noble by the honor he receives,
As if in a golden cloud. The son restores
The father. He hides his ancient blue beneath

His own bright red. But he bears him out of love,
His life made double by his father's life,
Ascending the humane. This is the form
Tradition wears, the clear, the single form
The solid shape, Æneas seen, perhaps,
By Nicholas Poussin, yet nevertheless
A tall figure upright in a giant's air.

The father keeps on living in the son, the world
Of the father keeps on living in the world
Of the son. These survivals out of time and space
Come to us every day. And yet they are
Merely parts of the general fiction of the mind:

Survivals of a good that we have loved,
Made eminent in a reflected seeming-so.

◇◇◇

THIS AS INCLUDING THAT

This rock and the dry birds
Fluttering in blue leaves,

This rock and the priest,
The priest of nothingness who intones—

It is true that you live on this rock
And in it. It is wholly you.

It is true that there are thoughts
That move in the air as large as air,

That are almost not our own, but thoughts
To which we are related,

In an association like yours
With the rock and mine with you.

The iron settee is cold.
A fly crawls on the balustrades.

MEMORANDUM

The katy-dids at Ephrata return
But this time at another place.
It is the same sound, the same season,
But it is not Ephrata.

You said the dew falls in the blood.
The dew falls deep in the mind
On life itself and there the katy-dids
Keep whanging their brass wings. . . .

Say this to Pravda, tell the damned rag
That the peaches are slowly ripening.
Say that the American moon comes up
Cleansed clean of lousy Byzantium.

Say that in the clear Atlantic night
The plums are blue on the trees. The katy-dids
Bang cymbals as they used to do.
Millions hold millions in their arms.

❂❁

FIRST WARMTH

I wonder, have I lived a skeleton's life,
As a questioner about reality,

A countryman of all the bones of the world?
Now, here, the warmth I had forgotten becomes

Part of the major reality, part of
An appreciation of a reality;

And thus an elevation, as if I lived
With something I could touch, touch every way.

◇◇◇

THE SICK MAN

Bands of black men seem to be drifting in the air,
In the South, bands of thousands of black men,
Playing mouth-organs in the night or, now, guitars.

Here in the North, late, late, there are voices of men,
Voices in chorus, singing without words, remote and deep,
Drifting choirs, long movements and turnings of sounds.

And in a bed in one room, alone, a listener
Waits for the unison of the music of the drifting bands
And the dissolving chorals, waits for it and imagines

The words of winter in which these two will come together,
In the ceiling of the distant room, in which he lies,
The listener, listening to the shadows, seeing them,

Choosing out of himself, out of everything within him,
Speech for the quiet, good hail of himself, good hail, good hail,
The peaceful, blissful words, well-tuned, well-sung, well-spoken.

AS AT A THEATRE

Another sunlight might make another world,
Green, more or less, in green and blue in blue,
Like taste distasting the first fruit of a vine,
Like an eye too young to grapple its primitive,
Like the artifice of a new reality,
Like the chromatic calendar of time to come.

It might be the candle of another being,
Ragged in unkempt perceptions, that stands
And meditates an image of itself,
Studies and shapes a tallowy image, swarmed
With slight, prismatic reeks not recollected,
A bubble without a wall on which to hang.

The curtains, when pulled, might show another whole,
An azure outre-terre, oranged and rosed,
At the elbow of Copernicus, a sphere,
A universe without life's limp and lack,
Philosophers' end . . . What difference would it make,
So long as the mind, for once, fulfilled itself?

THE DESIRE TO MAKE LOVE IN A PAGODA

Among the second selves, sailor, observe
The rioter that appears when things are changed,

Asserting itself in an element that is free,
In the alien freedom that such selves degustate:

In the first inch of night, the stellar summering
At three-quarters gone, the morning's prescience,

As if, alone on a mountain, it saw far-off
An innocence approaching toward its peak.

◇◇

NUNS PAINTING WATER-LILIES

These pods are part of the growth of life within life:
Part of the unpredictable sproutings, as of

The youngest, the still fuzz-eyed, odd fleurettes,
That could come in a slight lurching of the scene,

A swerving, a tilting, a little lengthening,
A few more hours of day, the unravelling

Of a ruddier summer, a birth that fetched along
The supernatural of its origin.

Inside our queer chapeaux, we seem, on this bank,
To be part of a tissue, a clearness of the air,

That matches, today, a clearness of the mind.
It is a special day. We mumble the words

Of saints not heard of until now, unnamed,
In aureoles that are over-dazzling crests . . .

We are part of a fraicheur, inaccessible
Or accessible only in the most furtive fiction.

❖◇

THE ROLE OF THE IDEA IN POETRY

Ask of the philosopher why he philosophizes,
Determined thereto, perhaps by his father's ghost,
Permitting nothing to the evening's edge.

The father does not come to adorn the chant.
One father proclaims another, the patriarchs
Of truth. They stride across and are masters of

The chant and discourse there, more than wild weather
Or clouds that hang lateness on the sea. They become
A time existing after much time has passed.

Therein, day settles and thickens round a form—
Blue-bold on its pedestal—that seems to say,
"I am the greatness of the new-found night."

◊⟩◊⟨◊⟩◊⟨◊⟩◊⟨◊⟩◊⟨◊⟩◊⟨◊⟩◊⟨◊⟩◊⟨◊⟩◊⟨◊⟩◊⟨◊⟩◊⟨◊⟩◊⟨◊⟩◊⟨◊⟩◊⟨◊⟩◊⟨◊⟩◊⟨◊⟩◊⟩

AMERICANA

The first soothsayers of the land, the man
In a field, the man on the side of a hill, all men
In a health of weather, knowing a few, old things,

93

(Remote from the deadly general of men,
The over-populace of the idea, the voices
Hard to be told from thoughts, the repeated drone

Of other lives becoming a total drone,
A sense separate that receives and holds the rest,
That which is human and yet final, like

A man that looks at himself in a glass and finds
It is the man in the glass that lives, not he.
He is the image, the second, the unreal,

The abstraction. He inhabits another man,
Other men, and not this grass, this valid air.
He is not himself. He is vitally deprived . . .)

These things he thinks of, as the buckskin hoop-la,
In a returning, a seeming of return,
Flaunts that first fortune, which he wanted so much.

◇◇

THE SOULS OF WOMEN AT NIGHT

Now, being invisible, I walk without mantilla,
In the much-horned night, as its chief personage.
Owls warn me and with tuft-eared watches keep

Distance between me and the five-times-sensed,
In these stations, in which nothing has been lost,
Sight least, but metaphysical blindness gained,

The blindness in which seeing would be false,
A fantastic irruption. Salute you, cata-sisters,
Ancient amigas, knowing partisans—

Or is it I that, wandering, know, one-sensed,
Not one of the five, and keep a rendezvous,
Of the loftiest amour, in a human midnight?

❀◇

A DISCOVERY OF THOUGHT

At the antipodes of poetry, dark winter,
When the trees glitter with that which despoils them,
Daylight evaporates, like a sound one hears in sickness.

One is a child again. The gold beards of waterfalls
Are dissolved as in an infancy of blue snow.
It is an arbor against the wind, a pit in the mist,

A trinkling in the parentage of the north,
The cricket of summer forming itself out of ice.
And always at this antipodes, of leaden loaves

Held in the hands of blue men that are lead within,
One thinks that it could be that the first word spoken,
The desire for speech and meaning gallantly fulfilled,

The gathering of the imbecile against his motes
And the wry antipodes whirled round the world away—
One thinks, when the houses of New England catch the first
  sun,

95

The first word would be of the susceptible being arrived,
The immaculate disclosure of the secret no more obscured.
The sprawling of winter might suddenly stand erect,

Pronouncing its new life and ours, not autumn's prodigal re-
    turned,
But an antipodal, far-fetched creature, worthy of birth,
The true tone of the metal of winter in what it says:

The accent of deviation in the living thing
That is its life preserved, the effort to be born
Surviving being born, the event of life.

❀❀❀❀❀❀❀❀❀❀❀❀❀❀❀❀❀❀❀❀❀❀❀❀❀❀❀❀❀❀❀❀❀❀

THE COURSE OF A PARTICULAR

Today the leaves cry, hanging on branches swept by wind,
Yet the nothingness of winter becomes a little less.   1
It is still full of icy shades and shapen snow.

The leaves cry . . . One holds off and merely hears the cry.
It is a busy cry, concerning someone else.
And though one says that one is part of everything,

There is a conflict, there is a resistance involved;
And being part is an exertion that declines:
One feels the life of that which gives life as it is.

The leaves cry. It is not a cry of divine attention,
Nor the smoke-drift of puffed-out heroes, nor human cry.
It is the cry of leaves that do not transcend themselves,

In the absence of fantasia, without meaning more
Than they are in the final finding of the air, in the thing
Itself, until, at last, the cry concerns no one at all.

◇◇◇

HOW NOW, O, BRIGHTENER . . .

Something of the trouble of the mind
Remains in the sight, and in sayings of the sight,
Of the spring of the year,

Trouble in the spillage and first sparkle of sun,
The green-edged yellow and yellow and blue and blue-edged
    green—
The trouble of the mind

Is a residue, a land, a rain, a warmth,
A time, an apparition and nourishing element
And simple love,

In which the spectra have dewy favor and live
And take from this restlessly unhappy happiness
Their stunted looks.

✿◈

THE DOVE IN SPRING

Brooder, brooder, deep beneath its walls—
A small howling of the dove
Makes something of the little there,

The little and the dark, and that
In which it is and that in which
It is established. There the dove

Makes this small howling, like a thought
That howls in the mind or like a man
Who keeps seeking out his identity

In that which is and is established . . . It howls
Of the great sizes of an outer bush
And the great misery of the doubt of it,

Of stripes of silver that are strips
Like slits across a space, a place
And state of being large and light.

There is this bubbling before the sun,
This howling at one's ear, too far
For daylight and too near for sleep.

❀❀❀❀❀❀❀❀❀❀❀❀❀❀❀❀❀❀❀❀❀❀❀❀❀❀❀

FAREWELL WITHOUT A GUITAR

Spring's bright paradise has come to this.
Now the thousand-leaved green falls to the ground.
Farewell, my days.

The thousand-leaved red
Comes to this thunder of light
As its autumnal terminal—

A Spanish storm,
A wide, still Aragonese,
In which the horse walks home without a rider,

Head down. The reflections and repetitions,
The blows and buffets of fresh senses
Of the rider that was,

Are a final construction,
Like glass and sun, of male reality
And of that other and her desire.

<hr />

THE SAIL OF ULYSSES

Under the shape of his sail, Ulysses,
Symbol of the seeker, crossing by night
The giant sea, read his own mind.
He said, "As I know, I am and have
The right to be." Guiding his boat
Under the middle stars, he said:

I

"If knowledge and the thing known are one
So that to know a man is to be
That man, to know a place is to be
That place, and it seems to come to that;
And if to know one man is to know all
And if one's sense of a single spot
Is what one knows of the universe,

99

Then knowledge is the only life,
The only sun of the only day,
The only access to true ease,
The deep comfort of the world and fate.

II

There is a human loneliness,
A part of space and solitude,
In which knowledge cannot be denied,
In which nothing of knowledge fails,
The luminous companion, the hand,
The fortifying arm, the profound
Response, the completely answering voice,
That which is more than anything else
The right within us and about us,
Joined, the triumphant vigor, felt,
The inner direction on which we depend,
That which keeps us the little that we are,
The aid of greatness to be and the force.

III

This is the true creator, the waver
Waving purpling wands, the thinker
Thinking gold thoughts in a golden mind,
Loftily jingled, radiant,
The joy of meaning in design
Wrenched out of chaos . . . The quiet lamp
For this creator is a lamp
Enlarging like a nocturnal ray
The space in which it stands, the shine
Of darkness, creating from nothingness
Such black constructions, such public shapes
And murky masonry, one wonders

At the finger that brushes this aside
Gigantic in everything but size.

IV

The unnamed creator of an unknown sphere,
Unknown as yet, unknowable,
Uncertain certainty, Apollo
Imagined among the indigenes
And Eden conceived on Morningside,
The center of the self, the self
Of the future, of future man
And future place, when these are known,
A freedom at last from the mystical,
The beginning of a final order,
The order of man's right to be
As he is, the discipline of his scope
Observed as an absolute, himself.

V

A longer, deeper breath sustains
The eloquence of right, since knowing
And being are one: the right to know
And the right to be are one. We come
To knowledge when we come to life.
Yet always there is another life,
A life beyond this present knowing,
A life lighter than this present splendor,
Brighter, perfected and distant away,
Not to be reached but to be known,
Not an attainment of the will
But something illogically received,
A divination, a letting down
From loftiness, misgivings dazzlingly

IOI

Resolved in dazzling discovery.
There is no map of paradise.
The great Omnium descends on us
As a free race. We know it, one
By one, in the right of all. Each man
Is an approach to the vigilance
In which the litter of truths becomes
A whole, the day on which the last star
Has been counted, the genealogy
Of gods and men destroyed, the right
To know established as the right to be.
The ancient symbols will be nothing then.
We shall have gone behind the symbols
To that which they symbolized, away
From the rumors of the speech-full domes,
To the chatter that is then the true legend,
Like glitter ascended into fire.

VI

Master of the world and of himself,
He came to this by knowledge or
Will come. His mind presents the world
And in his mind the world revolves.
The revolutions through day and night,
Through wild spaces of other suns and moons,
Round summer and angular winter and winds,
Are matched by other revolutions
In which the world goes round and round
In the crystal atmospheres of the mind,
Light's comedies, dark's tragedies,
Like things produced by a climate, the world
Goes round in the climates of the mind
And bears its floraisons of imagery.

The mind renews the world in a verse,
A passage of music, a paragraph
By a right philosopher: renews
And possesses by sincere insight
In the John-begat-Jacob of what we know,
The flights through space, changing habitudes.

In the generations of thought, man's sons
And heirs are powers of the mind,
His only testament and estate.
He has nothing but the truth to leave.
How then shall the mind be less than free
Since only to know is to be free?

VII

The living man in the present place,
Always, the particular thought
Among Plantagenet abstractions,
Always and always, the difficult inch,
On which the vast arches of space
Repose, always, the credible thought
From which the incredible systems spring,
The little confine soon unconfined
In stellar largenesses—these
Are the manifestations of a law
That bends the particulars to the abstract,
Makes them a pack on a giant's back,
A majestic mother's flocking brood,
As if abstractions were, themselves
Particulars of a relative sublime.
This is not poet's ease of mind.
It is the fate that dwells in truth.
We obey the coaxings of our end.

VIII

What is the shape of the sibyl? Not,
For a change, the englistered woman, seated
In colorings harmonious, dewed and dashed
By them: gorgeous symbol seated
On the seat of halidom, rainbowed,
Piercing the spirit by appearance,
A summing up of the loftiest lives
And their directing sceptre, the crown
And final effulgence and delving show.
It is the sibyl of the self,
The self as sibyl, whose diamond,
Whose chiefest embracing of all wealth
Is poverty, whose jewel found
At the exactest central of the earth
Is need. For this, the sibyl's shape
Is a blind thing fumbling for its form,
A form that is lame, a hand, a back,
A dream too poor, too destitute
To be remembered, the old shape
Worn and leaning to nothingness,
A woman looking down the road,
A child asleep in its own life.
As these depend, so must they use.
They measure the right to use. Need makes
The right to use. Need names on its breath
Categories of bleak necessity,
Which, just to name, is to create
A help, a right to help, a right
To know what helps and to attain,
By right of knowing, another plane.
The englistered woman is now seen
In an isolation, separate

From the human in humanity,
A part of the inhuman more,
The still inhuman more, and yet
An inhuman of our features, known
And unknown, inhuman for a little while,
Inhuman for a little, lesser time."

The great sail of Ulysses seemed,
In the breathings of this soliloquy,
Alive with an enigma's flittering . . .
As if another sail went on
Straight forwardly through another night
And clumped stars dangled all the way.

❖❖

PRESENCE OF AN EXTERNAL MASTER
OF KNOWLEDGE

Under the shape of his sail, Ulysses,
Symbol of the seeker, crossing by night
The giant sea, read his own mind.
He said, "As I know, I am and have
The right to be." He guided his boat
Beneath the middle stars and said:

"Here I feel the human loneliness
And that, in space and solitude,
Which knowledge is: the world and fate,
The right within me and about me,
Joined in a triumphant vigor,
Like a direction on which I depend . . .

A longer, deeper breath sustains
This eloquence of right, since knowing
And being are one—the right to know
Is equal to the right to be.
The great Omnium descends on me,
Like an absolute out of this eloquence."

The sharp sail of Ulysses seemed,
In the breathings of that soliloquy,
Alive with an enigma's flittering,
And bodying, and being there,
As he moved, straightly, on and on,
Through clumped stars dangling all the way.

A CHILD ASLEEP IN ITS OWN LIFE

Among the old men that you know,
There is one, unnamed, that broods
On all the rest, in heavy thought.

They are nothing, except in the universe
Of that single mind. He regards them
Outwardly and knows them inwardly,

The sole emperor of what they are,
Distant, yet close enough to wake
The chords above your bed to-night.

TWO LETTERS

I

A Letter From

Even if there had been a crescent moon
On every cloud-tip over the heavens,
Drenching the evening with crystals' light,

One would have wanted more—more—more—
Some true interior to which to return,
A home against one's self, a darkness,

An ease in which to live a moment's life,
The moment of life's love and fortune,
Free from everything else, free above all from thought.

It would have been like lighting a candle,
Like leaning on the table, shading one's eyes,
And hearing a tale one wanted intensely to hear,

As if we were all seated together again
And one of us spoke and all of us believed
What we heard and the light, though little, was enough.

II

A Letter To

She wanted a holiday
With someone to speak her dulcied native tongue,

In the shadows of a wood . . .
Shadows, woods . . . and the two of them in speech,

In a secrecy of words
Opened out within a secrecy of place,

Not having to do with love.
A land would hold her in its arms that day

Or something much like a land.
The circle would no longer be broken but closed.

The miles of distance away
From everything would end. It would all meet.

❖◈❖

CONVERSATION WITH THREE WOMEN
OF NEW ENGLAND

The mode of the person becomes the mode of the world,
For that person, and, sometimes, for the world itself.
The contents of the mind become solid show
Or almost solid seem show—the way a fly bird
Fixes itself in its inevitable bush . . .
It follows that to change modes is to change the world.

Now, you, for instance, are of this mode: You say
That in that ever-dark central, wherever it is,
In the central of earth or sky or air or thought,
There is a drop that is life's element,
Sole, single source and minimum patriarch,

The one thing common to all life, the human
And inhuman same, the likeness of things unlike.

And you, you say that the capital things of the mind
Should be as natural as natural objects,
So that a carved king found in a jungle, huge
And weathered, should be part of a human landscape,
That a figure reclining among columns toppled down,
Stiff in eternal lethargy, should be,
Not the beginning but the end of artifice,
A nature of marble in a marble world.

And then, finally, it is you that say
That only in man's definitions of himself,
Only encompassed in humanity, is he
Himself. The author of man's canons is man,
Not some outer patron and imaginer.

In which one of these three worlds are the four of us
The most at home? Or is it enough to have seen
And felt and known the differences we have seen
And felt and known in the colors in which we live,
In the excellences of the air we breathe,
The bouquet of being—enough to realize
That the sense of being changes as we talk,
That talk shifts the cycle of the scenes of kings?

DINNER BELL IN THE WOODS

He was facing phantasma when the bell rang.
The picnic of children came running then,

In a burst of shouts, under the trees
And through the air. The smaller ones

Came tinkling on the grass to the table
Where the fattest women belled the glass.

The point of it was the way he heard it,
In the green, outside the door of phantasma.

◆◆◆

REALITY IS AN ACTIVITY OF THE MOST AUGUST IMAGINATION

Last Friday, in the big light of last Friday night,
We drove home from Cornwall to Hartford, late.

It was not a night blown at a glassworks in Vienna
Or Venice, motionless, gathering time and dust.

There was a crush of strength in a grinding going round,
Under the front of the westward evening star,

The vigor of glory, a glittering in the veins,
As things emerged and moved and were dissolved,

Either in distance, change or nothingness,
The visible transformations of summer night,

An argentine abstraction approaching form
And suddenly denying itself away.

There was an insolid billowing of the solid.
Night's moonlight lake was neither water nor air.

❖◇

SOLITAIRE UNDER THE OAKS

In the oblivion of cards
One exists among pure principles.

Neither the cards nor the trees nor the air
Persist as facts. This is an escape

To principium, to meditation.
One knows at last what to think about

And thinks about it without consciousness,
Under the oak trees, completely released.

◇+

LOCAL OBJECTS

He knew that he was a spirit without a foyer
And that, in his knowledge, local objects become
More precious than the most precious objects of home:

The local objects of a world without a foyer,
Without a remembered past, a present past,
Or a present future, hoped for in present hope,

III

Objects not present as a matter of course
On the dark side of the heavens or the bright,
In that sphere with so few objects of its own.

Little existed for him but the few things
For which a fresh name always occurred, as if
He wanted to make them, keep them from perishing,

The few things, the objects of insight, the integrations
Of feeling, the things that came of their own accord,
Because he desired without knowing quite what,

That were the moments of the classic, the beautiful.
These were that serene he had always been approaching
As toward an absolute foyer beyond romance.

ARTIFICIAL POPULATIONS

The center that he sought was a state of mind,
Nothing more, like weather after it has cleared—
Well, more than that, like weather when it has cleared
And the two poles continue to maintain it

And the Orient and the Occident embrace
To form that weather's appropriate people,
The rosy men and the women of the rose,
Astute in being what they are made to be.

This artificial population is like
A healing-point in the sickness of the mind:

Like angels resting on a rustic steeple
Or a confect of leafy faces in a tree—

A health—and the faces in a summer night.
So, too, of the races of appropriate people
Of the wind, of the wind as it deepens, and late sleep,
And music that lasts long and lives the more.

<hr>

A CLEAR DAY AND NO MEMORIES

No soldiers in the scenery,
No thoughts of people now dead,
As they were fifty years ago,
Young and living in a live air,
Young and walking in the sunshine,
Bending in blue dresses to touch something,
Today the mind is not part of the weather.

Today the air is clear of everything.
It has no knowledge except of nothingness
And it flows over us without meanings,
As if none of us had ever been here before
And are not now: in this shallow spectacle,
This invisible activity, this sense.

BANJO BOOMER

The mulberry is a double tree.
Mulberry, shade me, shade me awhile.

A white, pink, purple berry tree,
A very dark-leaved berry tree.
Mulberry, shade me, shade me awhile.

A churchyard kind of bush as well,
A silent sort of bush, as well.
Mulberry, shade me, shade me awhile.

It is a shape of life described
By another shape without a word.
Mulberry, shade me, shade me awhile—

With nothing fixed by a single word.
Mulberry, shade me, shade me awhile.

JULY MOUNTAIN

We live in a constellation
Of patches and of pitches,
Not in a single world,
In things said well in music,
On the piano, and in speech,

As in a page of poetry—
Thinkers without final thoughts
In an always incipient cosmos,
The way, when we climb a mountain,
Vermont throws itself together.

❖◇

THE REGION NOVEMBER

It is hard to hear the north wind again,
And to watch the treetops, as they sway.

They sway, deeply and loudly, in an effort,
So much less than feeling, so much less than speech,

Saying and saying, the way things say
On the level of that which is not yet knowledge:

A revelation not yet intended.
It is like a critic of God, the world

And human nature, pensively seated
On the waste throne of his own wilderness.

Deeplier, deeplier, loudlier, loudlier,
The trees are swaying, swaying, swaying.

ON THE WAY TO THE BUS

A light snow, like frost, has fallen during the night.
Gloomily, the journalist confronts

Transparent man in a translated world,
In which he feeds on a new known,

In a season, a climate of morning, of elucidation,
A refreshment of cold air, cold breath,

A perception of cold breath, more revealing than
A perception of sleep, more powerful

Than a power of sleep, a clearness emerging
From cold, slightly irised, slightly bedazzled,

But a perfection emerging from a new known,
An understanding beyond journalism,

A way of pronouncing the word inside of one's tongue
Under the wintry trees of the terrace.

AS YOU LEAVE THE ROOM

You speak. You say: Today's character is not
A skeleton out of its cabinet. Nor am I.

That poem about the pineapple, the one
About the mind as never satisfied,

The one about the credible hero, the one
About summer, are not what skeletons think about.

I wonder, have I lived a skeleton's life,
As a disbeliever in reality,

A countryman of all the bones in the world?
Now, here, the snow I had forgotten becomes

Part of a major reality, part of
An appreciation of a reality

And thus an elevation, as if I left
With something I could touch, touch every way.

And yet nothing has been changed except what is
Unreal, as if nothing had been changed at all.

OF MERE BEING

The palm at the end of the mind,
Beyond the last thought, rises
In the bronze distance,

A gold-feathered bird
Sings in the palm, without human meaning,
Without human feeling, a foreign song.

You know then that it is not the reason
That makes us happy or unhappy.
The bird sings. Its feathers shine.

The palm stands on the edge of space.
The wind moves slowly in the branches.
The bird's fire-fangled feathers dangle down.

❀❀❀❀❀❀❀❀❀❀❀❀❀❀❀❀❀❀❀❀❀❀❀❀❀❀❀❀❀❀❀

A MYTHOLOGY REFLECTS ITS REGION

A mythology reflects its region. Here
In Connecticut, we never lived in a time
When mythology was possible—But if we had—
That raises the question of the image's truth.
The image must be of the nature of its creator.
It is the nature of its creator increased,
Heightened. It is he, anew, in a freshened youth
And it is he in the substance of his region,
Wood of his forests and stone out of his fields
Or from under his mountains.

MOMENT OF LIGHT

(Translated from the French of Jean Le Roy)

I feel an apparition,
at my back,
an ebon wrack,
of more than man's condition,
that leans upon me there;
and then in back, one more;
and then, still farther back,
still other men aligned;
and then, toujours plus grands, immensities of night,
who, less and less defined
by light
stretch off in the black:

ancestors from the first days of the world.

Before me, I know more,
one smaller at the first, and then one smaller still,
and more and more, that are my son and then his sons.

They lie buried in dumb sleep,
or bury themselves in the future.

And for the time, just one exists:
I.
Just one exists and I am time,
the whole of time.
I am the whole of light.
My flesh alone, for the moment, lives,

my heart alone gives,
my eyes alone have sight.
I am emblazoned, the others, all, are black.
I am the whole of light!
And those behind and those before
are only routineers of rounding time.
In back, they lie perdu in the black: the breachless grime,
(just one exists and I am time)
of an incalculable ether that burns and stings.

My will alone commands me: I am time!
Behind they passed the point of man,
before they are not embryo—I, only, touch with prime.
And that will last long length of time,
think what you will!

I am between two infinite states
on the mid-line dividing,
between the infinite that waits
and the long-abiding,
at the golden spot, where the mid-line swells
and yields to a supple, quivering, deep
inundation.

What do we count? All is for us that live!
Time, even time, and the day's strength and beam.
My fellows, you that live around me,
are you not surprised to be supreme,
on the tense line, in this expanse
of dual circumstance?
And are you not surprised to be the base
to know that, without you, the scale of lives
on which the eternal poising turns

would sink upon death's pitty under-place?
And are you not surprised to be the very poles?

Let us make signals in the air and cry aloud.
We must leave a wide noise tolling
in the night;
and in the deep of time,
set the wide wind rolling.

THREE PARAPHRASES FROM
LÉON-PAUL FARGUE

I

In a quarter made drowsy by the odor of its gardens and of its
trees, the ramp of dreams, in the distance, accelerates and retards
its chords, a little, in the autumn weather . . .

What gorgeous aspects cluster over their pale Calvary! What
gestures evoke the chants of latent and unrealized dreams! What
hands have opened penetrations into landscapes where things
remembered come to sight like the perspectives of roofs seen by
lightning . . .

A road lamp bides its time at the end of the gravel walk that
leads to the villa lost beneath the leaves, in which a light rain
still drips.

The angel is there, no doubt, at the keyboard, under the
plume of the shade; and his noble visage, and his hands, on
which the rings put forth touches toward the light, are bright
with a steadfast flame.

L

The bird troubled by some secret of the Islands, and yet concealing it, picks up its song, in its basketry of gold!

A terrace of autumn. A white villa placed like something on the watch at the terminal of the walk in the bitter odor. A thought as of gold falls down with sad descent. The blinds have been drawn in the rooms in which the idylls are dead.

"Dans un quartier," Poèmes (1912)

II

A fragrance of night, not to be defined, that brings on an obscure doubt, exquisite, tender, comes by the open window into the room where I am at work . . .

My cat watches the darkness, as rigid as a jug. A fortune of subtle seeing looks at me through its green eyes . . .

The lamp sings its slight song quietly, subdued as the song one hears in a shell. The lamp reaches out its placating hands. In its aureole, I hear the litanies, the choruses and the responses of flies. It lights up the flowers at the edge of the terrace. The nearest ones come forward timidly to see me, like a troop of dwarfs that discover an ogre . . .

The minute violin of a mosquito goes on and on. One could believe that a person was playing alone in a house at a remote distance . . . Insects fall with a sidewise fall and writhe gently on the table. A butterfly yellow as a wisp of straw drags itself along the little yellow valley that is my book . . .

A big clock outdoors intones drearily. Memories take motion like children dancing in a ring . . .

The cat stretches itself to the uttermost. Its nose traces in the air an imperceptible evolution. A fly fastens its scissors in the lamp . . .

Kitchen clatter mounts in a back-yard. Argumentative voices play at pigeon-vole. A carriage starts up and away. A train chugs at the next station. A long whistle rises far-off . . .

I think of someone whom I love, who is so little to be so separated, perhaps beyond the lands covered by the night, beyond the profundities of water. I am not able to engage her glance . . .

"Un odeur nocturne," Poèmes (1912)

III

Between the things of these twenty years, between the sensations of these twenty years and the eyes of Segonzac, there have been exchanges, secret, puissant, unerring, which he has inscribed in lasting stone. His faces, his portraits, his Morin, whom he loves like a son, his strolls around circuses, his bathers of Saint-Tropez, his heads of calves, his willows and his harvests sometimes, for me, finish by having the documentary value of postage-stamps. What I want to say is that they illustrate messages of precise origin, well-defined sensations, about which it is impossible to be mistaken. For me, the true artist appears to be like that: he is a witness. Sometimes a guide. Through him should shine the time that inspired him, of which he has disengaged in traits of fire the special symbols, the forms, the views, the spiritual habit as well as the positions of trees or of villages that belong to this time round the carrousel. That the National Library has now hastened to recognize in Segonzac this social role and this talent compounded of instinct and authority, shows that our poor old country is far from being down and out.

I read recently in a review these lines over which I meditated: "What is left today of the misty sheets of water of Corot, of those glades where the gold of the sun filtered, rich and clear, through the foliage woven by Courbet, and of these celebrated slopes of the Seine, so Second Empire, of Renoir, of Manet, and of Monet? What is left of the rose and blue snows of Monet?

"Yes: but where are last year's snows?"

What is left? Well, for one thing, men like Segonzac, who carry on, quite simply, who lead tradition by the hand, up to the

123

point where it meets what is modern. A modernity which they pass through without becoming too splashed up, always to find again, on the appointed day, the durable, the classic, the incontestable.

"Segonzac, ou l'Artiste," Portraits de Famille (1947)

PLAYS

THREE TRAVELERS WATCH A SUNRISE

The characters are three Chinese, two negroes and a girl.

The scene represents a forest of heavy trees on a hilltop in eastern Pennsylvania. To the right is a road, obscured by bushes. It is about four o'clock of a morning in August, at the present time.

When the curtain rises, the stage is dark. The limb of a tree creaks. A negro carrying a lantern passes along the road. The sound is repeated. The negro comes through the bushes, raises his lantern and looks through the trees. Discerning a dark object among the branches, he shrinks back, crosses stage, and goes out through the woods to the left.

A second negro comes through the bushes to the right. He carries two large baskets, which he places on the ground just inside of the bushes. Enter three Chinese, one of whom carries a lantern. They pause on the road.

SECOND CHINESE

     All you need,
     To find poetry,
     Is to look for it with a lantern.
          [*The Chinese laugh.*]

THIRD CHINESE

     I could find it without,
     On an August night,

If I saw no more
Than the dew on the barns.

> [*The Second Negro makes a sound to attract their attention. The three Chinese come through the bushes. The first is short, fat, quizzical, and of middle age. The second is of middle height, thin and turning gray; a man of sense and sympathy. The third is a young man, intent, detached. They wear European clothes.*]

SECOND CHINESE [*glancing at the baskets*]

Dew is water to see,
Not water to drink:
We have forgotten water to drink.
Yet I am content
Just to see sunrise again.
I have not seen it
Since the day we left Pekin.
It filled my doorway,
Like whispering women.

FIRST CHINESE

And I have never seen it.
If we have no water,
Do find a melon for me
In the baskets.

> [*The Second Negro, who has been opening the baskets, hands the First Chinese a melon.*]

FIRST CHINESE

Is there no spring?

> [*The negro takes a water bottle of red porcelain from one of the baskets and places it near the Third Chinese.*]

128

SECOND CHINESE [*to Third Chinese*]

Your porcelain water bottle.

> [*One of the baskets contains costumes of silk, red, blue, and green. During the following speeches, the Chinese put on these costumes, with the assistance of the negro, and seat themselves on the ground.*]

THIRD CHINESE

This fetches its own water.

> [*Takes the bottle and places it on the ground in the center of the stage.*]

I drink from it, dry as it is,

As you from maxims, [*to Second Chinese*]

Or you from melons. [*to First Chinese*]

FIRST CHINESE

Not as I, from melons.

Be sure of that.

SECOND CHINESE

Well, it is true of maxims.

> [*He finds a book in the pocket of his costume, and reads from it.*]

"The court had known poverty and wretchedness; humanity had invaded its seclusion, with its suffering and its pity."

> [*The limb of the tree creaks.*]

Yes: it is true of maxims,

Just as it is true of poets,

Or wise men, or nobles,

Or jade.

FIRST CHINESE

Drink from wise men? From jade?

Is there no spring?

> [*Turning to the negro, who has taken a jug from one of the baskets.*]

129

Fill it and return.

> [*The negro removes a large candle from one of the baskets and hands it to the First Chinese; then takes the jug and the lantern and enters the trees to the left. The First Chinese lights the candle and places it on the ground near the water bottle.*]

THIRD CHINESE

There is a seclusion of porcelain
That humanity never invades.

FIRST CHINESE [*with sarcasm*]

Porcelain!

THIRD CHINESE

It is like the seclusion of sunrise,
Before it shines on any house.

FIRST CHINESE

Pooh!

SECOND CHINESE

This candle is the sun;
This bottle is earth:
It is an illustration
Used by generations of hermits.
The point of difference from reality
Is this:
That, in this illustration,
The earth remains of one color—
It remains red,
It remains what it is.
But when the sun shines on the earth,
In reality
It does not shine on a thing that remains
What it was yesterday.
The sun rises
On whatever the earth happens to be.

THIRD CHINESE

> And there are indeterminate moments
> Before it rises,
> Like this,
> > [*with a backward gesture*]
> Before one can tell
> What the bottle is going to be—
> Porcelain, Venetian glass,
> Egyptian . . .
> Well, there are moments
> When the candle, sputtering up,
> Finds itself in seclusion,
> > [*He raises the candle in the air.*]
> And shines, perhaps, for the beauty of shining.
> That is the seclusion of sunrise
> Before it shines on any house.
> > [*replacing the candle*]

FIRST CHINESE [*wagging his head*]

> As abstract as porcelain.

SECOND CHINESE

> Such seclusion knows beauty
> As the court knew it.
> The court woke
> In its windless pavilions,
> And gazed on chosen mornings,
> As it gazed
> On chosen porcelain.
> What the court saw was always of the same color,
> And well shaped,
> And seen in a clear light.
> > [*He points to the candle.*]
> It never woke to see,
> And never knew,
> The flawed jars,

The weak colors,
The contorted glass.
It never knew
The poor lights.
                    [*He opens his book significantly.*]
When the court knew beauty only,
And in seclusion,
It had neither love nor wisdom.
These came through poverty
And wretchedness,
Through suffering and pity.
                    [*He pauses.*]
It is the invasion of humanity
That counts.
                    [*The limb of the tree creaks. The First Chi-
                    nese turns, for a moment, in the direction of
                    the sound.*]
FIRST CHINESE [*thoughtfully*]
The light of the most tranquil candle
Would shudder on a bloody salver.
SECOND CHINESE [*with a gesture of disregard*]
It is the invasion
That counts.
If it be supposed that we are three figures
Painted on porcelain
As we sit here,
That we are painted on this very bottle,
The hermit of the place,
Holding this candle to us,
Would wonder;
But if it be supposed
That we are painted as warriors,
The candle would tremble in his hands;

Or if it be supposed, for example,
That we are painted as three dead men,
He could not see the steadiest light
For sorrow.
It would be true
If the emperor himself
Held the candle.
He would forget the porcelain
For the figures painted on it.

THIRD CHINESE [*shrugging his shoulders*]
Let the candle shine for the beauty of shining.
I dislike the invasion
And long for the windless pavilions.
And yet it may be true
That nothing is beautiful
Except with reference to ourselves,
Nor ugly,
Nor high,

       [*pointing to the sky*]

Nor low.

       [*pointing to the candle*]

No: not even sunrise.
Can you play of this

       [*mockingly to First Chinese*]

For us?

       [*He stands up.*]

FIRST CHINESE [*hesitatingly*]
I have a song
Called *Mistress and Maid.*
It is of no interest to hermits
Or emperors,
Yet it has a bearing;

133

For if we affect sunrise,
We affect all things.

THIRD CHINESE

It is a pity it is of women.
Sing it.

> [*He takes an instrument from one of the
> baskets and hands it to the First Chinese,
> who sings the following song, accompanying
> himself, somewhat tunelessly, on the instru-
> ment. The Third Chinese takes various
> things out of the basket for tea. He arranges
> fruit. The First Chinese watches him while
> he plays. The Second Chinese gazes at the
> ground. The sky shows the first signs of
> morning.*]

FIRST CHINESE

The mistress says, in a harsh voice,
"He will be thinking in strange countries
Of the white stones near my door,
And I—I am tired of him."
She says sharply, to her maid,
"Sing to yourself no more."

Then the maid says, to herself,
"He will be thinking in strange countries
Of the white stones near her door;
But it is me he will see
At the window, as before.

"He will be thinking in strange countries
Of the green gown I wore.
He was saying good-by to her."

134

The maid drops her eyes and says to her mistress,
"I shall sing to myself no more."

THIRD CHINESE

That affects the white stones,
To be sure.

[*They laugh.*]

FIRST CHINESE

And it affects the green gown.

SECOND CHINESE

Here comes our black man.

[*The Second Negro returns, somewhat agitated, with water but without his lantern. He hands the jug to the Third Chinese. The First Chinese from time to time strikes the instrument. The Third Chinese, who faces the left, peers in the direction from which the negro has come.*]

THIRD CHINESE

You have left your lantern behind you.
It shines, among the trees,
Like evening Venus in a cloud-top.

[*The Second Negro grins but makes no explanation. He seats himself behind the Chinese to the right.*]

FIRST CHINESE

Or like a ripe strawberry
Among its leaves.

[*They laugh.*]

I heard tonight
That they are searching the hill
For an Italian.
He disappeared with his neighbor's daughter.

135

SECOND CHINESE [*confidingly*]
> I am sure you heard
> The first eloping footfall
> And the drum
> Of pursuing feet.

FIRST CHINESE [*amusedly*]
> It was not an elopement.
> The young gentlemen was seen
> To climb the hill
> In the manner of a tragedian
> Who sweats.
> Such things happen in the evening.
> He was
> *Un miserable.*

SECOND CHINESE
> Reach the lady quickly.
>> [*The First Chinese strikes the instrument
>> twice as a prelude to his narrative.*]

FIRST CHINESE
> There are as many points of view
> From which to regard her
> As there are sides to a round bottle.
>> [*pointing to the water bottle*]
> She was represented to me
> As beautiful.
>> [*They laugh. The First Chinese strikes the
>> instrument, and looks at the Third Chinese,
>> who yawns.*]

FIRST CHINESE [*reciting*]
> She was as beautiful as a porcelain water bottle.
>> [*He strikes the instrument in an insinuating
>> manner.*]

136

FIRST CHINESE

> She was represented to me
> As young.
> Therefore my song should go
> Of the color of blood.
>> [*He strikes the instrument. The limb of the
>> tree creaks. The First Chinese notices it and
>> puts his hand on the knee of the Second
>> Chinese, who is seated between him and
>> the Third Chinese, to call attention to the
>> sound. They are all seated so that they do
>> not face the spot from which the sound
>> comes. A dark object, hanging to the limb of
>> the tree, becomes a dim silhouette. The sky
>> grows constantly brighter. No color is to be
>> seen until the end of the play.*]

SECOND CHINESE [*to First Chinese*]

> It is only a tree
> Creaking in the night wind.

THIRD CHINESE [*shrugging his shoulders*]

> There would be no creaking
> In the windless pavilions.

FIRST CHINESE [*resuming*]

> So far the lady of the present ballad
> Would have been studied
> By the hermit and his candle
> With much philosophy;
> And possibly the emperor would have cried,
> "More light!"
> But it is a way with ballads
> That the more pleasing they are
> The worse end they come to;

For here it was also represented
That the lady was poor—
The hermit's candle would have thrown
Alarming shadows,
And the emperor would have held
The porcelain in one hand . . .
She was represented as clinging
To that sweaty tragedian,
And weeping up the hill.

SECOND CHINESE [with a grimace]

It does not sound like an elopement.

FIRST CHINESE

It is a doleful ballad,
Fit for keyholes.

THIRD CHINESE

Shall we hear more?

SECOND CHINESE

Why not?

THIRD CHINESE

We came for isolation,
To rest in sunrise.

SECOND CHINESE [raising his book slightly]

But this will be a part of sunrise,
And can you tell how it will end?—
Venetian,
Egyptian,
Contorted glass . . .

> [He turns toward the light in the sky to the
> right, darkening the candle with his hands.]

In the meantime, the candle shines,

> [indicating the sunrise]

As you say,

> [to the Third Chinese]

For the beauty of shining.

FIRST CHINESE [*sympathetically*]

Oh! it will end badly.

The lady's father

Came clapping behind them

To the foot of the hill.

He came crying,

"Anna, Anna, Anna!"

[*imitating*]

He was alone without her,

Just as the young gentleman

Was alone without her:

Three beggars, you see,

Begging for one another.

[*The First Negro, carrying two lanterns, approaches cautiously through the trees. At the sight of him, the Second Negro, seated near the Chinese, jumps to his feet. The Chinese get up in alarm. The Second Negro goes around the Chinese toward the First Negro. All see the body of a man hanging to the limb of the tree. They gather together, keeping their eyes fixed on it. The First Negro comes out of the trees and places the lanterns on the ground. He looks at the group and then at the body.*]

FIRST CHINESE [*moved*]

The young gentleman of the ballad.

THIRD CHINESE [*slowly, approaching the body*]

And the end of the ballad.

Take away the bushes.

[*The negroes commence to pull away the bushes.*]

139

SECOND CHINESE
>   Death, the hermit,
>   Needs no candle
>   In his hermitage.

> [*The Second Chinese snuffs out the candle.
> The First Chinese puts out the lanterns. As
> the bushes are pulled away, the figure of a
> girl, sitting half stupefied under the tree, sud-
> denly becomes apparent to the Second Chi-
> nese and then to the Third Chinese. They
> step back. The negroes move to the left.
> When the First Chinese sees the girl, the in-
> strument slips from his hands and falls
> noisily to the ground. The girl stirs.*]

SECOND CHINESE [*to the girl*]
>   Is that you, Anna?

> [*The girl starts. She raises her head, looks
> around slowly, leaps to her feet and
> screams.*]

SECOND CHINESE [*gently*]
>   Is that you, Anna?

> [*She turns quickly toward the body, looks at
> it fixedly and totters up the stage.*]

ANNA [*bitterly*]
>   Go.
>   Tell my father:
>   He is dead.

> [*The Second and Third Chinese support
> her. The First Negro whispers to the First
> Chinese, then takes the lanterns and goes
> through the opening to the road, where he
> disappears in the direction of the valley.*]

FIRST CHINESE [*to Second Negro*]

> Bring us fresh water
> From the spring.

>> [*The Second Negro takes the jug and enters
>> the trees to the left. The girl comes gradually
>> to herself. She looks at the Chinese and at
>> the sky. She turns her back toward the body,
>> shuddering, and does not look at it again.*]

ANNA

> It will soon be sunrise.

SECOND CHINESE

> One candle replaces
> Another.

>> [*The First Chinese walks toward the bushes
>> to the right. He stands by the roadside, as if
>> to attract the attention of anyone passing.*]

ANNA [*simply*]

> When he was in his fields,
> I worked in ours—
> Wore purple to see;
> And when I was in his garden
> I wore gold ear-rings.
> Last evening I met him on the road.
> He asked me to walk with him
> To the top of the hill.
> I felt the evil,
> But he wanted nothing.
> He hanged himself in front of me.

>> [*She looks for support. The Second and
>> Third Chinese help her toward the road. At
>> the roadside, the First Chinese takes the
>> place of the Third Chinese. The girl and the*

141

> *two Chinese go through the bushes and*
> *disappear down the road. The stage is empty*
> *except for the Third Chinese. He walks*
> *slowly across the stage, pushing the instru-*
> *ment out of his way with his foot. It rever-*
> *berates. He looks at the water bottle.*]

THIRD CHINESE

Of the color of blood . . .
Seclusion of porcelain . . .
Seclusion of sunrise . . .

> [*He picks up the water bottle.*]

The candle of the sun
Will shine soon
On this hermit earth.

> [*indicating the bottle*]

It will shine soon
Upon the trees,
And find a new thing

> [*indicating the body*]

Painted on this porcelain,

> [*indicating the trees*]

But not on this.

> [*indicating the bottle*]
> [*He places the bottle on the ground. A nar-*
> *row cloud over the valley becomes red. He*
> *turns toward it, then walks to the right. He*
> *finds the book of the Second Chinese lying*
> *on the ground, picks it up and turns over*
> *the leaves.*]

Red is not only
The color of blood,
Or

> [*indicating the body*]

142

Of a man's eyes,
Or
                    [*pointedly*]
Of a girl's.
And as the red of the sun
Is one thing to me
And one thing to another,
So it is the green of one tree
                    [*indicating*]
And the green of another,
Without which it would all be black.
Sunrise is multiplied,
Like the earth on which it shines,
By the eyes that open on it,
Even dead eyes,
As red is multiplied by the leaves of trees.

> [*Toward the end of this speech, the Second Negro comes from the trees to the left, without being seen. The Third Chinese, whose back is turned toward the negro, walks through the bushes to the right and disappears on the road. The negro looks around at the objects on the stage. He sees the instrument, seats himself before it and strikes it several times, listening to the sound. One or two birds twitter. A voice, urging a horse, is heard at a distance. There is the crack of a whip. The negro stands up, walks to the right and remains at the side of the road. The curtain falls slowly.*]

CARLOS AMONG THE CANDLES

The stage is indistinguishable when the curtain rises.

The room represented is semi-circular. In the center, at the back, is a large round window, covered by long curtains. There is a door at the right and one at the left. Farther forward on the stage there are two long, low, wooden tables, one at the right and one at the left. The walls and the curtains over the window are of a dark reddish-purple, with a dim pattern of antique gold.

Carlos is an eccentric pedant of about forty. He is dressed in black. He wears close-fitting breeches and a close-fitting, tightly-buttoned, short coat with long tails. His hair is rumpled. He leaps upon the stage through the door at the right. Nothing is visible through the door. He has a long thin white lighted taper, which he holds high above his head as he moves, fantastically, over the stage, examining the room in which he finds himself.

When he has completed examining the room, he tip-toes to the table at the right and lights a single candle at the edge of the table nearest the front of the stage. It is a thin black candle, not less than two feet high. All the other candles are like it. They give very little light.

He speaks in a lively manner, but is over-nice in sounding his words.

As the candle begins to burn, he steps back, regarding it. Nothing else is visible on the table.

144

CARLOS:

How the solitude of this candle penetrates me! I light a candle in the darkness. It fills the darkness with solitude, which becomes my own. I become a part of the solitude of the candle . . . of the darkness flowing over the house and into it . . . This room . . . and the profound room outside . . . Just to go through a door, and the change . . . the becoming a part, instantly, of that profounder room . . . and equally to feel it communicating, with the same persistency, its own mood, its own influence . . . and there, too, to feel the lesser influences of the shapes of things, of exhalations, sounds . . . to feel the mood of the candle vanishing and the mood of the special night coming to take its place . . .

[*He sighs. After a pause he pirouettes, and then continues.*]

I was always affected by the grand style. And yet I have been thinking neither of mountains nor of morgues . . . To think of this light and of myself . . . it is a duty. . . . Is it because it makes me think of myself in other places in such a light . . . or of other people in other places in such a light? How true that is: other people in other places in such a light . . . If I looked in at that window and saw a single candle burning in an empty room . . . but if I saw a figure . . . If, now, I felt that there was someone outside . . . The vague influence . . . the influence that clutches . . . But it is not only here and now . . . It is in the morning . . . the difference between a small window and a large window . . . a blue window and a green window . . . It is in the afternoon and in the evening . . . in effects, so drifting, that I know myself to be incalculable, since the causes of what I am are incalculable . . .

[*He springs toward the table, flourishing his taper. At the end farthest from the front of the stage, he discovers a second candle,*]

145

which he lights. He goes back to his former
position.]

The solitude dissolves . . . The light of two candles has a
meaning different from the light of one . . . and an effect different from the effect of one . . . And the proof that that is so,
is that I feel the difference . . . The associations have drifted
a little and changed, and I have followed in this change . . . If
I see myself in other places in such a light, it is not as I saw
myself before. If I see other people in other places in such a
light, the people and places are different from the people and
places I saw before. The solitude is gone. It is as if a company
of two or three people had just separated, or as if they were
about to gather. These candles are too far apart.

> [*He flourishes his taper above the table and
> finds a third candle in the center of it, which
> he lights.*]

And yet with only two candles it would have been a cold and
respectable company; for the feeling of coldness and respecta-
bility persists in the presence of three, modified a little, as if a
kind of stateliness had modified into a kind of elegance . . .
How far away from the isolation of the single candle, as arrogant
of the vacancy around it as three are arrogant of association . . .
It is no longer as if a company had just separated. It is only
as if it were about to gather . . . as if one were soon to forget
the room because of the people in the room . . . people tem-
pered by the lights around them, affected by the lights around
them . . . sensible that one more candle would turn this formative elegance into formative luxury.

> [*He lights a fourth candle. He indulges his
> humor.*]

And the suggestion of luxury into the suggestion of magnificence.

> [*He lights a fifth candle.*]

And the beginning of magnificence into the beginning of splendor.

[*He lights a sixth candle. He sighs deeply.*]

In how short a time have I been solitary, then respectable—in a company so cold as to be stately, then elegant, then conscious of luxury, even magnificence; and now I come, gradually, to the beginning of splendor. Truly, I am a modern.

[*He dances around the room.*]

To have changed so often and so much . . . or to have been changed . . . to have been carried by the lighting of six candles through so many lives and to have been brought among so many people . . . This grows more wonderful. Six candles burn like an adventure that has been completed. They are established. They are a city . . . six common candles . . . seven . . .

[*He lights another and another, until he has lighted twelve, saying after them, in turn:*]

Eight, nine, ten, eleven, twelve.

[*Following this, he goes on tip-toe to the center of the stage, where he looks at the candles. Their brilliance has raised his spirits to the point of gaiety. He turns from the lighted table to face the dark one at the left. He holds his taper before him.*]

Darkness again . . . as if a night wind had come blowing . . . but too weakly to fling the cloth of darkness.

[*He goes to the window, draws one of the curtains a little and peers out. He sees nothing.*]

I had as lief look into night as look into the dark corner of a room. Darkness expels me.

[*He goes forward, holding his taper high above him, until he comes to the table at the left. He finds this covered with candles, like*]

147

the table at the right, and lights them, with
whimsical motions, one by one. When all
the candles have been lighted, he runs to the
center of the stage, holding his hands over
his eyes. Then he returns to the window and
flings aside the curtains. The light from the
window falls on the tall stalks of flowers
outside. The flowers are like hollyhocks, but
they are unnaturally large, of gold and silver.
He speaks excitedly.]

Where now is my solitude and the lonely figure of solitude?
Where now are the two stately ones that left their coldness
behind them? They have taken their bareness with them. Their
coldness has followed them. Here there will be silks and
fans . . . the movement of arms . . . rumors of Renoir . . .
coiffures . . . hands . . . scorn of Debussy . . . communications of body to body . . . There will be servants, as fat as
plums, bearing pineapples from the Azores . . . because of
twenty-four candles, burning together, as if their light had dispelled a phantasm, falling on silks and fans . . . the movement
of arms . . . The pulse of the crowd will beat out the shallow
pulses . . . it will fill me.

[*A strong gust of wind suddenly blows into*
the room, extinguishing several of the can-
dles on the table at the left. He runs to the
table at the left and looks, as if startled, at
the extinguished candles. He buries his head
in his arms.]

That, too, was phantasm . . . The night wind came into
the room . . . The fans are invisible upon the floor.

[*In a burst of feeling, he blows out all the*
candles that are still burning on the table at

the left. He crosses the stage and stands be-
fore the table at the right. After a moment
he goes slowly to the back of the stage and
draws the curtains over the window. He re-
turns to the table at the right.]

What is there in the extinguishing of light? It is like twelve wild birds flying in autumn.

[*He blows out one of the candles.*]

It is like an eleven-limbed oak tree, brass-colored in frost. . . . Regret . . .

[*He blows out another candle.*]

It is like ten green sparks of a rocket, oscillating in air . . . The extinguishing of light . . . how closely regret follows it.

[*He blows out another candle.*]

It is like the diverging angles that follow nine leaves drifting in water, and that compose themselves brilliantly on the polished surface.

[*He blows out another candle.*]

It is like eight pears in a nude tree, flaming in twilight . . . The extinguishing of light is like that. The season is sorrowful. The air is cold.

[*He blows out another candle.*]

It is like the six Pleiades, and the hidden one, that makes them seven.

[*He blows out another candle.*]

It is like the seven Pleiades, and the hidden one, that makes them six.

[*He blows out another candle.*]

The extinguishing of light is like the five purple palmations of cinquefoil withering . . . It is full of incipiencies of darkness . . . of desolation that rises as a feeling rises . . . Imagination wills the five purple palmations of cinquefoil. But in this light they have the appearance of withering . . . To feel and, in the midst of feeling, to imagine . . .

> [*He blows out another candle.*]

The extinguishing of light is like the four posts of a cadaver, two at its head and two at its feet, to-wit: its arms and legs.

> [*He blows out another candle.*]

It is like three peregrins, departing.

> [*He blows out another candle.*]

It is like heaven and earth in the eye of the disbeliever.

> [*He blows out another candle. He dances around the room. He returns to the single candle that remains burning.*]

The extinguishing of light is like that old Hesper, clapped upon by clouds.

> [*He stands in front of the candle, so as to obscure it.*]

The spikes of his light bristle around the edge of the bulk. The spikes bristle among the clouds and behind them. There is a spot where he was bright in the sky . . . It remains fixed a little in the mind.

> [*He opens the door at the right. Outside, the night is as blue as water. He crosses the stage and opens the door at the left. Once more he flings aside the curtains. He extinguishes his taper. He looks out. He speaks with elation.*]

Oh, ho! Here is matter beyond invention.

> [*He springs through the window. Curtain.*]

A CEREMONY

In the sixteen hundreds, three brothers left Holland to seek their fortunes. One found his way to Ceylon where he took up life with a herd of elephants. In his discourse before the elephants, he said that he was human, believing that this alone would be enough to establish himself among them. But the tradition of men among elephants was not the same as it was among men themselves; and the elephants concluding that man in general was less worthy of his tradition among other men than of his tradition among elephants condemned him and trampled him to death.

The second brother went to Brazil. Leaving the Dutch fort near Belem and pushing up the Amazon to a remote position, he was attacked by Indians, who had never before seen a Dutchman. When taken prisoner, he tried to procure his liberty by indicating, as best he could, that he was not an enemy, that in spite of many differences he and they were or could be friends and allies. The Indians, notwithstanding a tradition among them respecting Spaniards, determined to spare his life. They disarmed him and kept him a prisoner until his death. They held off from him, since they had no single tradition in common; and when they buried him they built a mound for him far from their own.

The third brother came to New Netherland and bought a farm at New Utrecht. He became a neighbor of people who had left Holland when he was a boy, to whom he brought letters and news from home and word of parents and friends. He had come from Leyden and was welcome, as any one from an old land is welcome among those that have left it and know him. His merely being what he was composed of him and for him a tradition that was recognized. On his death he was buried under the altar of his church.

The ghosts of these three men met at dinner a long time later. The first ghost said of his discourse before the elephants that the appeal to tradition is not an appeal that can be made to barbarians, whether elephants or otherwise, since it is predicated on something that is held in common honor; and that it is this holding in common honor that gives it compulsion. The second ghost said of his dumb-show in the presence of the Indians that tradition is not ourselves imitating ourselves. If it was that, it would be what is left of the past and nothing more. Tradition is more than the memory and the customs of the memory. It is life's experiment made knowingly. The third ghost said that tradition is something that awakens a sense not only of that to which it relates but of itself. Thus when he had brought news of the university at Leyden to the fiscaal in New Amsterdam, when he had delivered messages from the many uncles who had stayed at home, when he had described the new banners in the old church, it was not only that the exiles to whom he spoke were back in Holland again, but that they felt a pride in having been, or of being still, a part of that of which such things could be said. The third ghost said that it is that pride, that warmth of feeling about many things, not only great things but also things small and dear to us, things held in common honor by those that have gone before us and by ourselves, that awaken a sense that tradition is like the revelations of an instinct.

At this moment, there entered into the room in which the

three ghosts were having their dinner, together with a much larger company of persons dining there, as if they were a single body or society, a group of men carrying a kind of litter, on which they bore an ancient bird of lead, a cock desperate to be abroad with all his feathers fighting the wind. At this gallant sight, the whole company rose to salute the procession waving their napkins in the air in a storm, in the midst of which the three ghosts suddenly vanished.

FANFARE IN THE MODE

OF

MYNHEER VAN DONK

PROCESSION

ADAGIA

ADAGIA

Happiness is an acquisition.

Progress in any aspect is a movement through changes of terminology.

The highest pursuit is the pursuit of happiness on earth.

Each age is a pigeon-hole.

The stream of consciousness is individual; the stream of life is total. Or, the stream of consciousness is individual, the stream of life, total.

To give a sense of the freshness or vividness of life is a valid purpose for poetry. A didactic purpose justifies itself in the mind of the teacher; a philosophical purpose justifies itself in the mind of the philosopher. It is not that one purpose is as justifiable as another but that some purposes are pure, others impure. Seek those purposes that are purely the purposes of the pure poet.

The poet makes silk dresses out of worms.

Merit in poets is as boring as merit in people.

Authors are actors, books are theatres.

An attractive view: The aspects of earth of interest to a poet are the casual ones, as light or color, images.

Definitions are relative. The notion of absolutes is relative.

Life is an affair of people not of places. But for me life is an affair of places and that is the trouble.

Wisdom asks nothing more.

Parfait Martinique: coffee mousse, rum on top, a little cream on top of that.

Literature is the better part of life. To this it seems inevitably necessary to add, provided life is the better part of literature.

Thought is an infection. In the case of certain thoughts it becomes an epidemic.

It is life that we are trying to get in poetry.

After one has abandoned a belief in god, poetry is that essence which takes its place as life's redemption.

Art, broadly, is the form of life or the sound or color of life. Considered as form (in the abstract) it is often indistinguishable from life itself.

The poet seems to confer his identity on the reader. It is easiest to recognize this when listening to music—I mean this sort of thing: the transference.

Accuracy of observation is the equivalent of accuracy of thinking.

A poem is a meteor.

An evening's thought is like a day of clear weather.

The loss of a language creates confusion or dumbness.

The collecting of poetry from one's experience as one goes along is not the same thing as merely writing poetry.

The relation of art to life is of the first importance especially in a skeptical age since, in the absence of a belief in God, the mind turns to its own creations and examines them, not alone from the aesthetic point of view, but for what they reveal, for what they validate and invalidate, for the support that they give.

A grandiose subject is not an assurance of a grandiose effect but, most likely, of the opposite.

Art involves vastly more than the sense of beauty.

Life is the reflection of literature.

As life grows more terrible, its literature grows more terrible.

Poetry and materia poetica are interchangeable terms.

Usage is everything (*"Les idées sont destinées à être deformées à l'usage. Reconnâitre ce fait est une preuve de désinteressement."* Georges Braque. *Verve* No. 2).

The imagination wishes to be indulged.

A new meaning is the equivalent of a new word.

Poetry is not personal.

The earth is not a building but a body.

Manner is an additional element.

A dead romantic is a falsification.

The romantic cannot be seen through: it is for the moment willingly not seen through.

Poetry is a means of redemption.

Poetry is a form of melancholia. Or rather, in melancholy, it is one of the *"aultres choses solatieuses."*

The poet must come at least as the miraculous beast and, at his best, as the miraculous man.

The real is only the base. But it is the base.

Life cannot be based on a thesis, since by nature, it is based on instinct. A thesis, however, is usually present and living in the struggle between thesis and instinct.

The poem reveals itself only to the ignorant man.

The relation between the poetry of experience and the poetry of rhetoric is not the same thing as the relation between the poetry of reality and that of the imagination. Experience, at least in the case of a poet of any scope, is much broader than reality.

To a large extent, the problems of poets are the problems of painters, and poets must often turn to the literature of painting for a discussion of their own problems.

Weather is a sense of nature. Poetry is a sense.

Abstraction is a part of idealism. It is in that sense that it is ugly.

In poetry at least the imagination must not detach itself from reality.

Not all objects are equal. The vice of imagism was that it did not recognize this.

The poet must put the same degree of intentness into his poetry as, for example, the traveler into his adventure, the painter into his painting.

All poetry is experimental poetry.

The bare image and the image as a symbol are the contrast: the image without meaning and the image as meaning. When the image is used to suggest something else, it is secondary. Poetry as an imaginative thing consists of more than lies on the surface.

Politics is the struggle for existence.

One has a sensibility range beyond which nothing really exists for one. And in each this is different.

In poetry, you must love the words, the ideas and the images and rhythms with all your capacity to love anything at all.

The individual partakes of the whole. Except in extraordinary cases he never adds to it.

It is the belief and not the god that counts.

A journey in space equals a journey in time.

Things seen are things as seen.

What we see in the mind is as real to us as what we see by the eye.

Poetry must be irrational.

The purpose of poetry is to make life complete in itself.

Poetry increases the feeling for reality.

The mind is the most powerful thing in the world.

There is nothing in life except what one thinks of it.

There is nothing beautiful in life except life.

There is no wing like meaning.

Consider: I. That the whole world is material for poetry; II. That there is not a specifically poetic material.

One reads poetry with one's nerves.

The poet is the intermediary between people and the world in which they live and also, between people as between themselves; but not between people and some other world.

Sentimentality is a failure of feeling.

The imagination is the romantic.

Poetry is not the same thing as the imagination taken alone. Nothing is itself taken alone. Things are because of interrelations or interactions.

The final belief is to believe in a fiction, which you know to be a fiction, there being nothing else. The exquisite truth is to know that it is a friction and that you believe in it willingly.

All of our ideas come from the natural world: trees = umbrellas.

There is nothing so oppressive to a man of intellectual principle as unprincipled thinking.

Wine and music are not good until afternoon. But poetry is like prayer in that it is most effective in solitude and in the times of solitude as, for example, in the earliest morning.

Intolerance respecting other people's religion is toleration itself in comparison with intolerance respecting other people's art.

The great objective is the truth not only of the poem but of poetry.

Poetry is a poetic conception, however expressed. A poem is poetry expressed in words. But in a poem there is a poetry of words. Obviously, a poem may consist of several poetries.

The exposition of a theory of poetry involves a comparison with other theories and the analysis of all.

Ethics are no more a part of poetry than they are of painting.

The ideal is the actual become anaemic. The romantic is often pretty much the same thing.

As the reason destroys, the poet must create.

The exquisite environment of fact. The final poem will be the poem of fact in the language of fact. But it will be the poem of fact not realized before.

We live in the mind.

A poet must have something by nature and he must know more about the world by reason thereof.

The poet feels *abundantly* the poetry of everything.

To live in the world but outside of existing conceptions of it.

It is the explanations of things that we make to ourselves that disclose our character: The subjects of one's poems are the symbols of one's self or of one of one's selves.

Poetry has to be something more than a conception of the mind. It has to be a revelation of nature. Conceptions are artificial. Perceptions are essential.

A poem should be part of one's sense of life.

To read a poem should be an experience, like experiencing an act.

There is no difference between god and his temple.

War is the periodical failure of politics.

164

Money is a kind of poetry.

Poetry is an effort of a dissatisfied man to find satisfaction through words, occasionally of the dissatisfied thinker to find satisfaction through his emotions.

It is not every day that the world arranges itself in a poem.

The death of one god is the death of all.

In the presence of extraordinary actuality, consciousness takes the place of imagination.

Everything tends to become real; or everything moves in the direction of reality.

There is an intensely pejorative aspect of the idea of the real. The opposite should be the case. Its own poetry is actual.

One does not write for any reader except one.

Every man dies his own death.

The writer who is content to destroy is on a plane with the writer who is content to translate. Both are parasites.

The thing said must be the poem not the language used in saying it. At its best the poem consists of both elements.

A poet looks at the world as a man looks at a woman.

To have nothing to say and to say it in a tragic manner is not the same thing as to have something to say.

The poem is a nature created by the poet.

The aesthetic order includes all other orders but is not limited to them.

Religion is dependent on faith. But aesthetics is independent of faith. The relative positions of the two might be reversed. It is possible to establish aesthetics in the individual mind as immeasurably a greater thing than religion. Its present state is the result of the difficulty of establishing it except in the individual mind.

Perhaps there is a degree of perception at which what is real and what is imagined are one: a state of clairvoyant observation, accessible or possibly accessible to the poet or, say, the acutest poet.

The ultimate value is reality.

Realism is a corruption of reality.

Perhaps it is of more value to infuriate philosophers than to go along with them.

The world is the only thing fit to think about.

All history is modern history.

Poetry is the sum of its attributes.

I don't think we should insist that the poet is normal or, for that matter, that anybody is.

This happy creature— It is he that invented the Gods. It is he that put into their mouths the only words they have ever spoken!

Poetry is a purging of the world's poverty and change and evil and death. It is a present perfecting, a satisfaction in the irremediable poverty of life.

Poetry is the scholar's art.

The thing seen becomes the thing unseen. The opposite is, or seems to be, impossible.

To study and to understand the fictive world is the function of the poet.

When one is young everything is physical; when one is old everything is psychic.

Which is correct: whether, if I respect my ancestors I am bound to respect myself, or, if I respect myself I am bound to respect my ancestors?

The most beautiful thing in the world is, of course, the world itself. This is so not only logically but categorically.

The tongue is an eye.

God is a symbol for something that can as well take other forms, as, for example, the form of high poetry.

The time will come when poems like Paradise will seem like very *triste* contraptions.

The great conquest is the conquest of reality. It is not enough to present life, for a moment, as it might have been.

A poem is a pheasant.

How has the human spirit ever survived the terrific literature with which it has had to contend?

The gold dome of things is the perfected spirit.

Reality is a vacuum.

All men are murderers.

The word must be the thing it represents; otherwise, it is a symbol. It is a question of identity.

When the mind is like a hall in which thought is like a voice speaking, the voice is always that of someone else.

In dramatic poetry the imagination attaches itself to a heightened reality.

It is necessary to propose an enigma to the mind. The mind always proposes a solution.

There must be something of the peasant in every poet.

Aristotle is a skeleton.

The body is the great poem.

The purpose of poetry is to contribute to man's happiness.

There is a basic literature of which poetry is an essential part.

How things seem now is always a question of sensibility.

Man is an eternal sophomore.

It is necessary to any originality to have the courage to be an amateur.

Life is the elimination of what is dead.

The fundamental difficulty in any art is the problem of the normal.

The poet is the priest of the invisible.

Society is a sea.

Metaphor creates a new reality from which the original appears to be unreal.

The transition from make believe for one's self to make believe for others is the beginning, or the end, of poetry in the individual.

The acquisitions of poetry are fortuitous; *trouvailles*. (Hence, its disorder.)

Exhibitionism attaches and is not inherent.

Romanticism is to poetry what the decorative is to painting.

The great poem is the disengaging of (a) reality.

The eye sees less than the tongue says. The tongue says less than the mind thinks.

Reality is the motif.

We have to step boldly into man's interior world or not at all.

Genealogy is the science of correcting other genealogists' mistakes.

The poet must not adapt his experience to that of the philosopher.

Description is an element, like air or water.

The reading of a poem should be an experience. Its writing must be all the more so.

A poem is a café. (Restoration.)

Poets acquire humanity.

Thought tends to collect in pools.

The reason is a part of nature and is controlled by it.

Life is not people and scene but thought and feeling.

In the world of words, the imagination is one of the forces of nature.

Life is not free from its forms.

The poet comes to words as nature comes to dry sticks.

Words are the only melodeon.

Bringing out the music of the eccentric sounds of words is no different in principle from bringing out their form and its eccentricities (Cummings): language as the material of poetry not its mere medium or instrument.

We have made too much of life. A journal of life is rarely a journal of happiness.

Since men made the world, the inevitable god is the beggar.

Poetry sometimes crowns the search for happiness. It is itself a search for happiness.

God is a postulate of the ego.

Esthetique is the measure of a civilization: not the sole measure, but a measure.

Poetry must resist the intelligence almost successfully.

The romantic exists in precision as well as in imprecision.

Literature is based not on life but on propositions about life, of which this is one.

Life is a composite of the propositions about it.

A change of style is a change of subject.

Poetry is the statement of a relation between a man and the world.

The feeling or the insight is that which quickens the words, not the other way round.

A man cannot search life for unprecedented experiences.

In children it is not the imitation that pleases us, but our perception of it. In later life, the pejorative aspect of imitation discloses its inherent unpleasantness. To give pleasure an imitation must have been studied as an imitation and then it pleases us as art.

Everything accomplishes itself: fulfills itself.

The romantic is the first phase of (a non-pejorative) lunacy.

The full flower of the actual, not the California fruit of the ideal.

In the end, the aesthetic is completely crushed and destroyed by the inability of the observer who has himself been crushed to have any feeling for it left.

The world is myself. Life is myself.

God is in me or else is not at all (does not exist).

The world is a force, not a presence.

Loss of faith is growth.

172

People take the place of thoughts.

Life lived on the basis of opinion is more nearly life than life lived without opinion.

Thought is life.

Everyone takes sides in social change if it is profound enough.

Poetry is not limited to a single effect, as, for example, overt reality.

Poetry is a search for the inexplicable.

Poems are new subjects.

Ignorance is one of the sources of poetry.

Poetry is a pheasant disappearing in the brush.

We never arrive intellectually. But emotionally we arrive constantly (as in poetry, happiness, high mountains, vistas).

The imagination consumes and exhausts some element of reality.

The poet is a god, or, the young poet is a god. The old poet is a tramp.

If the mind is the most terrible force in the world, it is also the only force that defends us against terror. Or, the mind is the most terrible force in the world principally in this, that it is the only force that can defend us against itself. The modern world is based on this pensée.

The poet represents the mind in the act of defending us against itself.

Quære, whether the residual satisfaction in a poem is the intellectual one.

No man is a hero to anyone that knows him.

On the bearing of the poet: 1. The prestige of the poet is part of the prestige of poetry. 2. The prestige of poetry is essential to the prestige of the poet.

The world is at the mercy of the strongest mind in it whether that strength is the strength of sanity or insanity, cunning or good-will.

Every poem is a poem within a poem: the poem of the idea within the poem of the words.

The poetic view of life is larger than any of its poems (a larger thing than any poem); and to recognize this is the beginning of the recognition of the poetic spirit.

On the death of some men the world reverts to ignorance.

Poetry is the gaiety (joy) of language.

Words are everything else in the world.

Only a noble people evolve a noble God.

If the answer was frivolous, the question was frivolous.

Unless life is interesting, there is nothing left (or, unless life is made interesting).

The interest of life is experienced by participating and by being part, not by observing nor by thinking.

Eventually an imaginary world is entirely without interest.

To be at the end of fact is not to be at the beginning of imagination but it is to be at the end of both.

To sit in a park and listen to the locusts; to sit in a park and hear church-bells—two pasts or one present and one past?

What is meant by interest? Is it a form of liking?

One cannot spend one's time in being modern when there are so many more important things to be.

The man who asks questions seeks only to reach a point where it will no longer be necessary for him to ask questions.

I have no life except in poetry. No doubt that would be true if my whole life was free for poetry.

The more intensely one feels something that one likes the more one is willing for it to be what it is.

The mind is not equal to the demands or oratory, poetry, etc. . . .

There is a nature that absorbs the mixedness of metaphors.

The world of the poet depends on the world that he has contemplated.

Poetry is a health.

Poetry is great only as it exploits great ideas or what is the same thing great feelings.

Imagination applied to the whole world is vapid in comparison to imagination applied to a detail.

It is easier to copy than to think, hence fashion. Besides a community of originals is not a community.

There must be some wing on which to fly.

Poetry is a cure of the mind.

Most modern reproducers of life, even including the camera, really repudiate it. We gulp down evil, choke at good.

We like the world because we do.

The mind that in heaven created the earth and the mind that on earth created heaven were, as it happened, one.

Nothing could be more inappropriate to American literature than its English source since the Americans are not British in sensibility.

Poetry is a response to the daily necessity of getting the world right.

A poem should stimulate some sense of living and of being alive.

Reality is the spirit's true center.

A poem need not have a meaning and like most things in nature often does not have.

Newness (not novelty) may be the highest individual value in poetry. Even in the meretricious sense of newness a new poetry has value.

The essential fault of surrealism is that it invents without discovering. To make a clam play an accordion is to invent not to discover. The observation of the unconscious, so far as it can be observed, should reveal things of which we have previously been unconscious, not the familiar things of which we have been conscious plus imagination.

There is nothing in the world greater than reality. In this predicament we have to accept reality itself as the only genius.

Man is the imagination or rather the imagination is man.

To "subtilize experience" is to apprehend the complexity of the world, to perceive the intricacy of appearance.

Poetry is often a revelation of the elements of appearance.

Literature is the abnormal creating an illusion of the normal.

Poetry is a renovation of experience.

Originality is an escape from repetition.

The theory of poetry is the life of poetry.

Feed my lambs (on the bread of living) . . . The glory of god is the glory of the world . . . To find the spiritual in reality . . . To be concerned with reality.

The theory of poetry is the theory of life.

Reality is the object seen in its greatest common sense.

Poetry constantly requires a new relation.

Reality is not what it is. It consists of the many realities which it can be made into.

What reality lacks is a *nœud vital* with life.

French and English constitute a single language.

One's ignorance is one's chief asset.

Proposita: 1. God and the imagination are one. 2. The thing imagined is the imaginer.
The second equals the thing imagined and the imaginer are one. Hence, I suppose, the imaginer is God.

The greatest piece of fiction: Greek mythology. Classical mythology but Greek above Latin.

Poetry is (and should be) for the poet a source of pleasure and satisfaction, not a source of honors.

Gaiety in poetry is a precious characteristic but it should be a characteristic of diction.

Reality is a cliché from which we escape by metaphor. It is only *au pays de la métaphore qu'on est poète.*

The degrees of metaphor. The absolute object slightly turned is a metaphor of the object.

Some objects are less susceptible to metaphor than others. The whole world is less susceptible to metaphor than a tea-cup is.

There is no such thing as a metaphor of a metaphor. One does not progress through metaphors. Thus reality is the indispensable element of each metaphor. When I say that man is a god it is very easy to see that if I also say that a god is something else, god has become reality.

Poetry seeks out the relation of men to facts.

The imagination is man's power over nature.

Imagination is the only genius.

The momentum of the mind is all toward abstraction.

The effect of the imagination on the works of artists is a different subject from that in which I am interested. In art its effect is the production of qualities: as strength (Pater, Michelangelo) and its value is a question of the value of those qualities. In life it produces things and its value is a question of the value of those things as, for example, the value of works of art.

The imagination is the liberty of the mind and hence the liberty of reality.

Success as the result of industry is a peasant ideal.

Success is to be happy with the wise.

Suppose any man whose spirit has survived had consulted his contemporaries as to what to do, or what to think, or what music to write, and so on.

In the long run the truth does not matter.

It should be said of poetry that it is essentially romantic as if one were recognizing the truth about poetry for the first time. Although the romantic is referred to, most often, in a pejorative sense, this sense attaches, or should attach, not to the romantic in general but to some phase of the romantic that has become stale. Just as there is always a romantic that is potent, so there is always a romantic that is impotent.

Poetry creates a fictitious existence on an exquisite plane. This definition must vary as the plane varies, an exquisite plane being merely illustrative.

PROSE

A COLLECT OF PHILOSOPHY

It is often the case that concepts of philosophy are poetic. I thought, therefore, that you might like to consider the poetic nature of at least a few philosophic ideas. I have in mind ideas that are inherently poetic, as, for example, the concept of the infinity of the world. But when I wrote to Jean Wahl, who is both a poet and a philosopher, about ideas that are inherently poetic, he said immediately that no ideas are inherently poetic, that the poetic nature of any idea depends on the mind through which it passes. This is as true of the poetic aspect of nature as it is of the poetic aspect of ideas. The sun rises and sets every day and yet it brings to few men and to those men only infrequently a sense of the universe of space. However, the idea of the infinity of the world, which is the same thing as a sense of the universe of space, is an idea that we are willing to accept as inherently poetic even at moments when it means nothing at all, just as we are willing to assume that the rising and the setting of the sun are inherently poetic, even at moments when we are indifferent to them. The idea of the infinity of the world is a poetic idea because it gives the imagination sudden life. Bruno became the orator of the Copernican theory. He said,

By this knowledge we are loosened from the chains of a most narrow dungeon, and set at liberty to rove in a more august empire; we are removed from presumptuous boundaries and poverty to the innumerable riches of an infinite space, of so worthy a field, and of such beautiful worlds. . . . It is not reasonable to believe that any part of the world is without a soul, life, sensation and organic structure. From this infinite All, full of beauty and splendor, from the vast worlds which circle above us to the sparkling dust of stars beyond, the conclusion is drawn that there are an infinity of creatures, a vast multitude, which, each in its degree, mirrors forth the splendor, wisdom and excellence of the divine beauty. . . . There is but one celestial expanse, where the stars choir forth unbroken harmony.

If this is sixteenth-century philosophy, it is, equally, sixteenth-century poetry. One understands why Victor Hugo said, in his time, that the stars are no longer mentionable in poetry. The remark also illustrates Jean Wahl's point that that is poetic which the mind conceives to be so.

I

It will help to define what is intended by the poetic nature of concepts of philosophy to speak of a few of the things that are not intended. One of these things is a poetic way of thinking on the part of the philosopher. For the moment, I do not refer to a poetic way of writing as, for example, in the case of Plato and in modern times of Nietzsche, say, or Bergson. There is a poetic style or way of thinking. A poet's natural way of thinking is by way of figures, and while this includes figures of speech it also includes examples, illustrations and parallel cases generally. Take Leibniz, for instance. The following passage from his *Theodicy* is a compact of figurations:

We know a very small part of eternity, which is immeasurable in its extent. . . . Nevertheless from so slight an experience we rashly judge regarding the immeasurable and eternal, like men who, having been born and brought up in prison, or perhaps in the subterranean salt mines of the Sarmatians, should think that there is no other light in the world than that of the feeble lamp which hardly suffices to direct their steps. If you look at a very beautiful picture, having covered up the whole of it except a very small part, what will it present to your sight . . . but a confused mass of colors,

184

laid on without selection and without art? . . . The experience of the eyes in painting corresponds to that of the ears in music. Eminent composers very often mingle discords with harmonies so as . . . to prick the hearer, who becomes anxious as to what is going to happen, and is so much the more pleased when presently all is restored to order; just as . . . we delight in the show of danger that is connected with performances on the tight-rope, or sword-dancing; and we ourselves in jest half let go a little boy, as if about to throw him from us, like the ape which carried Christiern, king of Denmark, while still an infant in swaddling clothes, and then, as in jest, relieved the anxiety of everyone by bringing him safely back to his cradle.

We associate the name of Leibniz with his *Monadology*. He held that reality consists of a mass of monads, like bees clinging to a branch, although for him the branch was merely a different set of monads. Bertrand Russell said that Leibniz's monads were gods. Monad by monad, then, by way of the course of an immense unity, he achieved God. The concept of this monadic creation seems to be the disappointing production of a poet *manqué*. Leibniz had a poet's manner of thinking but there was something a little too methodical about it. He had none of the enthusiasm of Bruno. There are those who regard a world of monads as poetic. Certainly the idea transforms reality. Moreover, in a system of monads, we come, in the end, to a man who is not only a man but sea and mountain, too, and to a God who is not only all these: man and sea and mountain but a God as well. Yet the idea seems to be completely lacking in anything securely lofty. Leibniz was a poet without flash. It is worth while stopping to think about him a moment because with all the equipage of a poet he never exposed any of a poet's brilliant excess in accomplishment. This may be because he was too intent on exposing something else and because he wanted his figures of speech to be the most understandable that would serve. It is worth while stopping to think of him because he stands for a class: the philosopher afraid of ornament. Men engaged in the elucidation of obscurity might well feel a horror of the metaphor. But the class I have in mind is the class to which metaphor is native and inescapable, which chooses to make its metaphors plain, and thinks from the true abundance of its thought. The disposition to metaphor cannot be kept concealed by the choice of metaphor; and one cannot help thinking that the presence of discipline is as much of an intrusion as the absence of it and, in the case of a man of genius, a deprivation and destruction. For a comparison between thinking like a philosopher and thinking like a poet, compare the quality of the image of the resemblance between the tension produced by a composer and the tension produced by a performer on the tight-rope with the quality of the image used by Jowett in his introduction to the *Phaedo*:

Is the soul related to the body as sight to the eye, or as the boatman to his boat?

Poets and philosophers often think alike, as we shall see. For the present, we must deny ourselves the definitions of poetry which are exceeded only by the definitions of philosophy. Leibniz, to sum it up, was a man who thought like a poet but did not write like one, although that seems strangely impossible; and, in consequence, his *Monadology* instead of standing as one of the world's revelations looks like a curious machine, several centuries old.

Another thing not intended is a poetic way of writing. If thinking in a poetic way is not the same thing as writing in a poetic way, so writing in a poetic way is not the same thing as having ideas that are inherently poetic conceptions. This is an accurate statement in the sense in which I mean it. Yet Plato wrote in a poetic way and certainly the doctrines of which he was so constantly prolific are with great frequency concepts poetic

186

per se. When I say that writing in a poetic way is not the same thing as having ideas that are inherently poetic concepts, I mean that the formidable poetry of Nietzsche, for example, ultimately leaves us with the formidable poetry of Nietzsche and little more. In the case of Bergson, we have a poetry of language, which made William James complain of its incessant euphony. But we also have the *élan vital*. In the case of Santayana, who was an exquisite and memorable poet in the days when he was, also, a young philosopher, the exquisite and memorable way in which he has always said things has given so much delight that we accept what he says as we accept our own civilization. His pages are part of the *douceur de vivre* and do not offer themselves for sensational summary.

Nor are we interested in philosophic poetry, as, for example, the poetry of Lucretius, some of the poetry of Milton and some of the poetry of Pope, and those pages of Wordsworth, which have done so much to strengthen the critics of poetry in their attacks on the poetry of thought. Theoretically, the poetry of thought should be the supreme poetry. Hegel called poetry the art of arts, specifically because in poetry the material of which the poem is made, that is to say, the language of the poem, is wholly subordinated to the idea. A poem in which the poet has chosen for his subject a philosophic theme should result in the poem of poems. That the wing of poetry should also be the rushing wing of meaning seems to be an extreme aesthetic good; and so in time and perhaps, in other politics, it may come to be. It is very easy to imagine a poetry of ideas in which the particulars of reality would be shadows among the poem's disclosures. If we are to dismiss from poetry expectations of that nature, we might equally well dismiss from philosophy all the profound expectations on which it is based. Of course, poems like the *De Rerum Natura* and the *Essay on Man* do not stir us particularly one way or the other, that is to say, either as poetry or philosophy. The great poetry I have projected is a compensation of time to come. In our consideration of the poetic aspect of philosophy it is enough to dismiss the philosophic poem as irrelevant and yet, at the same time, to point out the perfection latent in it. After all, Socrates left descendants, and one of them, in his youth, may choose to be concerned with the self, not in the sense common to youthful poets, but in the major sense common to the descendants of Socrates. Paul Weiss says in his *Nature and Man* that every object in the universe has some pertinence to the self. That is the sense of the self common to the descendants of Socrates.

When one says that the poetry of thought should be the supreme poetry and when one considers with what thought has been concerned throughout so many ages, the themes of supreme poetry are not hard to identify. Dr. Weiss, who was kind enough to write several letters to me last summer in relation to this paper, sent me a formulation of central doctrines to assist in the selecting of ideas which I have described as inherently poetic. I quote from one of these letters because to do so is like turning the pages of one of those books of the future about which I have been speculating. He said,

Plato: all things participate in the good; all beings love what they do not have, to wit, the good. Aristotle: all beings strive to realize their peculiar goods, already exemplified in some being somewhere in the natural world. St. Francis and St. Bonaventure: all beings have at least a trace of God in them. St. Thomas Aquinas: all existence is owed to God. Descartes: all bodies are machines. Leibniz: the world is at once the best and most rational of worlds; all the things we know in experience are combinations of spirits. Spinoza: all things happen by necessity; all things are in God. Kant: to be free is to be moral, and to be moral is to be free. Hegel: negation is a force; the absolute works out its own destiny; what comes to be is right.

Dr. Weiss did not limit himself to these formulations. He recognized that they were over-simplified. He said,

If by a poetic view we mean one which probes beneath those used in daily living, or one which cuts across the divisions which are normative to ordinary discourse, then all philosophy must be said to be poetic in conception and doctrine. It writes a cosmic poetry in prose, making use of such abstract terms as being, individuality, causality, etc. in order to talk about the presuppositions of all there is.

That all philosophy is poetic in conception and doctrine is no more true than that all poetry is philosophic in conception and doctrine. But if it was true, it would not mean that the object of all philosophic study is to achieve poetry. It would only mean what I have intended from the beginning and that is that it is often the case that the concepts of philosophy are poetic. Dr. Weiss's last remark is a statement of one of the reasons why that is true. Certainly a sense of the infinity of the world is a sense of something cosmic. It is cosmic poetry because it makes us realize in the same way in which an escape from all our limitations would make us realize that we are creatures, not of a part, which is our everyday limitation, but of a whole for which, for the most part, we have as yet no language. This sudden change of a lesser life for a greater one is like a change of winter for spring or any other transmutation of poetry. Not all philosophy probes beneath daily living. Does the philosophy of science? Not all the abridgements of abstraction draw us away into metaphysical spheres. Was John Locke a mystic? It is true that philosophy is poetic in conception and doctrine to the extent that the ideas of philosophy may be described as poetic concepts. It is true all the way and not merely to an extent as Dr. Weiss puts it. To the extent stated, however, it demonstrates itself and nothing more is required. A realization of the infinity of the world is equally a perception of philosophy and a typical metamorphosis of poetry.

Essentially what I intend is that it shall be as if the philosophers had no knowledge of poetry and suddenly discovered it in their search for whatever it is that they are searching for and gave the name of poetry to that which they discovered. Whether one arrives at the idea of God as a philosopher or as a poet matters greatly. The philosopher if he sees God himself as a philosopher, and he usually does, adorns him with the regalia and immanences with which it would be natural for a poet to adorn him. There are levels of thought or vision where everything is poetic. But there are levels of philosophy and for that matter of poetry where nothing is poetic. Our object is to stay on the levels where everything is poetic and to give attention to what we find there, that is to say, to identify at least a few philosophic ideas that are inherently poetic and to comment on them, one by one and, then, in general. We have already noticed the idea of the infinity of the world and the somewhat furious poetry that it brought about in Bruno and we have spoken of Leibniz's world of monads or spirits. Before we stop to look at another eccentric philosophic apparatus on the grand scale in the *World as Will* of Schopenhauer, let us take a look or two at some of the poetic concepts that have resulted from the study of perception.

According to the traditional views of sensory perception, we do not see the world immediately but only as the result of a process of seeing and after the completion of that process, that is to say, we never see the world except the moment after. Thus we are constantly observing the past. Here is an idea, not the result of poetic thinking and entirely without poetic intention, which instantly changes the face of the world. Its effect is that of an almost inappreciable change of which, nevertheless, we remain acutely conscious. The material world, for all the assurances of the eye, has become immaterial. It has become an image in the mind. The solid earth disappears and the whole atmosphere is subtilized not by the arrival of some venerable beam of light from an almost hypothetical star but by a breach of reality. What we see is not an external world but an image of it and hence an internal world. Berkeley rushed into this breach. He said,

It is indeed an opinion strangely prevailing amongst men, that houses, mountains, rivers, and in a word all sensible objects, have an existence, natural or real, distinct from their being perceived by the understanding. But with how great an assurance and acquiescence soever this principle may be entertained in the world, yet whoever shall find in his heart to call it in question may, if I mistake not, perceive it to involve a manifest contradiction. For what are the fore-mentioned objects but the things we perceive by sense? And what do we perceive besides our own ideas or sensations? And is it not plainly repugnant that any one of these, or any combination of them, should exist unperceived?

This was only one phase of Berkeley's philosophy. We are not interested, here, in following it beyond this stage. The point is that poetry is to a large extent an art of perception and that the problems of perception as they are developed in philosophy resemble similar problems in poetry. It may be said that to the extent that the analysis of perception in philosophy leads to ideas that are poetic the problems are identical. Whitehead has an important chapter related to this, "The Romantic Reaction," in his *Science and the Modern World*. He refers particularly to Wordsworth and Shelley. We have time only to mention this and, for the sake of disclosing another part of what he calls "the perceptual field," to quote one or two sentences, as follows:

191

My theory involves the entire abandonment of the notion that simple location is the primary way in which things are involved in space-time. In a certain sense, everything is everywhere at all times, for every location involves an aspect of itself in every other location. Thus every spatio-temporal standpoint mirrors the world.

These words are pretty obviously words from a level where everything is poetic, as if the statement that every location involves an aspect of itself in every other location produced in the imagination a universal iridescence, a dithering of presences and, say, a complex of differences.

I spoke a moment ago of the *World as Will*. Many of the ideas with which we are concerned have been very briefly summarized by Rogers in his *A Student's History of Philosophy*. I shall make use of his summary of Schopenhauer, as I have made use, elsewhere in this paper, of others of his summaries. He says,

While the world is illusion, mere appearance, there exists behind it a reality which appears—the thing-in-itself of Kant. . . . Is this thing really unknowable, however, as Kant had claimed? . . . Schopenhauer . . . agrees that we cannot reach it by the pathway of the reason. . . . Our insight into its nature is rather the outcome of a direct intuition of genius. . . . Now the inner essence of man's nature is *will*. It is as will that the reality of his own body comes home to him immediately. The various parts of the body are the visible expression of desires; teeth, throat and bowels are objectified hunger; the brain is the will to know, the foot the will to go, the stomach the will to digest. It is only as a secondary outcome of this original activity that the thought life arises. We think in order to do; the active impulse precedes, and is the necessary basis for, any conscious motion. And this insight, once attained, throws a flood of light on the outer world. The eternally striving, energizing power which is working everywhere in the universe— in the instinct of the animal, the life process of the plant, the blind force of inorganic matter—what is this but the will that underlies all existence? . . . Reality, then, is will. . . . We must leave out of our conception of the universal will that action for intelligent

ends which characterizes human willing. . . . The will is
deeper seated than the intellect; it is the blind man carrying
his shoulders the lame man who can see.

These words depict, in the imagination, a text of the grotesque, both human and inhuman. It is the text of a poem
although not a happy one. It is, in a way, the same poem as the
poem of Leibniz although the terms are different. It is the
cosmic poem of the ascent into heaven. I suppose that some
kinds of faith require logical, even though fantastic, structures
of this kind to support them on the way of that ascent. The
number of ways of passing between the traditional two fixed
points of man's life, that is to say, of passing from the self
to God, is fixed only by the limitations of space, which is
limitless. The eternal philosopher is the eternal pilgrim on that
road. It is difficult to take him seriously when he relies on the
evidence of the teeth, the throat and the bowels. Yet in the one
poem that is unimpeachably divine, the poem of the ascent
into heaven, it is possible to say that there can be no faults, since
it is precisely the faults of life that this poem enables us to
leave behind. If the idea of God is the ultimate poetic idea,
then the idea of the ascent into heaven is only a little below
it. Conceding that not all philosophy is concerned with this
particular poem, nevertheless a great deal of it is, and always
has been, and the philosophy of Schopenhauer is. The poets of
that theme find things on the way and what they find on the
way very often interests as much as what they find in the end.
Thus, Samuel Alexander in *Space, Time and Deity* finds the
order of compresence. He says,

What is of importance is the recognition that in any experience
the mind enjoys itself and contemplates its object or its object is
contemplated, and that these two existences, the act of the mind
and the object as they are in the experience, are distinct existences
united by the relation of compresence. The experience is a piece

ıg of these two existences in their togetherness.
the enjoyed, enjoys itself, or experiences itself
the other existence, the contemplated, is experi-
ıjoyed. The enjoyed and the contemplated are to-

...ler expresses himself with the same straining for the
utı. ...actness in the words he uses as the straining of a poet
for like exactness.

As a matter of fact, it is what philosophers find on the way
that constitutes the body of philosophy for if the end is appointed in advance neither logic nor the lack of it can affect
their passage. Jean Wahl wrote to me, saying

I am just now reading the *Méditations Cartesiennes* by Husserl.
Very dry. But he affirms that there is an enormous (ungeheueres)
a priori in our minds, an inexhaustible infinity of a priori. He speaks
of the approach to the unapproachable.

This enormous a priori is potentially as poetic a concept as
the idea of the infinity of the world. Jean Wahl spoke, also, of
other things in which you might be interested: of Pascal in a
frightened mood saying "*Le silence de ces espaces infinis
m'effraie*," adding appropriately that in Victor Hugo one might
find echoes of that idea. He quoted again from Pascal: "*La
sphère dont le centre est partout et la circonférence est nulle
part*," as a concept belonging to our category. He spoke of the
idea of the *ricorsi* of Vico; the idea of the *Ewiges Wiederkehr*
of Nietzsche; the idea of freedom as developed in the French
philosopher Lequier; the idea of "*les verités éternelles*" of
Malebranche. He particularly suggested the poems of Traherne.
We have, however, excluded poems of philosophical intentions
from our discussion. He had spoken in an earlier letter of Novalis
influenced by the ideas of Fichte; Hölderlin influencing, in his

opinion, the young Hegel; Shelley influenced by Plato; Blake; Mallarmé influenced by the Kabbala and Hegel. But these were all poets and I was approaching the subject the other way and with a different end in view. I was not interested in the philosophy of poets but in the poetry of philosophers. He made many other suggestions which I am happy to acknowledge for there is no one, what with his immense reading, to whom I could be more easily or more willingly indebted. I am not a philosopher.

Jean Paulhan sent some notes. He said,

It seems to me that the old psychological theory of perception considered as a true hallucination is the very type of the call to poetry. . . . The first word of the philosophy of the sciences, today, is that science has no value execpt its effectiveness and that nothing, absolutely nothing, constitutes an assurance that the external world resembles the idea that we form of it. Is that a poetic idea? Antipoetic, rather, in that it is opposite to the confidence which the poet, by nature, reposes, and invites us to repose, in the world. Let us say that it needs poetry to rise above itself; hence that it is an invitation to much poetry. It is an indirect way of being poetic.

Later on, he expressed himself as thinking that the philosophy of the sciences would lend itself better to the kind of poetry that I am trying to specify. His attitude toward the problem was not that of a man looking at the past but that of a man looking at the present and asking himself whether the concepts of the philosophy of the sciences are poetic. He said,

It is admitted, since Planck, that determinism—the relation of cause to effect—exists, or so it seems, on the human scale, only by means of an aggregate of statistical compensations and as the physicists say, by virtue of macroscopic approximations. (There is much to dream about in these macroscopic approximations.) As to the true nature of corpuscular or quantic phenomena, well, try to imagine them. No one has yet succeeded. But the poets—it is possible.

And later, because his mind had been engaged by the subject, he sent a last word. He said,

It comes to this that philosophers (particularly the philosophers of science) make, not discoveries but hypotheses that may be called poetic. Thus Louis de Broglie admits that progress in physics is, at the moment, in suspense because we do not have the words or the images that are essential to us. But to create illuminations, images, words, that is the very reason for being of poets.

III

Let us see, now, what deductions can be made from all this material.

First of all, since a similarity has been established between poets and philosophers and since it can no longer be necessary to argue that a measure of identity exists between them, what is the fundamental respect that separates them. The habit of forming concepts unites them. The use to which they put their ideas separates them. By the habit of forming concepts, I do not, of course, mean merely thinking, for all men have in common the habit of thinking. The habit of forming concepts is a habit of the mind by which it probes for an integration. Where we see the results of that habit in the works of philosophers we may think that it is a habit which they share with no one else. This is untrue. The habit of probing for an integration seems to be part of the general will to order. We must, therefore, go a step farther and look for the respect that separates the poet and the philosopher in the kind of integrations for which they search. The philosopher searches for an integration for its own sake, as, for example, Plato's idea that knowledge is recollection or that the soul is a harmony; the poet searches for an integration that shall be not so much sufficient in itself as sufficient for some quality that it possesses, such as its insight, its evocative power or its appearance in the eye of the imagination. The philosopher intends his integration to be fateful; the poet intends his to be effective.

And yet these integrations, although different from each other, have something in common, such as, say, a characteristic of the depth or distance at which they have been found, a facture of the level or position of the mind or, if you like, of a level or position of the feelings, because in the excitement of bringing things about it is not always easy to say whether one is thinking or feeling or doing both at the same time. The probing of the philosopher is deliberate, as the history of the part that logic has played in philosophy demonstrates. Yet one finds it simple to assume that the philosopher more or less often experiences the same miraculous shortenings of mental processes that the poet experiences. The whole scheme of the world as will may very well have occurred to Schopenhauer in an instant. The time he spent afterward in the explication of that instant is another matter. The idea of the Hegelian state, one of the masterpieces of idealism, may very well have come into Hegel's mind effortlessly and as a whole, as distinct from its details, in the same way that the gist of a poem comes into the poet's mind and takes possession of it. It remains true, however, that the probing of the philosopher is deliberate. On the other hand, the probing of the poet is fortuitous. I am speaking of the time before he has found his subject, because, once he has found his subject, that is to say, once he has achieved the integration for which he has been probing, he becomes as deliberate, in his own way, as the philosopher. Up to the point at which he has found his subject, the state of vague receptivity in which he goes about resembles one part of something that is dependent on another part, which he is not quite able to specify. In any case, it is misleading to speak of the depth or distance at which their integrations are found, or of the level or position of the mind or feelings, if the fact is that they probe in different spheres and if, in their different spheres, they move about by means of different motions. It may be said that the philosopher probes the sphere or spheres of perception and that he moves about therein like someone intent on making sure of every foot of the way. If the poet moves about in the same sphere or spheres, and occasionally he may, he is light-footed. He is intent on what he sees and hears and the sense of the certainty of the presences about him is as nothing to the presences themselves. The philosopher's native sphere is only a metaphysical one. The poet's native sphere is the sphere of which du Bellay wrote: "my village . . . my own small house . . .

> My Gaulish Loire more than the Latin Tiber,
> My tiny Lyré more than the Palatine hill,
> And more than sea-salt air, the sweet air of Anjou."

This seductive quotation takes one away from the sphere of perception a little too abruptly and too completely; for, after all, the philosopher, also, has a solid land that he loves. The poet's native sphere, to speak more accurately, is what he can make of the world.

The uses to which the philosopher and the poet put the world are different and the ends that they have in mind are different. This statement raises the question of the final cause of philosophy and the final cause of poetry. The answers to this question are as countless as the definitions of philosophy and poetry. The other day I read a phrase of Alain: "the history of doctrines." These words give us a single sense and an inadequate sense of what philosophy is. If I say poetry constantly requires a new station, it is a way, and an inadequate way, of saying what poetry is. To define philosophy and to define poetry are parts of the repertory of the mind. They are classic exercises.
ot be true if the definitions were adequate. In view
ilty about definitions, any discussion of the final

causes of philosophy and poetry must be limited, here, to pointing out the relation between the question of purposes and the miscellany of definitions. And yet for all the different kinds of philosophy it is possible to generalize and to say that the philosopher's world is intended to be a world, which yet remains to be discovered and which, at bottom, the philosophers probably hope will always remain to be discovered and that the poet's world is intended to be a world, which yet remains to be celebrated and which, at bottom, the poets probably hope will always remain to be celebrated. If the philosopher's world is this present world plus thought, then the poet's world is this present world plus imagination. If we think of the philosopher and the poet as raised to their highest exponents and made competent to realize everything that the figures of the philosopher and the poet, as projected in the mind of their creator, were capable of or, in other words, if we magnify them, what would they compose, by way of fulfilling not only themselves but also by way of fulfilling the aims of their creator? This brings us face to face once more with all the definitions. But whatever they composed, they could not compose the same thing and, perhaps, we should wonder what had ever led us to believe that they were close together.

Yet we should never be able to get away, even under this extreme magnifying, from the sense that they had in common the idea of creating confidence in the world:

> la confiance que le poète fait naturellement—
> et nous invite à faire—au monde.

The confidence of the philosopher might be a certainty with respect to something to be left behind. The confidence of the poet might be a more immediate certainty. These are ancient routines. The means used by philosophers and poets alike change and disappear. Other means take their place. An immense amount of philosophy is no longer part of our thought and yet perpetuates itself. The soul and Leibniz's swarms of spirits and Schopenhauer's manifestations of will, which appear to us to be eccentric conceptions, are not junk. Thus the soul lives as the self. When we read the *Phaedo*, we stand in the presence of Socrates, in the chamber in which he is shortly to die and we listen to him as he expounds his ideas concerning immortality. We observe that the confidence in the immortality of what was really Socrates was no less a confidence in the world, in which he reclined and spoke, a hostile and a fatal world. When we look over the shoulder of Jean Paulhan, in Paris, while he writes of *"la confiance . . . au monde"* and stop to consider what a happy phrase that is, we wonder whether we shall have the courage to repeat it, until we understand that there is no alternative. So many words other than confidence might have been used—words of understanding, words of reconciliation, of enchantment, even of forgetfulness. But none of them would have penetrated to our needs more surely than the word confidence.

The most significant deduction possible relates to the question of supremacy as between philosophy and poetry. If we say that philosophy is supreme, this means that the reason is supreme over the imagination. But is it? Does not philosophy carry us to a point at which there is nothing left except the imagination? If we rely on the imagination (or, say, intuition), to carry us beyond that point, and if the imagination succeeds in carrying us beyond that point (as in respect to the idea of God, if we conceive of the idea of God as this world's capital idea), then the imagination is supreme, because its powers have shown themselves to be greater than the powers of the reason. Philosophers, however, are not limited to the reason and, as the concepts, to which I have referred, show, their ideas are often triumphs of the imagination. To call attention to ideas in which the reason and the imagination have been acting in concert is a way of saying that when they act in concert they are supreme and is not the same thing as to say that one is supreme over the other. I might have cited the idea of God when I was speaking of the infinity of the world, of the infinite spaces, which terrified Pascal, the most devout of believers and, in the same abandonment to the superlative, the most profound of thinkers; and it would have been possible, in that case, to conclude what I have to say by placing here at the end a figure which would leave the question of supremacy a question too difficult to attempt to solve. In his words about the sphere of which the center is everywhere and the circumference nowhere, which I quoted a moment ago, we have an instance of words in which traces of the reason and traces of the imagination are mingled together.

However, instead of placing at the end the figure of Pascal, let me place here the figure of Planck. I recognize that Pascal was a much greater human being. On the other hand, Planck, who died only four years ago at Göttingen, at the age of ninety, was a much truer symbol of ourselves; and in that true role is a more significant figure for us than the remote and almost fictitious figure of Pascal. I referred to him earlier and in relation to the quantum theory. There has recently been published in Europe a group of his posthumous texts, of which one is a thesis on *The Concept of Causality in Physics*. He was, of course, the patriarch of all modern physicists. André George published a note on these last writings of this great scholar in *Les Nouvelles Littéraires*, which I summarize to the extent that it is in point, particularly in respect to the thesis on causality. He says:

. . . The last pages of the thesis are quite curious. One feels there, as it were, a supreme hesitation; the believer henceforth is no longer able to conceal a certain trouble. The most convinced determinist, Planck declares, in so many words, is not able to satisfy himself entirely with such an intepretation. For, in the end, a universal principle like the rigorous causal bond between two successive events ought to be independent of man. It is a principle of cosmic importance, it ought to be an absolute. Now, Planck not only recognizes that it is part of human aptitude to foresee events but to foresee them by means of science, "the provisional and changing creation of the power of the imagination." How then liberate the concept from such an anthropomorphic hypothesis? Only an intelligence external to man, "not constituting a part of nature," would be able to liberate it. This supra-natural intelligence would act through the deterministic power . . . Planck thereupon concludes that the law of casuality is neither true nor false. It is a working hypothesis.

George says, finally, that this conclusion is far away from the rigid concept, firmly determinist, which seemed up to now to constitute Planck's belief. He calls it a nuance but a nuance of importance, worth being signalized.

I think we may fairly say that it is a nuance of the imagination, one of those unwilled and innumerable nuances of the imagination that we find so often in the works of philosophers and so constantly in the works of poets. It is unexpected to have to recognize even in Planck the presence of the poet. It is as if in a study of modern man we predicated the greatness of poetry as the final measure of his stature, as if his willingness to believe beyond belief was what had made him modern and was always certain to keep him so.

❀◇

TWO OR THREE IDEAS

My first proposition is that the style of a poem and the poem itself are one.

One of the better known poems in *Fleurs du Mal* is the one (XII) entitled "La Vie Antérieure" or "Former Life." It begins with the line

J'ai longtemps habité sous de vastes portiques

or

A long time I lived beneath tremendous porches.

It continues:

Which the salt-sea suns tinged with a thousand fires
And which great columns, upright and majestic,
At evening, made resemble basalt grottoes.

The poem concerns the life among the images, sounds and colors of those calm, sensual presences.

At the center of azure, of waves, of brilliances,

and so on. I have chosen this poem to illustrate my first proposition, because it happens to be a poem in which the poem itself is immediately recognizable without reference to the manner in which it is rendered. If the style and the poem are one, one ought to choose, for the purpose of illustration, a poem that illustrates this as, for example, Yeats' *Lake-Isle of Innisfree*. To choose a French poem which has to be translated is to choose an example in which the style is lost in the paraphrase of translation. On the other hand, Baudelaire's poem is useful because it identifies what is meant by the poem itself. The idea of an earlier life is like the idea of a later life, or like the idea of a different life, part of the classic repertory of poetic ideas. It is part of one's inherited store of poetic subjects. Precisely, then, because it is traditional and because we understand its romantic nature and know what to expect from it, we are suddenly and profoundly touched when we hear it declaimed by a voice that says:

I lived, for long, under huge porticoes.

It is as if we had stepped into a ruin and were startled by a flight of birds that rose as we entered. The familiar experience is made unfamiliar and from that time on, whenever we think of that particular scene, we remember how we held our breath and how the hungry doves of another world rose out of nothingness and whistled away. We stand looking at a remembered habitation. All old dwelling-places are subject to these transmogrifications and the experience of all of us includes a succession of old dwelling-places: abodes of the imagination, ancestral or memories of places that never existed. It is plain that when, in this world of weak feeling and blank thinking, in which we are face to face with the poem every moment of time, we encounter some integration of the poem that pierces and dazzles us, the effect is an effect of style and not of the poem itself or at least not of the poem alone. The effective integration is not a disengaging of the subject. It is a question of the style in which the subject is presented.

Although I have limited myself to an instance of the relation between style and the familiar, one gets the same result in considering the relation between style and its own creations, that is between style and the unfamiliar. What we are really considering here are the creations of modern art and modern literature. If one keeps in mind the fact that most poets who have something to say are content with what they say and that most poets who have little or nothing to say are concerned primarily with the way in which they say it, the importance of this discussion becomes clear. I do not mean to imply that the poets who have something to say are the poets that matter; for obviously if it is true that the style of a poem and the poem itself are one, it follows that, in considering style and its own is to say, the relation between style and the may be, or become, that the poets who have little say are, or will be, the poets that matter. Today, painters who have something to say are less admired than painters who seem to have little or nothing to say but who do at least believe that style and the painting are one. The inclination toward arbitrary or schematic constructions in poetry is, from the point of view of style, very strong; and certainly if these constructions were effective it would be true that the style and the poem were one.

In the light of this first idea the prejudice in favor of plain English, for instance, comes to nothing. I have never been able to see why what is called Anglo-Saxon should have the right to higgle and haggle all over the page, contesting the right of other words. If a poem seems to require a hierophantic phrase, the phrase should pass. This is a way of saying that one of the consequences of the ordination of style is not to limit it, but to enlarge it, not to impoverish it, but to enrich and liberate it.

The second idea relates to poetry and the gods, both ancient and modern, both foreign and domestic. To simplify, I shall speak only of the ancient and the foreign gods. I do not mean to refer to them in their religious aspects but as creations of the imagination; and I suppose that as with all creations of the imagination I have been thinking of them from the point of view of style, that is to say of their style. When we think of Jove, while we take him for granted as the symbol of omnipotence, the ruler of mankind, we do not fear him. He does have a superhuman size, but at least not so superhuman as to amaze and intimidate us. He has a large head and a beard and is a relic, a relic that makes a kindly impression on us and reminds us of stories that we have heard about him. All of the noble images of all of the gods have been profound and most of them have been forgotten. To speak of the origin and end of gods is not a light matter. It is to speak of the origin and end of eras of human belief. And while it is easy to look back on those that have disappeared as if they were the playthings of cosmic make-believe, and on those that made petitions to them and honored them and received their benefits as legendary innocents, we are bound, nevertheless, to concede that the gods were personae of a peremptory elevation and glory. It would be wrong to look back to them as if they had existed in some indigence of the spirit. They were in fact, as we see them now, the clear giants of a vivid time, who in the style of their beings made the style of the gods and the gods themselves one.

This brings me to the third idea, which is this: In an age of disbelief, or, what is the same thing, in a time that is largely humanistic, in one sense or another, it is for the poet to supply the satisfactions of belief, in his measure and in his style. I say in his measure to indicate that the figures of the philosopher, the artist, the teacher, the moralist and other figures, including the poet, find themselves, in such a time, to be figures of an importance greatly enhanced by the requirements both of the individual and of society; and I say in his style by way of confining the poet to his role and thereby of intensifying that role. It is this that I want to talk about today. I want to try to formulate a conception of perfection in poetry with reference to the present time and the near future and to speculate on the activities possible to it as it deploys itself throughout the lives of men and women. I think of it as a role of the utmost seriousness. It is, for one thing, a spiritual role. One might stop to draw an ideal portrait of the poet. But that would be parenthetical. In any case, we do not say that the philosopher, the artist or the teacher is to take the place of the gods. Just so, we do not say that the poet is to take the place of the gods.

To see the gods dispelled in mid-air and dissolve like clouds is one of the great human experiences. It is not as if they had gone over the horizon to disappear for a time; nor as if they had been overcome by other gods of greater power and profounder knowledge. It is simply that they came to nothing. Since we have always shared all things with them and have always had a part of their strength and, certainly, all of their knowledge, we shared likewise this experience of annihilation. It was their annihilation, not ours, and yet it left us feeling that in a measure, we, too, had been annihilated. It left us feeling dispossessed and alone in a solitude, like children without parents, in a home that seemed deserted, in which the amical rooms and halls had taken on a look of hardness and emptiness. What was most extraordinary is that they left no momentoes behind, no thrones, no mystic rings, no texts either of the soil or of the soul. It was as if they had never inhabited the earth. There was no crying out for their return. They were not forgotten because they had been a part of the glory of the earth. At the same time, no man ever muttered a petition in his heart for the restoration of those unreal shapes. There was always in every man the increasingly human self, which instead of remaining the observer, the non-participant, the delinquent, became constantly more and more all there was or so it seemed; and whether it was so or merely seemed so still left it for him to resolve life and the world in his own terms.

Thinking about the end of the gods creates singular attitudes in the mind of the thinker. One attitude is that the gods of classical mythology were merely aesthetic projections. They were not the objects of belief. They were expressions of delight. Perhaps delight is too active a word. It is true that they were engaged with the future world and the immortality of the soul. It is true, also, that they were the objects of veneration and therefore of religious dignity and sanctity. But in the blue air of the Mediterranean these white and a little colossal figures had a special propriety, a special felicity. Could they have been created for that propriety, that felicity? Notwithstanding their divinity, they were close to the people among whom they moved. Is it one of the normal activities of humanity, in the solitude of reality and in the unworthy treatment of solitude, to create companions, a little colossal as I have said, who, if not superficially explicative, are, at least, assumed to be full of the secret of things and who in any event bear in themselves even, if they do not always wear it, the peculiar majesty of mankind's sense of worth, neither too much nor too little? To a people of high intelligence, whose gods have benefited by having been accepted and addressed by the superior minds of a superior world, the symbolic paraphernalia of the very great becomes unnecessary and the very great become the very natural. However all that may be, the celestial atmosphere of these deities, their ultimate remote celestial residences are not matters of chance. Their fundamental glory is the fundamental glory of men and women, who being in need of it create it, elevate it, without too much searching of its identity.

The people, not the priests, made the gods. The personages of immortality were something more than the conceptions of priests, although they may have picked up many of the conceits of priests. Who were the priests? Who have always been the high priests of any of the gods? Certainly not those officials or generations of officials who administered rites and observed rituals. The great and true priest of Apollo was he that composed the most moving of Apollo's hymns. The really illustrious archimandrite of Zeus was the one that made the being of Zeus people the whole of Olympus and the Olympian land, just as the only marvelous bishops of heaven have always been those that made it seem like heaven. I said a moment ago that we had not forgotten the gods. What is it that we remember of them? In the case of those masculine do we remember their ethics or is it their port and mien, their size, their color, not to speak of their adventures, that we remember? In the case of those feminine do we remember, as in the case of Diana, their fabulous chastity or their beauty? Do we remember those masculine in any way differently from the way in which we remember Ulysses and other men of supreme interest and excellence? In the case of those feminine do we remember Venus in any way differently from the way in which we remember Penelope and other women of much mark and feeling? In short, while the priests helped to realize the gods, it was the people that spoke of them and to them and heard their replies.

Let us stop now and restate the ideas which we are considering in relation to one another. The first is that the style of a poem and the poem itself are one; the second is that the style of the gods and the gods themselves are one; the third is that in an age of disbelief, when the gods have come to an end, when we think of them as the aesthetic projections of a time that has passed, men turn to a fundamental glory of their own and from that create a style of bearing themselves in reality. They create a new style of a new bearing in a new reality. This third idea, then, may be made to conform to the way in which the other two have been expressed by saying that the style of men and men themselves are one. Now, if the style of a poem and poem itself are one; if the style of the gods and the gods themselves are one; and if the style of men and men themselves are one; and if there is any true relation between these propositions, it might well be the case that the parts of these propositions are interchangeable. Thus, it might be true that the style of a poem and the gods themselves are one; or that the style of the gods and the style of men are one; or that the style of a poem and the style of men are one. As we hear these things said, without having time to think about them, it sounds as if they might be true, at least as if there might be something to them. Most of us are prepared to listen patiently to talk of the identity of the gods and men. But where does the poem come in? And if my answer to that is that I am concerned primarily with the poem and that my purpose this morning is to elevate the poem to the level of one of the major significances of life and to equate it, for the purpose of discussion, with gods and men, I hope it will be clear that it comes in as the central interest, the fresh and foremost object.

If in the minds of men creativeness was the same thing as creation in the natural world, if a spiritual planet matched the sun, or if without any question of a spiritual planet, the light and warmth of spring revitalized all our faculties, as in a measure they do, all the bearings one takes, all the propositions one formulates would be within the scope of that particular domination. The trouble is, however, that men in general do not create in light and warmth alone. They create in darkness and coldness. They create when they are hopeless, in the midst of antagonisms, when they are wrong, when their powers are no longer subject to their control. They create as the ministers of evil. Here in New England at this very moment nothing but good seems to be returning; and in that good, particularly if we ignore the difference between men and the natural world, how easy it is suddenly to believe in the poem as one has never believed in it before, suddenly to require of it a meaning beyond what its words can possibly say, a sound beyond any giving of the ear, a motion beyond our previous knowledge of feeling. And, of course, our three ideas have not only to be thought of as deriving what they have in common from the intricacies of human nature as distinguished from what the things of the natural world have in common, derived from strengths like light and warmth. They have to be thought of with reference to the meaning of style. Style is not something applied. It is something inherent, something that permeates. It is of the nature of that in which it is found, whether the poem, the manner of a god, the bearing of a man. It is not a dress. It may be said to be a voice that is inevitable. A man has no choice about his style. When he says I am my style the truth reminds him that it is his style that is himself. If he says, as my poem is, so are my gods and so am I, the truth remains quiet and broods on what he has said. He knows that the gods of China are always Chinese; that the gods of Greece are always Greeks and that all gods are created in the images of their creators; and he sees in these circumstances the operation of a style, a basic law. He observes the uniform enhancement of all things within the category of the imagination. He sees, in the struggle between the perfectible and the imperfectible, how the perfectible prevails, even though it falls short of perfection.

It is no doubt true that the creative faculties operate alike on poems, gods and men up to a point. They are always the same faculties. One might even say that the things created are always the same things. In case of a universal artist, all of his productions are his peculiar own. When we are dealing with racial units of the creative faculties all of the productions of one unit resemble one another. We say of a painting that it is Florentine. But we say the same thing and with equal certainty of a piece of sculpture. There is no difficulty in arguing about the poems, gods and men of Egypt or India that they look alike. But if the gods of India disappeared would not the poems of India and the men of India still remain alike. And if there were no poems, a new race of poets would produce poems that would take the place of the gods that had disappeared. What, then, is the nature of poetry in a time of disbelief? The truistic nature of some of the things that I have said shows how the free-will of the poet is limited. They demonstrate that the poetry of the future can never be anything purely eccentric and dissociated. The poetry of the present cannot be purely eccentric and dissociated. Eccentric and dissociated poetry is poetry that tries to exist or is intended to exist separately from the poem, that is to say in a style that is not identical with the poem. It never achieves anything more than a shallow mannerism, like something seen in a glass. Now, a time of disbelief is precisely a time in which the frequency of detached styles is greatest. I am not quite happy about the word detached. By detached, I mean the unsuccessful, the ineffective, the arbitrary, the literary, the non-umbilical, that which in its highest degree would still be words. For the style of the poem and the poem itself to be one there must be a mating and a marriage, not an arid love-song.

Yes: but the gods—now they come into it and make it a delicious subject, as if we were here together wasting our time on something that appears to be whimsical but turns out to be essential. They give to the subject just that degree of effulgence and excess, no more, no less, that the subject requires. Our first proposition, that the style of a poem and the poem itself are one was a definition of perfection in poetry. In the presence of the gods, or of their images, we are in the presence of perfection in created beings. The gods are a definition of perfection in ideal creatures. These remarks expound the second proposition that the style of the gods and the gods themselves are one. The exhilaration of their existence, their freedom from fate, their access to station, their liberty to command fix them in an atmosphere which thrills us as we share it with them. But these are merely attributes. What matters is their manner, their style, which tells us at once that they are as we wished them to be, that they have fulfilled us, that they are us but purified, magnified, in an expansion. It is their style that makes them gods, not merely privileged beings. It is their style most of all that fulfills themselves. If they lost all their privileges, their freedom from fate, their liberty to command, and yet still retained their style, they would still be gods, however destitute. That alone would destroy them, which deprived them of their style. When the time came for them to go, it was a time when their aesthetic had become invalid in the presence not of a greater aesthetic of the same kind, but of a different aesthetic, of which from the point of view of greatness, the difference was that of an intenser humanity. The style of the gods is derived from men. The style of the gods is derived from the style of men.

One has to pierce through the dithyrambic impressions that talk of the gods makes to the reality of what is being said. What is being said must be true and the truth of it must be seen. But the truth about the poet in a time of disbelief is not that he must turn evangelist. After all, he shares the disbelief of his time. He does not turn to Paris or Rome for relief from the monotony of reality. He turns to himself and he denies that reality was ever monotonous except in comparison. He asserts that the source of comparison having been eliminated, reality is returned, as if a shadow had passed and drawn after it and taken away whatever coating had concealed what lay beneath it. Yet the revelation of reality is not a part peculiar to a time of disbelief or, if it is, it is so in a sense singular to that time. Perhaps, the revelation of reality takes on a special meaning, without effort or consciousness on the part of the poet, at such a time. Why should a poem not change in sense when there is a fluctuation of the whole of appearance? Or why should it not change when we realize that the indifferent experience of life is the unique experience, the item of ecstasy which we have been isolating and reserving for another time and place, loftier and more secluded. There is inherent in the words *the revelation of reality* a suggestion that there is a reality of or within or beneath the surface of reality. There are many such realities through which poets constantly pass to and fro, without noticing the imaginary lines that divide one from the other. We were face to face with such a transition at the outset, for Baudelaire's line

A long time I passed beneath an entrance roof

opens like a voice heard in a theatre and a theatre is a reality within a reality. The most provocative of all realities is that

213

reality of which we never lose sight but never see solely as it is. The revelation of that particular reality or of that particular category of realities is like a series of paintings of some natural object affected, as the appearance of any natural object is affected, by the passage of time, and the changes that ensue, not least in the painter. That the revelation of reality has a character or quality peculiar to this time or that or, what is intended to be the same thing, that it is affected by states of mind, is elementary. The line from Baudelaire will not have the same effect on everyone at all times, any more than it will continue to have the same effect on the same person constantly. I remember that when a friend of mine in Ireland quoted the line, a few years ago, in a letter, my feeling about it was that it was a good instance of the value of knowing people of different educations. The chances are that my friend in Dublin and I have done much the same reading. The chances are, also, that we have retained many different things. For instance, this man had chosen Giorgione as the painter that meant most to him. For my own part, Giorgione would not have occurred to me. I should like you to be sure that in speaking of the revelation of reality I am not attempting to forecast the poetry of the future. It would be logical to conclude that, since a time of disbelief is also a time of truth-loving and since I have emphasized that I recognize that what I am trying to say is nothing unless it is true and that the truth of it must be seen, I think that the main characteristic of the poetry of the future or the near future will be an absence of the poetic. I do not think that. I cannot see what value it would have if I did, except as a value to me personally. If there is a logic that controls poetry, which everything that I have been saying may illustrate, it is not the narrow logic that exists on the level of prophecy. That there is a larger logic I have no doubt. But certainly it has to be large enough to allow for a good many irrelevancies.

One of the irrelevancies is the romantic. It looks like something completely contemptible in the light of literary intellectualism and cynicism. The romantic, however, has a way of renewing itself. It can be said of the romantic, just as it can be said of the imagination, that it can never effectively touch the same thing twice in the same way. It is partly because the romantic will not be what has been romantic in the past that it is preposterous to think of confining poetry hereafter to the revelation of reality. The whole effort of the imagination is toward the production of the romantic. When, therefore, the romantic is in abeyance, when it is discredited, it remains true that there is always an unknown romantic and that the imagination will not be forever denied. There is something a little romantic about the idea that the style of a poem and the poem itself are one. It seems to be a much more broadly romantic thing to say that the style of the gods and the gods themselves are one. It is completely romantic to say that the style of men and men themselves are one. To collect and collate these ideas of disparate things may seem to pass beyond the romantic to the fantastic. I hope, however, that you will agree that if each one of these ideas is valid separately, or more or less valid, it is permissible to have brought them together as a collective source of suppositions. What is romantic in all of them is the idea of style which I have not defined in any sense uniformly common to all three. A poem is a restricted creation of the imagination. The gods are the creation of the imagination at its utmost. Men are a part of reality. The gradations of romance noticeable as the sense of style is used with reference to these three, one by one, are relevant to the difficulties of the imagination in a truth-loving time. These difficulties exist only as one foresees them. They may never exist at all. An age in which the imagination might be expected to become part of time's *rejectamenta* may behold it established and protected and enthroned on one of the few ever-surviving thrones; and, to our surprise, we may find posted in the portico of its eternal dwelling, on the chief portal, among the morning's ordinances, three regulations which if they were once rules of art will then have become rules of conduct. By that time the one that will matter most is likely to be the last, that the style of man is man himself, which is about what we have been saying.

It comes to this that we use the same faculties when we write poetry that we use when we create gods or when we fix the bearing of men in reality. That this is obvious does not make the statement less. On the contrary, it makes the statement more, because its obviousness is that of the truth. The three ideas are sources of perfection. They are of such a nature that they are instances of aesthetic ideas tantamount to moral ideas, a subject precious in itself but beyond our scope today. For today, they mean that however one time may differ from another, there are always available to us the faculties of the past, but always vitally new and strong, as the sources of perfection today and tomorrow. The unity of style and the poem itself is a unity of language and life that exposes both in a supreme sense. Its collation with the unity of style and the gods and the unity of style and men is intended to demonstrate this.

❀❀❀❀❀❀❀❀❀❀❀❀❀❀❀❀❀❀❀❀❀❀❀❀❀

THE IRRATIONAL ELEMENT IN POETRY

I

To begin with, the expression: the irrational element in poetry, is much too general to be serviceable. After one has thought about it a bit it spreads out. Then too we are at the moment so beset by the din made by the surrealists and surrationalists, and so preoccupied in reading about them that we may become confused by these romantic scholars and think of them as the sole exemplars of the irrational today. Certainly, they exemplify one aspect of it. Primarily, however, what I have in mind when I speak of the irrational element in poetry is the transaction between reality and the sensibility of the poet from which poetry springs.

II

I am not competent to discuss reality as a philosopher. All of us understand what is meant by the transposition of an objective reality to a subjective reality. The transaction between reality and the sensibility of the poet is precisely that. A day or two before Thanksgiving we had a light fall of snow in Hartford. It melted a little by day and then froze again at night, forming a thin, bright crust over the grass. At the same time, the moon was almost full. I awoke once several hours before daylight and as I lay in bed I heard the steps of a cat running over the snow under my window almost inaudibly. The faintness and strangeness of the sound made on me one of those impressions which one so often seizes as pretexts for poetry. I suppose that in such a case one is merely expressing one's sensibility and that the reason why this expression takes the form of poetry is that it takes whatever form one is able to give it. The poet is able to give it the form of poetry because poetry is the medium of his personal sensibility. This is not the same thing as saying that a poet writes poetry because he writes poetry, although it sounds much like it. A poet writes poetry because he is a poet; and he is not a poet because he is a poet but because of his personal sensibility. What gives a man his personal sensibility I don't know and it does not matter because no one knows. Poets continue to be born not made and cannot, I am afraid, be predetermined. While, on the one hand, if they could be predetermined, they might long since have become extinct, they might, on the other hand, have changed life from what it is today into one of those transformations in which they delight, and they might have seen to it that they greatly multiplied themselves there.

III

There is, of course, a history of the irrational element in poetry, which is, after all, merely a chapter of the history of the irrational in the arts generally. With the irrational in a pathological sense we are not concerned. Fuseli used to eat raw beef at night before going to bed in order that his dreams might attain a beefy violence otherwise lacking. Nor are we concerned with that sort of thing; nor with any irrationality provoked by prayer, whiskey, fasting, opium, or the hope of publicity. The Gothic novels of eighteenth-century England are no longer irrational. They are merely boring. What interests us is a particular process in the rational mind which we recognize as irrational in the sense that it takes place unaccountably. Or, rather, I should say that what interests us is not so much the Hegelian process as what comes of it. We should probably be much more intelligently interested if from the history of the irrational there had developed a tradition. It is easy to brush aside the irrational with the statement that we are rational beings, Aristotelians and not brutes. But it is becoming easier every day to say that we are irrational beings; that all irrationality is not of a piece and that the only reason why it does not yet have a tradition is that its tradition is in progress. When I was here at Harvard, a long time ago, it was a commonplace to say that all the poetry had been written and all the paintings painted. It may be something of that sort that first interested us in the irrational. One of the great figures in the world since then has been Freud. While he is responsible for very little in poetry, as compared, for example, with his effect elsewhere, he has given the irrational a legitimacy that it never had before. More portentous influences have been Mallarmé and Rimbaud.

IV

It may be that my subject expressed with greater nicety is irrational manifestations of the irrational element in poetry; for if the irrational element is merely poetic energy, it is to be found wherever poetry is to be found. One such manifestation is the disclosure of the individuality of the poet. It is unlikely that this disclosure is ever visible as plainly to anyone as to the poet himself. In the first of the poems that I shall read to you in a moment or two the subject that I had in mind was the effect of the depression on the interest in art. I wanted a confronting of the world as it had been imagined in art and as it was then in fact. If I dropped into a gallery I found that I had no interest in what I saw. The air was charged with anxieties and tensions. To look at pictures there was the same thing as to play the piano in Madrid this afternoon. I was as capable of making observations and of jotting them down as anyone else; and if that is what I had wished to do, I could have done it. I wanted to deal with exactly such a subject and I chose that as a bit of reality, actuality, the contemporaneous. But I wanted the result to be poetry so far as I was able to write poetry. To be specific, I wanted to apply my own sensibility to something perfectly matter-of-fact. The result would be a disclosure of my own sensibility or individuality, as I called it a moment ago, certainly to myself. The poem is called "The Old Woman and the Statue." The old woman is a symbol of those who suffered during the depression and the statue is a symbol of art, although in several poems of which *Owl's Clover*, the book from which I shall read, consists, the statue is a variable symbol. While there is nothing automatic about the poem, nevertheless it has an

219

automatic aspect in the sense that it is what I wanted it to be without knowing before it was written what I wanted it to be, even though I knew before it was written what I wanted to do. If each of us is a biological mechanism, each poet is a poetic mechanism. To the extent that what he produces is mechanical: that is to say, beyond his power to change, it is irrational. Perhaps I do not mean wholly beyond his power to change, for he might, by an effort of the will, change it. With that in mind, I mean beyond likelihood of change so long as he is being himself. This happens in the case of every poet.

V

I think, too, that the choice of subject-matter is a completely irrational thing, provided a poet leaves himself any freedom of choice. If you are an imagist, you make a choice of subjects that is obviously limited. The same thing is true if you are anything else in particular and profess rigidly. But if you elect to remain free and to go about in the world experiencing whatever you happen to experience, as most people do, even when they insist that they do not, either your choice of subjects is fortuitous or the identity of the circumstances under which the choice is made is imperceptible. Lyric poets are bothered by spring and romantic poets by autumn. As a man becomes familiar with his own poetry, it becomes as obsolete for himself as for anyone else. From this it follows that one of the motives in writing is renewal. This undoubtedly affects the choice of subjects as definitely as it affects changes in rhythm, diction and manner. It is elementary that we vary rhythms instinctively. We say that we perfect diction. We simply grow tired. Manner is something that has not yet been disengaged adequately. It does not mean style; it means the attitude of the writer, his bearing rather than his point of view. His bearing toward what? Not toward anything in particular, simply his pose. He hears the cat on the snow.

The running feet set the rhythm. There is no subject beyond the cat running on the snow in the moonlight. He grows completely tired of the thing, wants a subject, thought, feeling, his whole manner changes. All these things enter into the choice of subject. The man who has been brought up in an artificial school becomes intemperately real. The Mallarmiste becomes the proletarian novelist. All this is irrational. If the choice of subject was predictable it would be rational. Now, just as the choice of subject is unpredictable at the outset, so its development, after it has been chosen, is unpredictable. One is always writing about two things at the same time in poetry and it is this that produces the tension characteristic of poetry. One is the true subject and the other is the poetry of the subject. The difficulty of sticking to the true subject, when it is the poetry of the subject that is paramount in one's mind, need only be mentioned to be understood. In a poet who makes the true subject paramount and who merely embellishes it, the subject is constant and the development orderly. If the poetry of the subject is paramount, the true subject is not constant nor its development orderly. This is true in the case of Proust and Joyce, for example, in modern prose.

VI

Why does one write poetry? I have already stated a number of reasons, among them these: because one is impelled to do so by a personal sensibility and also because one grows tired of the monotony of one's imagination, say, and sets out to find variety. In his discourse before the Academy, ten years or more ago, M. Brémond elucidated a mystical motive and made it clear that, in his opinion, one writes poetry to find God. I should like to consider this in conjunction with what might better be considered separately, and that is the question of meaning in poetry. M. Brémond proposed the identity of poetry and prayer, and followed Bergson in relying, in the last analysis, on faith. M. Bré-

221

mond eliminated reason as the essential element in poetry. Poetry in which the irrational element dominated was pure poetry. M. Brémond himself does not permit any looseness in the expression pure poetry, which he confines to a very small body of poetry, as he should, if the lines in which he recognizes it are as precious to his spirit as they appear to be. In spite of M. Brémond, pure poetry is a term that has grown to be descriptive of poetry in which not the true subject but the poetry of the subject is paramount. All mystics approach God through the irrational. Pure poetry is both mystical and irrational. If we descend a little from this height and apply the looser and broader definition of pure poetry, it is possible to say that, while it can lie in the temperament of very few of us to write poetry in order to find God, it is probably the purpose of each of us to write poetry to find the good which, in the Platonic sense, is synonymous with God. One writes poetry, then, in order to approach the good in what is harmonious and orderly. Or, simply, one writes poetry out of a delight in the harmonious and orderly. If it is true that the most abstract painters paint herrings and apples, it is no less true that the poets who most urgently search the world for the sanctions of life, for that which makes life so prodigiously worth living, may find their solutions in a duck in a pond or in the wind on a winter night. It is conceivable that a poet may arise of such scope that he can set the abstraction on which so much depends to music. In the meantime we have to live by the literature we have or are able to produce. I say live by literature, because literature is the better part of life, provided it is based on life itself. From this point of view, the meaning of poetry involves us profoundly. It does not follow that poetry that is irrational in origin is not communicable poetry. The pure poetry of M. Brémond is irrational in origin. Yet it communicates so much that M. Brémond regards it as supreme. Because most of us are incapable of sharing the experiences of M. Brémond, we have

to be content with less. When we find in poetry that which
gives us a momentary existence on an exquisite plane, is it
necessary to ask the meaning of the poem? If the poem had a
meaning and if its explanation destroyed the illusion, should we
have gained or lost? Take, for instance, the poem of Rimbaud,
one of *Les Illuminations*, entitled "Beaten Tracks." I quote Miss
Rootham's translation:

On the right the summer dawn wakes the leaves, the mists and
the sounds in this corner of the park. The slopes on the left clasp
in their purple shade the myriad deep-cut tracks of the damp high-
way. A procession from fairyland passes by. There are chariots
loaded with animals of gilded wood, with masts and canvas painted
in many colors, drawn by twenty galloping piebald circus-ponies;
and children and men on most astonishing beasts; there are twenty
vehicles, embossed, and decked with flags and flowers like coaches
of by-gone days, as coaches out of a fairytale; they are full of
children dressed up for a suburban pastoral. There are even coffins
under their night-dark canopies and sable plumes, drawn by trotting
mares, blue and black.

I do not know what images the poem has created. M. Delahaye
says that the poem was prompted by an American circus which
visited Charleville, where Rimbaud lived as a boy, in 1868 or
1869. What is the effect of this explanation? I need not answer
that. Miss Sitwell wrote the introduction to the collection of
Miss Rootham's translations of the poems of Rimbaud. Something that she said in the course of that introduction illustrates
the way the true subject supersedes the nominal subject. She
said:

How different was this life [of the slum] from that sheltered
and even rather stuffy life of perpetual Sundays that he had led
when he was a little boy in Charleville, and on these ever-recurring
days of tight clothing and prayer, when Madame Rimbaud had
escorted him, his brother and two sisters, to the eleven o'clock
Mass, along the bright light dust-powdery roads, under trees

whose great glossy brilliant leaves and huge pink flowers that seemed like heavenly transfigurations of society ladies, appeared to be shaking with laughter at the sober procession.

Miss Sitwell herself could not say whether the eleven o'clock Mass suggested the bright light flowers or whether the society ladies came into her mind with the great glossy brilliant leaves and were merely trapped there by the huge pink flowers, or whether they came with the huge pink flowers. It might depend upon whether, in Miss Sitwell's mind, society ladies are, on the one hand, great glossy and brilliant, or, on the other hand, huge and pink. Here the true subject was the brilliance and color of an impression.

VII

The pressure of the contemporaneous from the time of the beginning of the World War to the present time has been constant and extreme. No one can have lived apart in a happy oblivion. For a long time before the war nothing was more common. In those days the sea was full of yachts and the yachts were full of millionaires. It was a time when only maniacs had disturbing things to say. The period was like a stage-setting that since then has been taken down and trucked away. It had been taken down by the end of the war, even though it took ten years of struggle with the consequences of the peace to bring about a realization of that fact. People said that if the war continued it would end civilization, just as they say now that another such war will end civilization. It is one thing to talk about the end of civilization and another to feel that the thing is not merely possible but measurably probable. If you are not a communist, has not civilization ended in Russia? If you are not a Nazi, has it not ended in Germany? We no sooner say that it never can happen here than we recognize that we say it without

224

any illusions. We are preoccupied with events, even when we do not observe them closely. We have a sense of upheaval. We feel threatened. We look from an uncertain present toward a more uncertain future. One feels the desire to collect oneself against all this in poetry as well as in politics. If politics is nearer to each of us because of the pressure of the contemporaneous, poetry, in its way, is no less so and for the same reason. Does anyone suppose that the vast mass of people in this country was moved at the last election by rational considerations? Giving reason as much credit as the radio, there still remains the certainty that so great a movement was emotional and, if emotional, irrational. The trouble is that the greater the pressure of the contemporaneous, the greater the resistance. Resistance is the opposite of escape. The poet who wishes to contemplate the good in the midst of confusion is like the mystic who wishes to contemplate God in the midst of evil. There can be no thought of escape. Both the poet and the mystic may establish themselves on herrings and apples. The painter may establish himself on a guitar, a copy of *Figaro* and a dish of melons. These are fortifyings, although irrational ones. The only possible resistance to the pressure of the contemporaneous is a matter of herrings and apples or, to be less definite, the contemporaneous itself. In poetry, to that extent, the subject is not the contemporaneous, because that is only the nominal subject, but the poetry of the contemporaneous. Resistance to the pressure of ominous and destructive circumstance consists of its conversion, so far as possible, into a different, an explicable, an amenable circumstance.

VIII

M. Charles Mauron says that a man may be characterized by his obsessions. We are obsessed by the irrational. This is because we expect the irrational to liberate us from the rational. In a note on Picasso with the tell-tale title of "Social Fact and Cosmic Vision," Christian Zervos says:

The explosion of his spirit has destroyed the barriers which art . . . impressed on the imagination. Poetry has come forward with all that it has of the acute, the enigmatical, the strange sense which sees in life not only an image of reality but which conceives of life as a mystery that wraps us round everywhere.

To take Picasso as the modern one happens to think of, it may be said of him that his spirit is the spirit of any artist that seeks to be free. A superior obsession of all such spirits is the obsession of freedom. There is, however, no longer much excuse for explosions for, as in painting, so in poetry, you can do as you please. You can compose poetry in whatever form you like. If it seems a seventeenth-century habit to begin lines with capital letters, you can go in for the liquid transitions of greater simplicity; and so on. It is not that nobody cares. It matters immensely. The slightest sound matters. The most momentary rhythm matters. You can do as you please, yet everything matters. You are free, but your freedom must be consonant with the freedom of others. To insist for a moment on the point of sound. We no longer like Poe's tintinnabulations. You are free to tintinnabulate if you like. But others are equally free to put their hands over their ears. Life may not be a cosmic mystery that wraps us round everywhere. You have somehow to know the sound that is the exact sound; and you do in fact know, without knowing how. Your knowledge is irrational. In that sense life is mysterious; and if it is mysterious at all, I suppose that it is cosmically mysterious. I hope that we agree that it is at least mysterious. What is true of sounds is true of everything: the feeling for words, without regard to their sound, for example. There is, in short, an unwritten rhetoric that is always changing and to which the poet must always be turning. That is the book in which he learns that the desire for literature is the desire for life. The incessant desire for freedom in literature or in any of the arts is a desire for freedom in life. The desire is irrational. The result is the irrational searching the irrational, a conspicuously happy state of affairs, if you are so inclined.

Those who are so inclined and without reserve say: The least fastidiousness in the pursuit of the irrational is to be repudiated as an abomination. Rational beings are canaille. Instead of seeing, we should make excavations in the eye; instead of hearing, we should juxtapose sounds in an emotional clitter-clatter.

This seems to be freedom for freedom's sake. If we say that we desire freedom when we are already free, it seems clear that we have in mind a freedom not previously experienced. Yet is not this an attitude toward life resembling the poet's attitude toward reality? In spite of the cynicisms that occur to us as we hear of such things, a freedom not previously experienced, a poetry not previously conceived of, may occur with the suddenness inherent in poetic metamorphosis. For poets, that possibility is the ultimate obsession. They purge themselves before reality, in the meantime, in what they intend to be saintly exercises.

You will remember the letter written by Rimbaud to M. Delahaye, in which he said:

It is necessary to be a seer, to make oneself a seer. The poet makes himself a seer by a long, immense and reasoned unruliness of the senses. . . . He attains the unknown.

IX

Let me say a final word about the irrational as part of the dynamics of poetry. The irrational bears the same relation to the rational that the unknown bears to the known. In an age as harsh as it is intelligent, phrases about the unknown are quickly dismissed. I do not for a moment mean to indulge in mystical rhetoric, since for my part, I have no patience with that sort of thing. That the unknown as the source of knowledge, as the object of thought, is part of the dynamics of the known does not permit of denial. It is the unknown that excites the ardor of scholars, who, in the known alone, would shrivel up with boredom. We accept the unknown even when we are most skeptical. We may resent the consideration of it by any except the most lucid minds; but when so considered, it has seductions more powerful and more profound than those of the known.

Just so, there are those who, having never yet been convinced that the rational has quite made us divine, are willing to assume the efficacy of the irrational in that respect. The rational mind, dealing with the known, expects to find it glistening in a familiar ether. What it really finds is the unknown always behind and beyond the known, giving it the appearance, at best, of chiaroscuro. There are, naturally, charlatans of the irrational. That, however, does not require us to identify the irrational with the charlatans. I should not want to be misunderstood as having the poets of surrealism in mind. They concentrate their prowess in a technique which seems singularly limited but which, for all that, exhibits the dynamic influence of the irrational. They are extraordinarily alive and that they make it possible for us to read poetry that seems filled with gaiety and youth, just when we were beginning to despair of gaiety and youth, is immensely to the good. One test of their dynamic quality and, therefore, of their dynamic effect, is that they make other forms seem obsolete. They, in time, will be absorbed, with the result that what is now so concentrated, so inconsequential in the restrictions of a technique, so provincial, will give and take and become part of the process of give and take of which the growth of poetry consists.

Those who seek for the freshness and strangeness of poetry in fresh and strange places do so because of an intense need.

The need of the poet for poetry is a dynamic cause of the poetry that he writes. By the aid of the irrational he finds joy in the irrational. When we speak of fluctuations of taste, we are speaking of evidences of the operation of the irrational. Such changes are irrational. They reflect the effects of poetic energy; for where there are no fluctuations, poetic energy is absent. Clearly, I use the word irrational more or less indifferently, as between its several senses. It will be time enough to adopt a more systematic usage, when the critique of the irrational comes to be written, by whomever it may be that this potent subject ultimately engages. We must expect in the future incessant activity by the irrational and in the field of the irrational. The advances thus to be made would be all the greater if the character of the poet was not so casual and intermittent a character. The poet cannot profess the irrational as the priest professes the unknown. The poet's role is broader, because he must be possessed, along with everything else, by the earth and by men in their earthy implications. For the poet, the irrational is elemental; but neither poetry nor life is commonly at its dynamic utmost. We know Sweeney as he is and, for the most part, prefer him that way and without too much effulgence and, no doubt, always shall.

◇◇

THE WHOLE MAN: PERSPECTIVES, HORIZONS

The subject of "The Whole Man" would have excited the attention of Professor Whitehead. One of his constant concerns was with the effect of types of individuals or groups on society and, in the long run, this was a concern with civilization. For example, he said, "College faculties are going to want watching. . . . I don't need to tell you that there is a good deal of sniffing on this, the Harvard College and graduate schools side of the Charles River, sniffing at the new Harvard School of Business Administration on the opposite bank. . . . If the American universities were up to their job they would be taking business in hand and teaching it ethics and professional standards."

These remarks illustrate the existence of a relation between an imaginative thinker like Professor Whitehead and business. To consider the effect of his presence as a member of the board of directors of a corporation of national scope or, for that matter, as a member of the executive committee of one of the larger unions, makes a dazzling parenthesis. I am trying to make a point by citing Professor Whitehead as an example of an all-round man, because I do not think the definition of an all-round man necessarily includes a man of any actual technical business experience. He need not be a banker who collects books or a manufacturer who reads philosophy. It is a question of breadth of character and, say, diversity of faculties. In order to establish in your minds Professor Whitehead's right to the title, let me quote him again: "The mischief of elevating the type that has aptitude for economic advancement is that it denies the superior forms of aptitude which exist in quite humble people. Who shall say that to live kindly and graciously and meet one's problems bravely from day to day is not a great art, or that those who can do it are not great artists. Aesthetics are understood in too restricted a sense."

This sketches for you a man who did as much as any man can do to qualify as an all-around man. He began life as a mathematician and ended it as a philosopher. He is a wholly contemporaneous figure although no longer alive. My quotations are from his *Dialogues* as recorded by Lucien Price.

Last week I received a letter, greetings on my seventy-fifth birthday, from a young scholar, a Korean. When he was at New

Haven, he used to come up to Hartford and the two of us would go out to Elizabeth Park, in Hartford, and sit on a bench by the pond and talk about poetry. He did not wait for the ducks to bring him ideas but always had in mind questions that disclosed his familiarity with the experience of poetry. He spoke in the most natural English. He is now studying in Switzerland at Fribourg, from where his letter came. It was written in what appeared to be the most natural French. Apparently they prize all-round young men in Korea, too. In his letter, he said, "Seventy-five years is not a great deal, when one thinks that the poets and philosophers of the Far East, nourishing themselves only on the mist, have been able to prolong life up to one hundred and even one hundred and fifty years. Historians tell us that they have then been able to enter into fairyland, which is beyond our comprehension today."

That is my idea of a specialist. If these venerable men, by reducing themselves to skin and bones and by meditation prolonged year after year, could perceive final harmony in what all the world would concede to be final form, they would be supreme in life's most magnificent adventure. But they would still be specialists. They would, of course, be specialists in precisely that respect which led us to regard Professor Whitehead as a specimen of the all-round man.

There is no inevitable rapport between all men who seek the truth and who hope, thereby, to be made free and to remain free. I, for one, do not regard the all-round man as the apt opposite of the vertical man. It is illusory so to regard him. There is not the same contradistinction that would exist, say, between the horizontal and the vertical or between the latitudinal and the longitudinal. What really exists is the difference between the theorist and the technician, the difference between Hamlet and Horatio, the difference between the man who can talk about pictures and the man who can afford to buy them.

None of these differences involve direct and total opposites. The best technician, the purest mechanic, is necessarily something of a theorist. Hamlet was far more pushing than Horatio ever thought of being, when it came to the point. More often than the satirists admit, the man who can afford to buy pictures is entirely competent to take their measure and at the same time to take the measure both of the artist and of the dealer.

Admitting, however, that human nature contains no built-in iron curtains, the relation of the theorist to society is one thing and the relation of the technician is another. They do not make their impacts by what they have in common but by that in which they differ. The community does not reflect their likenesses but their unlikenesses. If we personalize a university, it corresponds to the all-round man. It is a complex of theorists and of some exceedingly vertical characters. As a whole, however, it is articulate only through its theorists. The world is the world through its theorists. Their function is to conceive of the whole and, from the center of their immense perspectives, to tell us about it. If we say that the basic consideration underlying this evening's discussion is that there are grades of importance in the multitude of man's concerns and that things of first importance must have precedence over things of secondary or lesser importance, it becomes clear that the man who applies himself to considerations of first importance must have precedence over the man who applies himself to things of secondary or lesser importance. This does not require demonstration. Let me try, nevertheless. Modern art often seems to be an attempt to bridge the gap between fact and miracle. To succeed in doing this, if it can be done at all, seems to be exclusively the task of the specialist, that is to say, the painter. If we want to build a bridge, we are bound to employ a bridge builder. It would not help us to invoke even the ghost of Professor Whitehead, which is, no doubt, an exceedingly able-bodied ghost. Sooner or later, however, some all-round man is going to think about this particular bit of bridge-building. He will say that there is a kind of corollary to the relation between the theorist and the technician (or if you prefer between the humanist and the scientist) and the relation between art, on the one hand, and painting, on the other. It seems likely that modern art will be affected more by what he has to say by way of approval, if he should approve, or by way of disapproval, if he should disapprove, than by what the painters themselves will have to say.

I suppose it is true that nothing keeps painting alive from one time to another except its form. What is true of painting is no less true of poetry and music. Form alone and of itself is an ever-youthful, ever-vital beauty. The vigor of art perpetuates itself through generations of form. But if the vigor of art is itself formless, and since it is merely a principle it must be, its form comes from those in whom the principle is active, so that generations of form come from generations of men. The all-round man is certain to scrutinize form as he scrutinizes men, that is to say, in relation to all past form. It is inevitable that, from his scrutiny of past form, some ideal should have been created, whether it is derived from something actual in the past or something desired to become actual in the future. Modern art is inescapably framed within these large horizons, which, certainly, are not the horizons of a school, whether of time or place. I repeat that what is true of painting is no less true of poetry and music. The principle of poetry is not confined to its form however definitely it may be contained therein. The principle of music would be an addition to humanity if it were not humanity itself, in other than human form, and while this hyperbole is certain to be repulsive to a good many people, still it may stand. This is the life of the arts which the all-round man thinks of in relation to life itself.

You may be saying that I am going beyond the intention of this evening's general subject, that I am changing the man with more interests than one into a figure slightly fabulous and also that I am changing the specialist, who is, after all, a creature of necessity, into an illiberal bigot; and that the figures with whom we are really concerned are the educated, intelligent, widely experienced man on the one hand, and the educated, intelligent, less widely experienced man on the other. The trouble is that a man's scope may be independent of his education, intelligence, and experience. Furthermore, one may at least express uncertainty about this scope always having a relation to his effect on society. Notwithstanding this, I prefer my slightly fabulous creature of thought and my technician. As to the latter, it may be said that the ever-increasing mass of people could not live together in the world without the technician and that the elevating of the level of life for people in general is, in all except its concept, a technical problem. The all-round man was in his heyday, in this country, a hundred and fifty or even two hundred years ago. Looking back at them, many of our original political philosophers seem to have been just such all-round men: Franklin, Washington, Jefferson, Madison. There were no technicians, or few. A city the size of New York today could not exist without technicians. We live here today by the aid of types living a century and more apart. What a many-sided man Dr. Benjamin Rush of Philadelphia seems to us to have been. In what a leisurely, spacious city he lived. Did Dr. Rush have much choice about it? Could Philadelphia have been anything but what it was? Could Franklin, Washington, Jefferson, Madison have lived different lives? If we account for our technicians by saying that they are part of the struggle for survival, can we account for our all-round men in any other way? Are the all-round men any less the result of pressure than the technicians? What pressure? What other pressure could it be than the pres-

234

sure of society itself, the developing forces, the demands and permissions of people adapting themselves to the circumstances in which they find themselves, devising the formulae of civilized existence? The human struggle, however, is immensely more than the mere struggle to survive than these questions suggest.

It is possible to conceive a neo-Platonic republic in which technicians would be political and moral neuters. In such a republic, one class would be the class of all-round men: the general thinkers, the over-all thinkers, men capable of different sights, the sturdy fathers of that very republic and the authors of its political and moral declarations. Since most of us are technicians on at least one side or, say, to some extent, those in whom we reposed the profoundest confidence would actually be few, perhaps a group composed of men with minds like the rapacious and benign mind of Professor Whitehead. To be ruled by thought, in reality to govern ourselves by the truth or to be able to feel that we were being governed by the truth, would be a great satisfaction, as things go. The great modern faith, the key to an understanding of our times, is faith in the truth and particularly in the idea that the truth is attainable, and that a free civilization based on the truth, in general and in detail, is no less attainable.

❖◆❖

ON POETIC TRUTH

Poetry has to do with reality in its most individual aspect. An isolated fact, cut loose from the universe, has no significance for the poet. It derives its significance from the reality to which it belongs. To see things in their true perspective, for example, we require to draw very extensively upon experiences that are past. All that we see and hear is given a meaning in this way. It is the function of science to complete this interpretation. The scientist can tell me much which I cannot know from ordinary observation. But however exhaustive information of this kind may be there is something which it does not cover and that is particularity here and now. There is in reality, whether we think of it as animate or inanimate, human or sub-human, an aspect of individuality at which many forms of rational explanation stop short.

For Plato the only reality that mattered is exemplified best for us in the principles of mathematics. The aim of our lives should be to draw ourselves away as much as possible from the unsubstantial fluctuating facts of the world about us and establish some communion with the objects which are apprehended by thought and not sense. This was the source of Plato's asceticism. It must suffice here to note the dismissal of the individual and particular facts of experience as of no importance in themselves. Plato would describe himself as a realist in the sense that it is by breaking away from the world of facts that we make contact with reality.

What do we learn? Just this; that poetry has to do with reality in that concrete and individual aspect of it which the mind can never tackle altogether on its own terms, with matter that is foreign and alien in a way in which abstract systems, ideas in which we detect an inherent pattern, a structure that belongs to the ideas themselves, can never be. It is never familiar to us in the way in which Plato wished the conquests of the mind to be familiar. On the contrary its function, the need which it meets and which has to be met in some way in every age that is not to become decadent or barbarous is precisely this contact with reality as it impinges on us from the outside, the sense that we can touch and feel a solid reality which does not wholly dissolve itself into the conceptions of our own minds. It is the individual and particular that does this. And the wonder and mystery of art, as indeed of religion in the last resort, is the revelation of something "wholly other" by which the inexpressible loneliness of thinking is broken and enriched. To know facts as facts in the ordinary way has, indeed, no particular power or worth. But a quickening of our awareness of the irrevocability by which a thing is what it is, has such power, and it is, I believe, the very soul of art. But no fact is a bare fact, no individual is a universe in itself. The artist exhibits affinities in the *actual* structure of objects by which their significance is deepened and enhanced. What I desire to stress is that there is a unity rooted in the individuality of objects and discovered in a different way from the apprehension of rational connections.

The extraction of a meaning from a poem and appraisement of it by rational standards of truth has mainly been due to enthusiasm for moral or religious truth. But that is not usual today. Politics is our culprit. It would be fantastic to suggest that the overt meaning, what the poem seems to say, contributes little to the artistic significance and merit of a poem. We merely protest against the abstraction of this content from the whole and appraisement of it by other than aesthetic standards. The "something said" is important, but it is important for the poem only in so far as the saying of that particular something in a special way is a revelation of reality. The form derives its significance from the whole. Form has no significance except in relation to the reality that is being revealed.

The genuine artist is never "true to life." He sees what is real, but not as we are normally aware of it. We do not go storming through life like actors in a play. Art is never real life. The poet sees with a poignancy and penetration that is altogether unique. What matters is that the poet must be true to his art and not "true to life," whether his art is simple or complex, violent or subdued. Emotion is thought to lie at the center of aesthetic experience. That, however, is not how the matter appears to me. If I am right, the essence of art is insight of a special kind into reality. But such insight is bound to be accompanied by remarkable emotions. A poem would be nothing without some meaning. The truth is that meaning is an awareness and a communication. But it is no ordinary awareness, no ordinary communication.

Novelty must be inspired. But there must be novelty. This crisis is most evident in religion. The theologians whose thought is most astir today do make articulate a supreme need, and one that has now become also imperative, as their urgency shows, the need to infuse into the ages of enlightenment an awareness of reality adequate to their achievements and such as will not be attenuated by them. There is one most welcome and authentic note; it is the insistence on a reality that forces itself upon our consciousness and refuses to be managed and mastered. It is here that the affinity of art and religion is most evident today. Both have to mediate for us a reality not ourselves. This is what the poet does. The supreme virtue here is humility, for the humble are they that move about the world with the love of the real in their hearts.

0+0+0+0+0+0+0+0+0+0+0+0+0+0+0+0+0+0+0+0+0+0+0+0+0+0+0+0+0+0+0+

HONORS AND ACTS

I

Poetic Acts

The act of conferring an honor on a poet is a poetic act. By a poetic act I mean an act that is a projection of poetry into reality. The act of conferring an academic honor on a poet is a poetic act specifically because it engages all those that participate in it with at least the idea of poetry, for at least a moment, that is to say it engages them with something that is unreal, as if they had opened a door and stepped into another dimension not immediately calculable. What is unreal here is the idea of poetry and the projection of that idea into this present place. To choose this immediate act as an illustration of the poetic act is a choice of expediency only.

The act should be observed for a moment. When we go to the corner to catch a bus or walk down the block to post a letter, our acts in doing these things are direct. But when we gather together and become engaged with something unreal our act is not so much the act of gathering together as it is the act of becoming engaged with something unreal. We do this sort of thing on a large scale when we go to church on Sunday, when we celebrate days like Christmas or the much more impressive days of the end of Lent. On Easter the great ghost of what we call the next world invades and vivifies this present world, so that Easter seems like a day of two lights, one the sunlight of the bare and physical end of winter, the other the double light. However, we find the poetic act in lesser and everyday things, as for example, in the mere act of looking at a photograph of someone who is absent or in writing a letter to a person at a distance, or even in thinking of a remote figure, as when Virgil, in the last lines of the last of the *Georgics*, thinks of Cæsar and of the fact that while the poet was writing his poem

> . . . great Cæsar fired his lightnings and conquered
> By deep Euphrates.

As to this last example, it is an instance of one of the commonplaces of the romantic. Just as in space the air envelops objects far away with an ever-deepening blue, so in the dimension of the poetic act the unreal increasingly subtilizes experience and varies appearance. The real is constantly being engulfed in the unreal. But I want to be quite sure that you recognize that I am talking about something existing, not about something purely poetic; and for that reason I add one or two more examples from actuality. The act of thinking of the life of the rich is a poetic act and this seems to be true whether one thinks of it with liking or with dislike. The same thing may be said of the act of thinking of the life of the poor. Most of us do not share the life of either the one or the other and for that reason both are unreal. It is possible, too, to think of the national economy as a poetico-economy; and surely for millions of men and women the act of joining the armed forces is measurably a poetic act, since for all of them it is a deviation from the normal, impelled by senses and necessities inoperative on the ordinary level of life. The activity of the unreal in reality, that is to say, the activities of poetry in everyday life, would be like the activity of an hallucination in the mind, except for this, that the examples cited have been cited as poetic acts in the course of the visible life about us. An awareness of poetic acts may change our sense of the texture of life, but it does not falsify the texture of life. When Joan of Arc said:

> Have no fear: what I do, I do by command.
> My brothers of Paradise tell me what I have to do.

those words were the words of an hallucination. No matter what her brothers of Paradise drove her to do, what she did was never a poetic act of faith in reality because it could not be.

The important question is: what is the significance of the poetic act or, in short, what is the philosophy of what we are talking about? I am thinking of it in terms of meaning and value for the poet. Ordinarily the poet is associated with the word, not with the act; and ordinarily the word collects its strength from the imagination or, with its aid, from reality. The poet finds that as between these two sources: the imagination and reality, the imagination is false, whatever else may be said of it, and reality is true; and being concerned that poetry should be a thing of vital and virile importance, he commits himself to reality, which then becomes his inescapable and ever-present difficulty and inamorata. In any event, he has lost nothing; for the imagination, while it might have led him to purities beyond definition, never yet progressed except by particulars. Having gained the world, the imaginative remains available to him in respect to all the particulars of the world. Instead of having lost anything, he has gained a sense of direction and a certainty of understanding. He has strengthened himself to resist the bogus. He has become like a man who can see what he wants to see and touch what he wants to touch. In all his poems with all their enchantments for the poet himself, there is the final enchantment that they are true. The significance of the poetic act then is that it is evidence. It is instance and illustration. It is an illumination of a surface, the movement of a self in the rock. Above all it is a new engagement with life. It is that miracle to which the true faith of the poet attaches itself.

(*Bard College*, 1948)

II

I am happy to receive this evening's medal and grateful that a society occupying the position of the Poetry Society of America should think me worthy of this award. Thank you. That the medal should be presented in the name of a young poet makes it all the more precious, since, among all the images of the poet, the purest is that of the young poet.

We are, here, a group of people who regard poetry as one of the sanctions of life. We believe it to be a vital engagement between the imagination and reality. The outcome of that engagement, if successful, is fulfillment. We say, also, that poetry is an instrument of the will to perceive the innumerable accords, whether of the imagination or of reality, that make life a thing different from what it would be without such insights. If we are right, then, from this serious point of view, the act of bestowing an honor on a poet is equal to the honor of receiving it.

The other day, in the middle of January, as I was taking a walk in Elizabeth Park, in Hartford, I saw at a little distance across the snow a group of automobiles that had pulled up on one side of the road. A dozen people or more got out of them. They took off their coats and threw them together in a pile on the asphalt. It was then possible to see that this was a wedding party. Often in the summer, particularly on Saturday mornings, one sees such parties there. They come to have photographs taken in the gardens. But these people had come in January. The bride stood up in white satin covered with a veil. An ornament in her hair caught the sunlight and sparkled brightly in the cold wind. The bridesmaids were dressed in dark crimson gowns with low necks. They carried armfuls of chrysanthemums. One of the men stood in the snow taking pictures of the bride, then of the bride surrounded by the bridesmaids, and so on, until nothing more was possible. Now, this bride with her gauze and glitter was the genius of poetry. The only thing wrong with her was that she was out of place.

What is the apt locale of the genius of poetry? As it happens, she creates her own locale as she goes along. Unlike the bride, she recognizes that she cannot impose herself on the scene. She is the spirit of visible and invisible change. She knows that if poetry is one of the sanctions of life, if it is truly a vital engagement between man and his environment of the world, if it is genuinely a means by which to achieve balance and measure in our circumstances, it is something major and not minor; and that if it is something major it must have its place with other major things. And knowing this and in consequence of it, she has herself chosen as her only apt locale in a final sense the love and thought of the poet, where everything she does is right and reasonable. Her power to change is so great that out of the love and thought of individual poets she makes the love and thought of the poet, the single image. Out of that which is often untutored and seemingly incapable of being tutored, insensible to custom and law, marginal, grotesque, without a past, the creation of unfortunate chance, she evolves a power that dominates life, a central force so subtle and so familiar that its presence is most often unrealized. Individual poets, whatever their imperfections may be, are driven all their lives by that inner companion of the conscience which is, after all, the genius of poetry in their hearts and minds. I speak of a companion of the conscience because to every faithful poet the faithful poem is an act of conscience.

The answer I have given to the question as to the apt locale of the genius of poetry is also the answer to the question as to the position of poetry in the world today. There is no doubt that poetry does in fact exist for the thoughtful young man in Basel or the votary in Naples. The Marxians, and for that matter a good many other people, think of it in terms of its social impact. In one direction it moves toward the ultimate things of pure poetry; in the other it speaks to great numbers of people of themselves, making extraordinary texts and memorable music out of what they feel and know. In both cases it makes itself manifest in a kind of speech that comes from secrecy. Its position is always an inner position, never certain, never fixed. It is to be found beneath the poet's word and deep within the reader's eye in those chambers in which the genius of poetry sits alone with her candle in a moving solitude.

(1951)

Not long ago I was listening to a conversation between two men about modern poetry. One said to the other, "Do you really think that any of these fellows are as good, say, as Sir Walter Scott?" Now, how many of you when you go home tonight are likely to sit down and read *The Lady of the Lake?* Sir Walter Scott's poetry is like the scenery of a play that has come to an end. It is scenery that has been trucked away and stored somewhere on the horizon or just a little below. In short, the world of Sir Walter Scott no longer exists. It means nothing to compare a modern poet with the poet of a century or more ago. It is not a question of comparative goodness. It is like comparing a modern soldier, say, with an ancient one, like comparing Eisenhower with Agamemnon.

I have just used the words "a modern poet." These words are intended to mean nothing more than a poet of the present time. The word "modern" to whatever it may be attached, as, for example, a modern publisher or a bookseller with a modern shop, usually implies a sense of modishness. A modern painter is more than likely to be the product of a movement. A modern musician sounds like one the moment you hear him. However that may be, what a modern poet desires, above everything else, is to be nothing more than a poet of the present time. I think it may be said that he considers his function to be this: to find, by means of his own thought and feeling, what seems to him to be the poetry of his time as differentiated from the poetry of the time of Sir Walter Scott, or the poetry of any other time, and to state it in a manner that effectively discloses it to his readers.

I say that he is to find it by his own thought and feeling; and the reason for this is that the only place for him to find it is in the thought and feeling of other people of which he becomes aware through his own thought and feeling. Becoming aware does not always mean becoming consciously aware. His awareness may be limited to instinct. There is about every poet a vast world of other people from which he derives himself and through himself his poetry. What he derives from his generation he returns to his generation, as best he can. His poetry is theirs and theirs is his, because of the interaction between the poet and his time, which publishers, booksellers and printers do more than any others in the world to broaden and deepen.

(*National Book Award*, 1951)

IV

When a poet comes out of his cavern or wherever it is that he secretes himself, even if it is a law office or a place of business, and suddenly finds himself confronted by a great crowd of people, the last thing in the world that enters his mind is to thank those who are responsible for his being there. And this is particularly true if the crowd has come not so much on his account as on account, say, of a novelist or some other figure, who is, as a rule, better known to it than any poet. And yet the crowd will have come, to some extent on his account, because the poet exercises a power over life, by expressing life, just as the novelist does; and I am by no means sure that the poet does not exercise this power at more levels than the novelist, with more colors, with as much perception and certainly with more music, not merely verbal music, but the rhythms and tones of human feeling.

I think then that the first thing that a poet should do as he comes out of his cavern is to put on the strength of his particular calling as a poet, to address himself to what Rilke called the mighty burden of poetry and to have the courage to say that, in his sense of things, the significance of poetry is second to none. We can never have great poetry unless we believe that

245

poetry serves great ends. We must recognize this from the beginning so that it will affect everything that we do. Our belief in the greatness of poetry is a vital part of its greatness, an implicit part of the belief of others in its greatness. Now, at seventy-five, as I look back on the little that I have done and as I turn the pages of my own poems gathered together in a single volume, I have no choice except to paraphrase the old verse that says that it is not what I am, but what I aspired to be that comforts me. It is not what I have written but what I should like to have written that constitutes my true poems, the uncollected poems which I have not had the strength to realize.

Humble as my actual contribution to poetry may be and however modest my experience of poetry has been, I have learned through that contribution and by the aid of that experience of the greatness that lay beyond, the power over the mind that lies in the mind itself, the incalculable expanse of the imagination as it reflects itself in us and about us. This is the precious scope which every poet seeks to achieve as best he can.

Awards and honors have nothing to do with this. The role of awards and honors in the life of a poet is simply to bring him back to reality, to remind him, in the midst of all his hopes for poetry, that he lives in the world of Darwin and not in the world of Plato. He does not accept them as a true satisfaction because there is no true satisfaction for the poet but poetry itself. He accepts them as tokens of the community that exists between poetry on the one hand and men and women on the other. He accepts them not for their immediate meaning but as symbols and it is their secondary value that makes him the richer for having received them.

And having said this much, I feel better able to express my obligation to this body and to the judges for the privilege of being here today and for the honor they have done me and to say that I am grateful to them and thank them. And I am grate-

ful to my publisher, Alfred Knopf, and his staff, and thank them
for the notably handsome job they made of the *Collected Poems*.
(*National Book Award,* 1955)

◇◇◇

A POET THAT MATTERS

(A REVIEW OF *Selected Poems,* BY MARIANNE MOORE)

The tall pages of *Selected Poems* by Marianne Moore are the
papers of a scrupulous spirit. The merely fastidious spirit *à la
mode* is likely to be on the verge of suffocation from hyper-
aesthesia. But Miss Moore's is an unaffected, witty, colloquial
sort of spirit. In "The Fish," for instance, the lines move with
the rhythm of sea-fans waving to and fro under water. They
are lines of exquisite propriety. Yet in this poem she uses what
appears, aesthetically, to be most inapposite language:

> All
> external
> marks of abuse are present on this
> defiant edifice—
> all the physical features of.

Everywhere in the book there is this enhancing diversity. In
consequence, one has more often than not a sense of invigora-
tion not usually communicated by the merely fastidious.

That Miss Moore is scrupulous, the lines just quoted demonstrate. *All* and *external* are rhymes enough for anyone that finds
full rhymes to be crude. The same thing is true of *this* and
edifice. Thus, the lines which at first glance appeared to contain
no rhymes whatever, have on a second look a more intricate
appearance. Moreover, the units of the lines are syllables and

247

not feet; the first line contains one syllable; the second three; the third nine; the fourth six; the last eight. This scheme is repeated with exactness throughout the poem. It is this scheme that requires Miss Moore to end the stanza with *of*, and that occasionally requires her to pass, elsewhere, from one line to the next in the middle of a word. If the verse is not to be free, its alternative is to be rigid. Finally, in printing the lines, the first two have been set well to the left, the next two have been set in a little to the right and the last has been set in still further to the right. Now, all these things contribute to the effect of the stanza. The light rhymes please one unconsciously. The exactness with which the syllables are repeated, the indentations which arrest the eye, even if slightly: all these things assist in creating and in modulating the rhythm. In addition, Miss Moore instinctively relates sounds. There is a relation between the groups of letters *ext, ks, phys*. The *i*'s in *defiant edifice* are related. As these relations change, not only the sounds change, but the colors, the texture, the effects also change.

The poem with which the book opens, "The Steeple-Jack," is highly characteristic. The lines and stanzas flow innocently. Nevertheless, throughout the dozen stanzas the lines repeat themselves, syllable by syllable, without variation. The stanzas are mechanisms. Yet instead of producing a mechanical effect, they produce an effect of ease. In one of her poems Miss Moore writes of

> . . . intermingled echoes
> struck from thin glasses successively at random—.

In "The Steeple-Jack" she writes of

> a sea the purple of the peacock's neck is
> paled to greenish azure as Dürer changed
> the pine green of the Tyrol to peacock blue.

248

The strong sounds of *the purple of the peacock's neck* contrast and intermingle with the lighter sounds of *paled to greenish azure* and return again to the strong sounds of the last line. The colors of the first and second lines acquire a quality from their association with the word *Dürer* and the image of Dürer and the *pine green* and *peacock blue* of the last line owe something to the word *Tyrol* and the image of the Tyrol. This is not at all going too finely into minutiae. For with Miss Moore these things lie on the surface.

"The Steeple-Jack" serves, too, to illustrate what interests Miss Moore. The point of the poem is a view of the common-place. The view is that of Dürer or of Miss Moore in the mask or mood of Dürer, or, more definitely, perhaps, under the stimulus of Dürer. The common-place is, say, a New England fishing-village. Whatever the poem may do for Dürer or for the village, it does many happy things for Miss Moore and for those who delight in her. Obviously, having in mind the subject-matter of the poem, Miss Moore *donne dans le romanesque.* Consciously, the point of the poem may have been something wholly casual. It may lie in the words

> it is a privilege to see so
> much confusion.

Consciously, it may have had no more point than the wish to make note of observations made while in the cloud of a mood. That is Miss Moore's method. Subject, with her, is often incidental. There are in "The Steeple-Jack" the following creatures: eight stranded whales, a fish, sea-gulls, the peacock of the peacock's neck referred to a moment ago, a guinea, a twenty-five pound lobster, an exotic serpent (by allusion), a ring-lizard, a snake (also by allusion), a crocodile, cats, cobras, rats, the diffident little newt and a spider. This is a modest collection. Miss

Moore makes the most lavish snake-charmer look like a visitor. The people in the poem are Dürer;

> The college student
> named Ambrose sits on the hill-side
> with his not-native books and hat
> and sees boats
>
> at sea progress white and rigid as if in
> a groove;

and C. J. Poole, Steeple-Jack, with one or two references to others. Poole is merely a sign on the sidewalk with his name on it. The last stanza is:—

> It could not be dangerous to be living
> in a town like this, of simple people,
> who have a steeple-jack placing danger signs by the church
> while he is gilding the solid-
> pointed star, which on a steeple
> stands for hope.

Stendhal in his *Pensées* said:

> *Le bel esprit comme on sait fut de tout*
> *temps l'ennemi le plus perfide du génie.*

Miss Moore's wit, however, does not in the least imperil what she is about. Out of her whales and the college student and Poole and the danger signs she composes a poem simple, radiant with imagination, contemporaneous, displaying everywhere her sensitive handling. The poem leaves one indubitably convinced that she leans to the romantic.

And so she should, with a difference. In "The Steeple-Jack" she observes the fog on the sea-side flowers and trees

> so that you have
> the tropics at first hand: the trumpet vine . . .
> or moon vines trained on fishing-twine.

She then writes

>   . . . There are no banyans, frangipani nor
> jack-fruit trees; nor an exotic serpent
> life.

If she had said in so many words that there were banyans, frangipani, and so on, she would have been romantic in the sense in which the romantic is a relic of the imagination. She hybridizes the thing by a negative. That is one way. Equally she hybridizes it by association. Moon-vines are moon-vines and tedious. But moon-vines trained on fishing-twine are something else and they are as perfectly as it is possible for anything to be what interests Miss Moore. They are an intermingling. The imagination grasps at such things and sates itself, instantaneously in them. Yet clearly they are romantic. At this point one very well might stop for definitions. It is clear enough, without all that, to say that the romantic in the pejorative sense merely connotes obsolescence, but that the word has, or should have, another sense. Thus, when A. E. Powell in *The Romantic Theory of Poetry* writes of the romantic poet

> He seeks to reproduce for us the feeling as it lives within himself; and for the sake of a feeling which he thinks interesting or important he will insert passages which contribute nothing to effect of the work as a whole,

she is surely not thinking of the romantic in a derogatory sense. True, when Professor Babbitt speaks of the romantic, he means the romantic. Romantic objects are things, like garden furniture or colonial lingerie or, not to burden the imagination, country millinery.

Yes, but for the romantic in its other sense, meaning always the living and at the same time the imaginative, the youthful, the delicate and a variety of things which it is not necessary to try to particularize at the moment, constitutes the vital element in poetry. It is absurd to wince at being called a romantic poet. Unless one is that, one is not a poet at all. That, of course, does not mean banyans and frangipani; and it cannot for long mean no banyans and no frangipani. Just what it means, Miss Moore's book discloses. It means, now-a-days, an uncommon intelligence. It means in a time like our own of violent feelings, equally violent feelings and the most skilful expression of the genuine. Miss Moore's lines,

> the shadows of the Alps
> imprisoning in their folds like flies in amber, the rhythms
> of the skating rink

might so easily have been pottered over and nullified; and how hilarious, how skilful they are! Only the other day there was a comment on "Samuel Prout's romantic renderings of mediaeval fountains." The commentator was far from meaning mediaeval renderings of romantic fountains. For him Prout's renderings were romantic because they delighted him and since the imagination does not often delight in the same thing twice, it may be assumed that by romantic he meant something that was, for his particular imagination, an indulgence and a satisfaction.

Professor Babbit says that

a thing is romantic when, as Aristotle would say, it is wonderful rather than probable. . . . A thing is romantic when it is strange, unexpected, intense, superlative, extreme, unique, etc.

It must also be living. It must always be living. It is in the sense of living intensity, living singularity that it is the vital element in poetry. The most brilliant instance of the romantic in this sense is Mr. Eliot, who incessantly revives the past and creates the future. It is a process of cross-fertilization, an immense process, all arts considered, of hybridization. Mr. Eliot's "Prelude" with the smell of steaks in passageways, is an instance, in the sense that the smell of steaks in the Parnassian air is

252

a thing perfectly fulfilling Professor Babbitt's specifications. Hamlet in modern dress is another instance of hybridization. Any playing of a well-known concerto by an unknown artist is another. Miss Moore's book is a collection of just that. It is not a matter of phrases, nor of odd-looking lines, nor of poems from which one must wholly take, giving anything whatsoever at one's peril. Poetry for her is "a place for the genuine." If the conception of the poet as a creature ferocious with ornamental fury survives anywhere except in the school books, it badly needs a few pungent footnotes. We do not want "high-sounding interpretation." We want to understand. We want, as she says,

> imaginary gardens with real toads in them.

The very conjunction of imaginary gardens and real toads is one more specimen of the romantic of Miss Moore. Above all things she demands

> the raw material of poetry in
> all its rawness.

She demands the romantic that is genuine, that is living, the enriching poetic reality.

Miss Moore's form is not the quirk of a self-conscious writer. She is not a writer. She is a woman who has profound needs. In any project for poetry (and one wishes that the world of tailors, plasterers, barkeepers could bring itself to accept poets in a matter-of-fact way) the first effort should be devoted to establishing that poets are men and women, not writers. Miss Moore may have had more than one reason for adding in the *Notes* appended to her book that in "Peter," the hero "built for the midnight grass-party," was a

> Cat owned by Miss Magdalen Heuber and
> Miss Maria Weniger.

253

But this amusing stroke is, after all, a bit of probity, whatever else it may be. That Miss Moore uses her wit is a bit of probity. The romantic that falsifies is rot and that is true even though the romantic inevitably falsifies: it falsifies but it does not vitiate. It is an association of the true and the false. It is not the true. It is not the false. It is both. The school of poetry that believes in sticking to the facts would be stoned if it was not sticking to the facts in a world in which there are no facts: or some such thing.

This brings one round to a final word. Miss Moore's *emportements* are few. Instead of being intentionally one of the most original of contemporary or modern poets, she is merely one of the most truthful. People with a passion for the truth are always original. She says:

> Truth is no Apollo.

She has thought much about people and about poetry, and the truth, and she has done this with all the energy of an intense mind and imagination and this book is the significant result. It contains the veritable thing.

❖◇❖

WILLIAMS

(PREFACE TO *Collected Poems*, 1921–1931)

The slightly tobaccoy odor of autumn is perceptible in these pages. Williams is past fifty.

There are so many things to say about him. The first is that he is a romantic poet. This will horrify him. Yet the proof is everywhere. Take the first poem, "All the Fancy Things." What

254

gives this its distinction is the image of the woman, once a girl in Puerto Rico in the old Spanish days, now solitary and growing old, not knowing what to do with herself, remembering. Of course, this is romantic in the accepted sense, and Williams is rarely romantic in the accepted sense.

The man has spent his life in rejecting the accepted sense of things. In that, most of all, his romantic temperament appears. But it is not enough merely to reject: what matters is the reason for rejection. The reason is that Williams has a romantic of his own. His strong spirit makes its own demands and delights to try its strength.

It will be observed that the lonely figure in "All the Fancy Things" and the person addressed in "Brilliant Sad Sun" have been slightly sentimentalized. In order to understand Williams at all, it is necessary to say at once that he has a sentimental side. Except for that, this book would not exist and its character would not be what it is. "The Cod Head" is a bit of pure sentimentalization; so is "The Bull." Sentiment has such an abhorrent name that one hesitates. But if what vitalizes Williams has an abhorrent name, its obviously generative function in his case may help to change its reputation. What Williams gives, on the whole, is not sentiment but the reaction from sentiment, or, rather, a little sentiment, very little, together with acute reaction.

His passion for the anti-poetic is a blood-passion and not a passion of the inkpot. The anti-poetic is his spirit's cure. He needs it as a naked man needs shelter or as an animal needs salt. To a man with a sentimental side the anti-poetic is that truth, that reality to which all of us are forever fleeing.

The anti-poetic has many aspects. The aspect to which a poet is addicted is a test of his validity. Its merely rhetorical aspect is valueless. As an affectation it is a commonplace. As a scourge it has a little more meaning. But as a phase of a man's spirit, as a source of salvation, now, in the midst of a baffled generation, as one looks out of the window at Rutherford or Passaic, or as one walks the streets of New York, the anti-poetic acquires an extraordinary potency, especially if one's nature possesses that side so attractive to the Furies.

Something of the unreal is necessary to fecundate the real; something of the sentimental is necessary to fecundate the anti-poetic. Williams, by nature, is more of a realist than is commonly true in the case of a poet. One might, at this point, set oneself up as the Linnæus of aesthetics, assigning a female role to the unused tent in "The Attic Which Is Desire," and a male role to the soda sign; and generally speaking one might run through these pages and point out how often the essential poetry is the result of the conjunction of the unreal and the real, the sentimental and the anti-poetic, the constant interaction of two opposites. This seems to define Williams and his poetry.

All poets are, to some extent, romantic poets. Thus, the poet who least supposes himself to be so is often altogether so. For instance, no one except a *surrealiste* himself would hesitate to characterize that whole school as romantic, dyed through and through with the most authentic purple. What, then, is a romantic poet now-a-days? He happens to be one who still dwells in an ivory tower, but who insists that life would be intolerable except for the fact that one has, from the top, such an exceptional view of the public dump and the advertising signs of Snider's Catsup, Ivory Soap and Chevrolet Cars; he is the hermit who dwells alone with the sun and moon, but insists on taking a rotten newspaper. While Williams shares a good deal of this with his contemporaries in the manner and for the reason indicated, the attempt to define him and his work is not to be taken as an attempt to define anyone or anything else.

So defined, Williams looks a bit like that grand old plaster

256

cast, Lessing's Laocoön: the realist struggling to escape from the serpents of the unreal.

He is commonly identified by externals. He includes here specimens of abortive rhythms, words on several levels, ideas without logic, and similar minor matters, which, when all is said, are merely the diversions of the prophet between morning and evening song. It will be found that he has made some veritable additions to the corpus of poetry, which certainly is no more sacred to anyone than to him. His special use of the anti-poetic is an example of this. The ambiguity produced by bareness is another. The implied image, as in "Young Syca-more," the serpent that leaps up in one's imagination at his prompting, is an addition to imagism, a phase of realism which Williams has always found congenial. In respect to manner he is a virtuoso. He writes of flowers exquisitely. But these things may merely be mentioned. Williams himself, a kind of Diogenes of contemporary poetry, is a much more vital matter. The truth is that, if one had not chanced to regard him as Laocoön, one could have done very well by him as Diogenes.

RUBBINGS OF REALITY

If a man writes a little every day, as Williams does, or used to do, it may be that he is merely practicing in order to make perfect. On the other hand he may be practicing in order to get at his subject. If his subject is, say, a sense, a mood, an integra-tion, and if his representation is faint or obscure, and if he practices in order to overcome his faintness or obscurity, what he really does is to bring, or try to bring, his subject into that degree of focus at which he sees it, for a moment, as it is and at which he is able to represent it in exact definition.

A man does not spend his life doing this sort of thing unless doing it is something he needs to do. One of the sanctions of the writer is that he is doing something that he needs to do. The need is not the desire to accomplish through writing something not incidental to the writing itself. Thus a political or a religious writer writes for political or religious reasons. Williams writes, I think, in order to write. He needs to write.

What is the nature of this need? What does a man do when he delineates the images of reality? Obviously, the need is a general need and the activity a general activity. It is of our nature that we proceed from the chromatic to the clear, from the unknown to the known. Accordingly the writer who practices in order to make perfect is really practicing to get at his subject and, in that exercise, is participating in a universal activity. He is obeying his nature. Imagism (as one of Williams's many involvements, however long ago) is not something superficial. It obeys an instinct. Moreover, imagism is an ancient phase of poetry. It is something permanent. Williams is a writer to whom writing is the grinding of a glass, the polishing of a lens by means of which he hopes to be able to see clearly. His delineations are trials. They are rubbings of reality.

The modern world is the result of such activity on a grand scale, not particularly in writing but in everything. It may be said, for instance, that communism is an effort to improve the human focus. The work of Picasso is an attempt to get at his subject, an attempt to achieve a reality of the intelligence. But the world of the past was equally the result of such activity. Thus the German pietists of the early 1700's who came to Pennsylvania to live in the caves of the Wissahickon and to dwell in solitude and meditation were proceeding in their way, from the chromatic to the clear. Is not Williams in a sense a literary pietist, chastening himself, incessantly, along the Passaic?

There is an intellectual *tenue*. It is easy to see how underneath the chaos of life today and at the bottom of all the disintegrations there is the need to see, to understand: and, in so far as one is not completely baffled, to re-create. This is not emotional. It springs from the belief that we have only our own intelligence on which to rely. This manifests itself in many ways, in every living art as in every living phase of politics or science. If we could suddenly re-make the world on the basis of our own intelligence, see it clearly and represent it without faintness or obscurity, Williams's poems would have a place there.

◇◇

JOHN CROWE RANSOM: TENNESSEAN

What John Crowe Ransom does is to make a legend of reality. One picks up a sense of his personality in its native condition without any of the trophies of his experience as an outsider. It might be clearer to say before any of the trophies, etc., instead of without, because the reality of which he makes a legend is the reality of Tennessee. They say that there are even more Ransoms in Tennessee than Tates in Kentucky. However that may be, the more there are of you, the more you possess and the more you are possessed. To be a Ransom in Tennessee is something more precious than it is easy to say.

There are scholars who have never been anybody anywhere and never will be. Mr. Ransom is not one of them. It is hard in speaking of this sort of thing to keep on the right side. When one speaks of the personality of the Tennessean, the exact sense one has of the words cannot be conveyed hastily. The Tennessean is not the New Englander. He is not the Westerner. He is not even the Southerner. He lives in a land of his own as endeared and as beloved as any in the world, and among a people, whose chief characteristic is its raciness. He would say that he lives in Tennessee and among the Tennesseans and it would be the same thing. I don't in the least mean anything romantic. On the contrary, I mean a real land and a real people and I mean Mr. Ransom as the instinct and expression of them.

One turns with something like ferocity toward a land that one loves, to which one is really and essentially native, to demand that it surrender, reveal, that in itself which one loves. This is a vital affair, not an affair of the heart (as it may be in one's first poems), but an affair of the whole being (as in one's last poems), a fundamental affair of life, or, rather, an affair of fundamental life; so that one's cry of O Jerusalem becomes little by little a cry to something a little nearer and nearer until at last one cries out to a living name, a living place, a living thing, and in crying out confesses openly all the bitter secretions of experience. This is why trivial things often touch us intensely. It is why the sight of an old berry patch, a new growth in the woods in the spring, the particular things on display at a farmers' market, as, for example, the trays of poor apples, the few boxes of black-eyed peas, the bags of dried corn, have an emotional power over us that for a moment is more than we can control.

There are men who are not content merely to acknowledge these emotions. There are men who must understand them, who isolate them in order to understand them. Once they understand them it may be said that they cease to be natives. They become outsiders. Yet it is certain that, at will, they become insiders again. In ceasing to be natives they have become insiders and outsiders at once. And where this happens to a man whose life is that of the thinker, the poet, the philosopher, the teacher, and in a broad generalized sense, the artist, while his activity may appear to be that of the outsider, the insider remains as the base of his character, the essential person, something fixed, the play of his thoughts, that on which he lavishes his sense of the prodigious and the legendary, the material of his imagination.

Mr. Ransom's poems are composed of Tennessee. It would not necessarily be the case that the poems of a native of another land would be composed of that land. But a Tennessean has no choice. O Jerusalem. O Appalachia. Above everything else Mr. Ransom's poems are not composed of the books he has read, of the academies he has seen, of the halls and columns and carvings on the columns, the stairs and towers and doorways and tombs, the wise old men and the weak young men of nowhere in particular, going nowhere at all. He himself comes out of a region dense with a life of its own, so individualized that he can tell a fellow countryman by a thousand things and not know how he does it. It is not a question of his being bold enough to be himself. He is of that hard stuff on which a mountain has been bearing down for a long time with such a weight that its impress on him has passed into everything he does and passes, through him, outward, a long distance.

But it is as a legend. As he grew into an outsider without ceasing to be an insider, it was as if everything to which he was native took on a special quality, an exact identity, a microscopic reality, which, only for what it was, had a value because it was wholly free from his outsidedness. This is what happens to things we love. He picked it up and took it with him. He drew a picture of it, many pictures of it, in his books. The greater the value he set on it, the dearer it became, the more closely he sought out its precise line and look, the more it became a legend, the peculiar legend of things as they are when they are as we want them to be, without any of the pastiche of which the presence

261

vulgarizes so many legends and possibly everything legendary in things, not as they are, but as we should like them to be.

❀❖❀❀

THE SHAPER

Paul Rosenfeld was a shaper who lived a life of shaping, that is to say, a *Schöpfer*, who lived for the sake of *Schöpfung*. Perhaps there existed for him an ideal *Schöpfung*, a world composed of music, but which did not whirl round in music alone; or of painting, but which did not expand in color and form alone; or of poetry, but which did not limit itself to the *explication orphique* of the poet. But whether or not there was an ideal *Schöpfung*, in which everything coalesced, toward which everything converged, the truth about him seems to be that he was incessantly engaged or involved or attracted by the activity of shaping.

This is the life of the artist, whether the artist be the young sculptor or the old politician, or, say, sociologist; whether the artist be the young Spanish painter or the barbarian statesman. Thus, if the uncertainty in the case of Rosenfeld suggested by the words "engaged or involved or attracted" had been a certainty, if the shaping had been the obsession of a single shape, if the fascinated interest had become a determination of the will to be executed with all the *Schöpferkraft* of which he was capable, we should have said, afterward, that this urbane and somewhat placid figure had not really surprised us. The uninterrupted activity of shaping dissipated the possibility of an ultimate shape.

This constant shaping, as distinguished from constancy of

shape, is characteristic of the poet. Rosenfeld appears to have been too eagerly sensitive to the figures about him to be able to isolate himself or to permit himself to be isolated, in any single shaping of his own. He was the young man (for a long time) of eager intelligence, conscious of the creative forces of his generation and delighting in them. In a way, he lived and spoke in constant praise of his generation. It may be that his generation as a whole was the ideal *Schöpfung* to which Rosenfeld has been related. He was conscious of his generation as a whole and while he may have praised it without thinking that that was what he was doing, he would have done it just the same had it occurred to him because, although he itemized, the sum of the items was his generation. In short, he saw the world in his character as poet. To be explicit, he delighted in and praised the poetry in the activity of the young sculptor, the young painter, and so on.

To be still more explicit, his character as poet made it easy and natural for him to give character to the young poet, the most inchoate of human beings and yet potentially the most choate. If it should not be quite true that poets are born, not made, it seems certain that if made they must be made shortly after being born. Even then they lose character quickly. The existence of certain figures checks this loss of character. The figure most likely to do this seems to be that of the perfectly normal creature who is touched by poetry, the man of intelligence who discloses by his interest and sympathy that poetry is something significant to him. Rosenfeld was such a character.

He was not the critic angered by the idea that poetry is so much twaddle fit for fools. He was a poet himself; and he would as soon have thought that philosophy is the nonsense of apt comedians. As a member of a group, as a familiar figure, without eccentricity, saying and writing things of understanding,

263

he communicated confidence and discipline, and a sense of the necessity of both; and in that, too, he was shaping, helping to give shape, to those to whom that meant becoming choate.

<hr>

A NOTE ON MARTHA CHAMPION

Miss Champion begins by being an artist. The trouble she takes about small letters in place of capitals and about the relations between her lines and about punctuation; the indifference to what she is writing about as compared to the way in which she writes about it; the pleasure she finds in lines like

> Intent and bright
> Like tenderness

and

> Wave-slap on the shore.
> Grief is slow,
> Which overtakes me here;

these things are manifestly the affairs of an artist. If it is the "Farewell of Meleager" translated by Mackail in *Select Epigrams* (8:XIV):

No longer will I . . . inhabit the hill-tops: what is there sweet, what desirable in the mountains? Daphnis is dead . . . I will dwell here in the city

that is the source of "After Meleager," Miss Champion's paraphrase which changes the tone of the Anthology to the tone of today is again the affair of an artist.

Youngish artists have a way of being melancholy. It may be

that this is merely a symptom of the distress they feel at the absence of definition. They have no very distinct outline of themselves or of the abstractions that bedevil them. They are, in short, likely to be a bit baffled. Thus to Miss Champion the idea of the twisting of love, which might involve all sorts of implications, has exclusively an artistic implication. The elaboration of the metaphor in "Fragmenta I" interests her without regard to its insignificance. In "Fragmenta II," a subject that might have been profoundly felt, there are, in the absence of feeling, the phrases:

> towering plains

> Divides the waves
> Like solitude

> sweet-crumbling pebbles;

and in "Perseid" the melancholy of what chance have we is confused with

> giddy Charlestoning deft houses.

If Miss Champion happened to be setting out to think about the twisting of love, or to think about farewells to Daphnis or Daphne or her Uncle Charles or Mrs. Mistlebacher, or about separation, or grief and its assuaging, or the oddity of man measuring himself against things which the Perseids do so poorly as, say the Hotel Pierre; or if she meant to feel these things to the depths or felt them whether or not she meant to do so; or if she did not mean to think about them or to be moved by them in the least but to use them for the sounds they might provoke, the sensations as of color or the opportunities for strange conjunctions to which they might give rise, as

> dark seas,
> And silly clouds

and

> feeble stars . . .
> bent, hatted chimneys;

if she meant to do any one of these things and meant it persistently so that her will involved everything for her, that would be one thing; but if she did not quite know what she meant to do and did a little of all of them, that would be something infinitely more complicated and difficult and defeating and discouraging. None of Miss Champion's themes is a clear theme lustily treated.

Yet there is nothing more delightful in poetry than the sort of sensitiveness that Miss Champion possesses when it is put to the lusty uses to which she seems capable of putting it. The

> crooked noises

and

> we finger a dead mouse in this house

of "Poem" are fascinating.

◇◇◇

A NOTE ON SAMUEL FRENCH MORSE

(INTRODUCTION TO *Time of Year*)

What is there about a book of first poems that immediately interests us? For one thing, it is possible that we are going to have a fresh opportunity to become aware that the people in the world, and the objects in it, and the world as a whole, are not absolute things, but, on the contrary, are the phenomena of perception. In short, it is possible that a new poet is that special person at our elbow with his special, possibly even extraordinary, perception, to whom Thoreau refers at the end of the passage from "Autumnal Tints," with which Mr. Morse introduces his collection. Since the perception of life is life itself, a book containing the first poems of a poet new to us has a natural and intense attraction.

This is true even if, as we turn the pages, we find them a little obstinate. But they could hardly be anything else. If we were all alike; if we were millions of people saying do, re, mi in unison, one poet would be enough and Hesiod himself would do very well. Everything he said would be in no need of expounding or would have been expounded long ago. But we are not all alike and everything needs expounding all the time because, as people live and die, each one perceiving life and death for himself, and mostly by and in himself, there develops a curiosity about the perceptions of others. This is what makes it possible to go on saying new things about old things. The fact is that the saying of new things in new ways is grateful to us. If a bootblack says that he was so tired that he lay down like a dog under a tree, he is saying a new thing about an old thing, in a new way. His new way is not a literary novelty; it is an unaffected statement of his perception of the thing.

Poems written with this in mind will often not possess, nor be intended to possess, either emotion or the music of emotion. Instead, they will possess, and be intended to possess, the "moral beauty" that Mr. Venturi spoke of recently as being present in the painting of Cézanne. As the writer of such poems becomes more and more the master of his own poetry: that is to say, as he becomes better able to realize his individual perceptions, and as he acquires faith in his function as poet, he is likely to project the rigors of his early work into what he does later. So that his early work really discloses his identity.

What, then, is the identity of Mr. Morse? It is something that he is serious about poetry. The passage from Thoreau demonstrates that, and so do the three or four words from Job which, in the Bible, follow the verse in which Job cries

> Or seest thou as man seeth?

But what is his exact character as a poet? One of his poems, "The Track into the Swamp," relates to one of the abandoned roads, the lost roads, of which New England is so full. We have been accustomed to think that at the far end of such roads the ghosts of the Transcendentalists still live. Obviously they do not live at this end. Mr. Morse is not the ghost of a Transcendentalist. If he has any use at all for Kant, it is to keep up the window in which the cord is broken. He is anti-transcendental. His subject is the particulars of experience. He is a realist; he tries to get at New England experience, at New England past and present, at New England foxes and snow and thunderheads. When he generalizes, as in "End of a Year," his synthesis is essentially a New England synthesis. He writes about his own people and his own objects as closely as possible according to his own perception. This rectitude characterizes everything that he does.

❧❧❧❧❧❧❧❧❧❧❧❧❧❧❧❧❧❧❧❧❧❧❧❧❧❧❧❧

TWO PREFACES

I

Gloire du long Désir, Idées

Denis Saurat refers to *Eupalinos* as Valéry's "prose masterpiece," not meaning more, however, than that it was one of a number of masterpieces by Valéry in prose, not to speak of his masterpieces in verse. He cites a brief passage or two and then says, "You have to go back to Bossuet to find such writing in prose." It is easy to believe this of *Eupalinos* if you give yourself up to some of the more rhetorical episodes. There is, for example, the passage in which Socrates speaks of the chance that had placed in his hands an object which became, for him, the source of reflections on the difference between constructing and knowing. Phaedrus asked him to help him to see the object, and thereupon Socrates said:

Well then, Phaedrus, this is how it was. I was walking on the very edge of the sea. I was following an endless shore. . . . This is not a dream I am telling you. I was going I know not whither, overflowing with life, half-intoxicated by my youth. The air, deliciously rude and pure, pressing against my face and limbs, confronted me— an impalpable hero that I must vanquish in order to advance. And this resistance, ever overcome, made of me, too, at every step an imaginary hero, victorious over the wind, and rich in energies that were ever reborn, ever equal to the power of the invisible adversary. . . . That is just what youth is. I trod firmly the winding beach, beaten and hardened by the waves. All things around me were simple and pure: the sky, the sand, the water.

Merely to share the balance and the imagery of these words is to share the particular exhilaration of the experience itself. Then, too, toward the close of the work, in the speech in which Socrates states the conclusions to which the speakers have been brought, he substitutes for oral exhilaration the exhilaration that comes from the progression of the mind. Only enough of this true apostrophe can be cited to identify it. Socrates says to Phaedrus:

O coeternal with me in death, faultless friend, and diamond of sincerity, hear then:
It served no purpose, I fear, to seek this God, whom I have tried all my life to discover, by pursuing him through the realm

of thought alone; by demanding him of that most variable and most ignoble sense of the just and the unjust, and by urging him to surrender to the solicitings of the most refined dialectic. The God that one so finds is but a word born of words, and returns to the word. For the reply we make to ourselves is assuredly never anything other than the question itself; and every question put by the mind to the mind is only, and can only be, a piece of simplicity. But on the contrary, it is in acts, and in the combination of acts, that we ought to find the most immediate feeling of the presence of the divine, and the best use for that part of our strength that is unnecessary for living, and seems to be reserved for the pursuits of an indefinable object that infinitely transcends us.

Valéry himself has commented on the work. In a letter to Paul Souday written in 1923, he said:

I was asked to write a text for the album *Architectures*, which is a collection of engravings and plans. Since this text was to be magnificently printed in folio format and fitted in exactly with the decoration and pagination of the work, I was requested to limit its size quite precisely to 115,800 *letters* . . . 115,800 characters! It is true, the characters were to be sumptuous.

I accepted. My dialogue was at first too long. I shortened it; and then a little too short—I lengthened it. I came to find these exigencies very interesting, though it is possible that the text itself may have suffered a little in consequence.

After all, the sculptors never complained who were obliged to house their Olympian personages inside the obtuse triangle of pediments! . . .

There is, also, a letter to Dontenville, *inspecteur d'Académie*, written in 1934. The letter to Paul Souday was written a few months after the composition of *Eupalinos*. The letter to Dontenville was written after the lapse of ten years. Valéry, referring again to the requirement of 115,800 characters, said:

This rigor, at first astounding and repellent, albeit required of a man accustomed enough to the rigor of poems in fixed form, made this man wonder at first—but then find that the peculiar condition proposed to him might be easily enough satisfied by employing the very elastic form of the *dialogue*. (An insignificant rejoinder, introduced or cut out, allows us a few fumblings to conform with fixed requirements of measurement.) The adjustment was, in effect, easily made in the proofs.

The vast proof sheets I received gave me the strange impression that I had in my hands a work of the sixteenth century and was 400 years dead.

The name of Eupalinos was taken by me from the article "Architecture" in the *Encyclopédie Berthelot*, when I was looking for the name of an architect. I since learned, from a study by the learned Hellenist Bidez (of Ghent), that Eupalinos, an engineer more than an architect, dug canals and built scarcely any temples; I gave him my ideas, as I did Socrates and Phaedrus. Moreover, I have never been in Greece; and as for Greek, I have unfortunately remained the most indifferent of scholars, getting lost in the original text of Plato and finding him, in the translations, terribly long and often boring. . . .

Since Valéry describes Eupalinos as of Megara, and since it was at Megara that the school of Euclid flourished, Valéry's ascription of the name of Eupalinos to the *Encyclopédie Berthelot* dispels the idea of any relation between Eupalinos and Euclid. Finally, to return to the letter to Paul Souday, Valéry said of "these dialogues":

They are works made to order, in which I have not managed or known how to establish a true thought in its most favorable light. I should have tried to show that pure thought and the search for truth in itself can only ever aspire to the discovery or the construction of some *form*.

What, then, are the ideas that Valéry has chosen to be discussed by the shades of Socrates and his friend Phaedrus, as they meet, in our time, in their "dim habitation" on the bank of Ilissus? They are alone and remain alone. Eupalinos does not appear and takes no part in the discussion, unless, as he is spoken of, an image of him passes, like the shade of a shade.

The talk is prolonged, and during its course, one or the other speaker propounds ideas. If we attempt to group a number of the ideas propounded, we have something like the following:

There are no details in execution.

Nothing beautiful is separable from life, and life is that which dies.

We must now know what is truly beautiful, what is ugly; what befits man; what can fill him with wonder without confounding him, possess him without stupefying him. . . . It is that which puts him, without effort, above his own nature.

By dint of constructing, . . . I truly believe that I have constructed myself. . . . To construct oneself, to know oneself—are these two distinct acts or not?

What is important for me above all else is to obtain from *that which is going to be,* that it should with all the vigor of its newness satisfy the reasonable requirements of *that which has been.*

O body of mine . . . keep watch over my work. . . . Grant me to find in thy alliance the feeling of what is true; temper, strengthen, and confirm my thoughts.

No geometry without the word.

Nothing can beguile, nothing attract us, . . . nothing by us is chosen from among the multitude of things, and causes a stir in our souls, that was not in some sort pre-existent in our being or secretly awaited by our nature.

An artist is worth a thousand centuries.

Man . . . fabricates by abstraction.

Man can act only because he can ignore.

That which makes and that which is made are indivisible.

The greatest liberty is born of the greatest rigor.

Man's deepest glances are those that go out to the void. They converge beyond the All.

272

If, then, the universe is the effect of some act; that act itself, the effect of a Being, and of a need, a thought, a knowledge, and a power which belong to that Being, it is then only by an act that you can rejoin the grand design, and undertake the imitation of that which has made all things. And that is to put oneself in the most natural way in the very place of the God.

Now, of all acts the most complete is that of constructing.

But the constructor whom I am now bringing to the fore . . . takes as the starting point of his act, the very point where the god had left off. . . . Here I am, says the Constructor, I am the act.

Must I be silent, Phaedrus?—So you will never know what temples, what theaters, I should have conceived in the pure Socratic style! . . . And exercising an ever stricter control over my mind, at the highest point I should have realized the operation of transforming a quarry and a forest into an edifice, into splendid equilibriums! . . .

Then out of raw materials I was going to put together my structures entirely ordained for the life and joy of the rosy race of men. . . . But you shall learn no more. You can conceive only the old Socrates, and your stubborn shade. . . .

This is the substance of the dialogue between Socrates and Phaedrus, or, at least, these sayings, taken from their talk, indicate what they have been talking about. And what in fact have they been talking about? And why is Valéry justified when, in his closing words, Socrates says: ". . . all that we have been saying is as much a natural sport of the silence of these nether regions as the fantasy of some rhetorician of the other world who has used us as puppets!" Have we been listening to the talk of men or of puppets? These questions are parts of the fundamental question, What should the shades of men talk about, or in any case what may they be expected, categorically, to talk about, in the Elysian fields? Socrates answers this question in the following manner:

Think you not that we ought now to employ this boundless leisure which death leaves us, in judging and rejudging ourselves unwearyingly, revising, correcting, attempting other answers to the events that took place, seeking, in fine, to defend ourselves by illusions against nonexistence, as the living do against their existence?

This Socratic question (and answer) seems empty. The Elysian fields would be the merest penal habitude, if existence in them was not as absolute as it is supposed to be eternal and if our disillusioned shades were dependent, there, on some fresh illusion to be engendered by them for themselves in that transparent realm. It cannot be said freely that Valéry himself fails to exhibit Socrates and Phaedrus engaged in any such discussion, for as the talk begins to reach its end, there emerges from it an Anti-Socrates, to whom an Anti-Phaedrus is listening, as if their conversation had been, after all, a process of judging and rejudging what they had done in the past, with the object of arriving at a state of mind equivalent to an illusion. The dialogue does not create this impression. It does not seem to us, as we read it, that we are concerned with the fortunes of the selves of Socrates and Phaedrus, notwithstanding that that would be a great concern.

We might well expect an existence after death to consist of the revelation of the truth about life, whether the revelation was instantaneous, complete, and dazzling, or whether it was a continuity of discoveries made at will. Hence when a conversation between Socrates and Phaedrus after death occurs, we somehow expect it to consist of resolutions of our severest philosophical or religious difficulties, or of some of them. The present dialogue, however, is a discussion of aesthetics. It may even be said to be the apotheosis of aesthetics, which is not at all what we have had in mind as that which phantoms talk about. It makes the scene seem more like a place in provincial France than either an archaeological or poetic afterworld. In view of

274

Valéry's reference to "the very admirable Stephanos," it is clear that the scene is the afterworld of today, since Mallarmé died in 1898. The trouble is that our sense of what ought to be discussed in the afterworld is derived from specimens that have fallen into disuse. Analysis of the point would be irrelevant. It seems enough to suppose that to the extent that the dead exist in the mind of the living, they discuss whatever the living discuss, although it cannot be said that they do it in quite the same way, since when Phaedrus told Socrates how Socrates, if he had been an architect, would have surpassed "our most famous builders," Eupalinos included, Socrates replied: "Phaedrus, I beg of you! . . . This subtle matter of which we are now made does not permit of our laughing. I feel I ought to laugh, but I cannot. . . . So refrain!"

This elevation of aesthetics is typical of Valéry's thought. It is itself an act of consruction. It is not an imbalance attributable to his nature as a poet. It is a consequence of reasonable conviction on his part. His partiality for architecture was instinctive and declared itself in his youthful *Introduction to the Method of Leonardo da Vinci*. It was not an artificiality contrived to please the company of architects who had commanded *Eupalinos*. It seems most natural that a thinker who had traced so much of man's art to man's body should extend man's art itself to the place of God and in that way should relate man's body to God, in the manner in which this is done in *Eupalinos*. Socrates said: "I cannot think that there exists more than one Sovereign Good."

Phaedrus then spoke of what Eupalinos had said concerning forms and appearances. He repeated the words of Eupalinos:

Listen, Phaedrus . . . that little temple, which I built for Hermes, a few steps from here, if you could know what it means to me!— There where the passer-by sees but an elegant chapel—'t is but a trifle: four columns, a very simple style—there I have enshrined the

275

memory of a bright day in my life. O sweet metamorphosis! This delicate temple, none knows it, is the mathematical image of a girl of Corinth, whom I happily loved. It reproduces faithfully the proportions that were peculiarly hers. It lives for me! It gives me back what I have given it. . . .

Eupalinos had then spoken of buildings that are mute, of others that speak, and of others that sing, for which he gave the reasons.

Socrates interrupted Phaedrus with a reference to his prison, which he called "a drab and indifferent place in itself." But he added, "In truth, dear Phaedrus, I never had a prison other than my body."

Eupalinos had gone on to speak to Phaedrus of the effect on the spirit of the sites of ports: ". . . the presence of the pure horizon, the waxing and the waning of a sail, the emotion that comes of being severed from the earth, the beginning of perils, the sparkling threshold of lands unknown." He did not profess to be able to connect up an analysis with an ecstasy. He said:

I feel my need of beauty, proportionate to my unknown resources, engendering of itself alone forms that give it satisfaction. I desire with my whole being. . . . The powers assemble. The powers of the soul, as you know, come strangely up out of the night. . . . By force of illusion they advance to the very borders of the real. I summon them, I adjure them by my silence. . . .

He continued:

O Phaedrus, when I design a dwelling (whether it be for the gods, or for a man), and when I lovingly seek its form, . . . I confess, how strange soever it may appear to you, *that it seems to me my body is playing its part in the game.*

Eupalinos ended with the prayer to his body, which Socrates called "an unexampled prayer," when Phaedrus repeated it. It is Socrates himself—in the apostophe to Phaedrus, beginning "O coeternal with me in death," in the closing pages of the dialogue—who says that man by his acts puts himself in the place of God, not meaning that he becomes God but that he puts himself in the very place of God: *la place même du Dieu.*

It follows that for Eupalinos and for men like him what they do is their approach to the divine and that the true understanding of their craft and the total need that they feel to try to arrive at a true understanding of it and also at an exact practice of it are immeasurably the most important things in the world, through which the world itself comes to the place of the divine. The present work has to be read with all this in mind. Any rigorous intellectual discipline in respect to something significant is a discipline in respect to everything significant. Valéry's own discipline appears in every page of the dialogue. The need to understand uncommon things and to manifest that understanding in common things shows itself constantly. The modeling of the cluster of roses is an instance. The comparison of the object found on the shore of the sea, a natural object, with an object made by man is another. The parable of the Phoenician and how he went about making a ship is a third. It is the parable of the artist. The image of the Phoenician's boat recalled to Socrates ". . . the black, loose-flapping sails of the vessel with its load of priests, which as it labored back from Delos, dragging on its oars. . . ."

At this, Phaedrus exclaimed, "How little you seem to relish living your beautiful life over again!"

Socrates then asked, "Is there anything vainer than the shadow of a sage?"

And Phaedrus said, "A sage himself." The image of the man of action makes the shade of the man of thought regret his life. It is, in a way, the triumphant image of the constructor as it faces the image of the man of thought. Perhaps on his own grounds, it was Valéry, for all his life of study, full of the sea,

277

watching the departure of the Phoenician's supreme boat on its maiden voyage: "Her scarlet cheeks took all the kisses that leapt up to meet her on her course; the well-stretched triangles of her full, hard sails held down her quarter to the wave. . . ."

Is it not possible that one of the most perceptive texts of modern times, although neither immense nor varied, and containing little of life and the nature of man, is yet a masterpiece? Within the limits of the work, Valéry expresses ideas relevant to the thought of his time as it came to consider, with an unprecedented interest, the problems of art. In the dialogue, Socrates speaks of these expatiations as if with a nuance of their triviality. As he continued to probe, his interest heightened to such an extent that he lost his own traditional character; and in this, he became part of the new time in which his shade comes close to us. The nuance of triviality had vanished by the time he reached the noble speech beginning "O coeternal with me in death," when he was ready to say:

The Demiurge was pursuing his own designs, which do not concern his creatures. The converse of this must come to pass. He was not concerned about the troubles that were bound to spring from that very separation which he diverted or perhaps bored himself with making. He has given you the means of living, and even of enjoying many things, but not generally those which you particularly want.

But I come after him. I am he who conceives what you desire a trifle more exactly than you do yourselves. . . . I shall make mistakes sometimes, and we shall have some ruins; but one can always very profitably look upon a work that has failed as a step which brings us nearer to the most beautiful.

In the end, Socrates had become the constructor, and if he had, then Valéry had. The thinker had become the creator. Jean Wahl might have diminished this to a defense mechanism. Perhaps it was an appearance of what Alain called the inimitable visage of the artist. To be a little more exact in quoting Alain, one should say that the creator had asserted its parentage of the thinker, for Alain had spoken of thought as the daughter of poetry in a passage peculiarly applicable to Valéry. He had said that of all the indicators of thought the most sensitive were poets, first because they take risks a little further than logic permits; also because the rule they adopt always carries them a little beyond what they hoped for. Mallarmé and Valéry announce a new climate of thought. They want clear enigmas, those that are developable, that is to say, mathematical. Alain says:

And if it is true, as I believe, that Thought, daughter of Poetry, resembles her mother, we shall see everywhere a clarity of details, a clarity won by conquest, in the place of our vague aspirations; and the young will make us see another manner of believing—which will be a refusal to believe.

Eupalinos is a work of this "clarity of details." This is its precise description. In it Valéry made language itself a constructor, until Socrates asked:

What is there more mysterious than clarity? . . . What more capricious than the way in which light and shade are distributed over hours and over men? . . . Orpheuslike we build, by means of the word, temples of wisdom and science that may suffice for all reasonable creatures. This great art requires of us an admirably exact language.

It has been said that Rilke, who translated so much of Valéry, including *Eupalinos*, felt an intense interest, as a poet, in the language of the work. The page on music—". . . a mobile edifice, incessantly renewed and reconstructed within itself, and entirely dedicated to the transformations of a soul"; the page on the sea shore—"This frontier between Neptune and Earth"; the page on in the beginning—"In the beginning . . .

there was what is: the mountains and the forests . . ."—are pages of true poetry. It was natural for such pages to give Rilke pleasure. But what impressed him was what he called the composure and finality of Valéry's language. Rilke read *Eupalinos* when it came out in the *Nouvelle Revue française*, and his translation of it was the last work he did before he died.

It seems sometimes, in the fluidity of the dialogue, as if the discussion was casual and fortuitous or, say, Socratic. But a discussion over which the mind of Socrates presides derives much of its vitality from this characteristic, so that when the talk is over, we have a sense of extended and noble unity, a sense of large and long-considered form.

II

Chose légère, ailée, sacrée

In 1930, Louis Séchan published a work on *La Danse grecque antique*, which contained a chapter on Valéry's *Dance and the Soul*. M. Séchan was Professor of Greek Language and Literature at the University of Montpellier. He sent a copy of this book to Valéry, who acknowledged it in a letter, which it seems worth while to copy at length, as follows:

I thank you greatly for your attention in sending me your fine work on Greek dancing. I learn from it many things I ignored—and even ignored about myself. Your kind chapter on my little dialogue generously attributes to me much more erudition than I ever possessed. Neither Callimachus nor Lucian, Xenophon nor the Parthenia was known to me; and would not in any case have been of much use to me. Documents in general impede rather than help me. They result in difficulties for me, and consequently in peculiar solutions, in all those compositions in which history must play some part.

In reality, I confined myself to dipping into Emmanuel at the

280

Library, and I left open on my table the book of Marey which I have had for the last thirty years. Those outline drawings of jumping and walking, some memories of ballets were my essential resources. The flutist does come from the Throne. The head compact like a pine cone from a living dancer.

The constant thought of the Dialogue is physiological—from the digestive troubles of the prelude-beginning to the final swoon. Man is slave to the sympathetic and pneumogastric nerves. Sumptuary sensations, the gestures of luxury, and spectacular thoughts exist only by the good favor of these tyrants of our vegetative life. Dance is the type of the runaway.

As for the form of the whole, I have tried to make of the Dialogue itself a sort of ballet of which the Image and the Idea are Coryphaeus in turn. The abstract and the sensible take the lead alternately and unite in the final vertigo.

To sum up: I in no degree strove for historic or technical rigor (and for very good reason). I freely introduced what I needed to maintain my Ballet and vary its figures. This extended to *the ideas themselves*. Here they are *means*. It is true that this idea (that ideas are means) is familiar to me, and perhaps *substantial*. It leads on, moreover, to wicked thoughts about philosophy (cf. "Leonardo and the Philosophers," which I published last year).

I should never have planned to write on the dance, to which I had never given serious thought. Moreover, I considered—and I still do—that Mallarmé had exhausted the subject in so far as it belongs to literature. This conviction made me first refuse the invitation of the *Revue musicale*. Other reasons made me resolve to accept it. What Mallarmé had prodigiously written then became a peculiar condition of my work. I must neither ignore him nor espouse his thought too closely. I adopted the line of introducing, amid the divers interpretations which the three characters give of the dance, the one whose formulation and incomparable demonstration through style are to be found in the *Divagations*.

I have explained myself at considerable length. But I feel I owe this to one who has been such an attentive and even fervent critic of my Dialogue. You have perfectly presented its spirit, which, in truth, is neither *this* nor *that*—neither with Plato, nor according to Nietzsche, but an act of transformation.

The nature of M. Séchan's book can be gathered from Valéry's comment on it. M. Séchan thought that Valéry's attitude toward *Dance and the Soul* as something fortuitous was typical of Valéry. He discussed Mallarmé's remarks in *Divagations* on the dance as corporeal writing or hieroglyphic, and he dwelt on the resemblance between the dance and the meditations of the spirit in moments of tension. He referred to the analysis of *Dance and the Soul* by Paul Souday in the latter's work on Valéry and, in particular, to the contrasting conceptions of the dance by the persons taking part in the present dialogue, thus: the conception of Eryximachus (the Eryximachus of Plato's *Symposium*) that the dance is purely sensory; the conception of Phaedrus (the Phaedrus of *Eupalinos*) that the dance is psychologically evocative; and the conception of Socrates, which reconciles the other two, that the dance is an interpretation of a secret and physical order. And finally M. Séchan speaks of the fact that both Schopenhauer and Nietzsche were influential forces at the time when Valéry was maturing. But he regards *Dance and the Soul* as Apollonian rather than Dionysian, because as Apollonian it corresponds better with the Greek genius. It is, in fact, possible, if only because Valéry published *Eupalinos* and *Dance and the Soul* together and because they seem to be inseparable companions, that Valéry had a sense that *Eupalinos* was Apollonian and that *Dance and the Soul* was Dionysian. On the other hand, it is certain that Valéry's own genius was Apollonian and that the Dionysian did not comport with it, and, with that, the subject may be dismissed.

Dance and the Soul is a lesser work than *Eupalinos*, since it does not contain the proliferation of ideas which characterizes *Eupalinos*. Socrates is always and everywhere proliferation. In this dialogue, however, he confines himself to the proliferation of a single idea. He asks repeatedly the question, "O my friends, what in truth is dance?" and again, "But what then is dance, and what can steps say?" and again, "O my friends, I am only asking you what is dance. . . ."

While these questions are being asked, a dance is going on, a ballet is being danced. The scene is a banqueting place with a banquet in course. There are servants serving food and no end of wine. The persons are Socrates, Phaedrus, and Eryximachus, great numbers of multicolored groups of smiling figures, whirling and dissolving in enchanted sequences, Athikte, the *première danseuse*, who is commencing, the *musiciennes*, one of whom, coral-rose, is blowing an enormous shell, another, a tall flute-player, who denotes the measure with her toe. Socrates is conscious of ideas that come to him as he watches Athikte and observes the majesty of her movements. Eryximachus exclaims: "Dear Socrates, she teaches us that which we do, showing clearly to our souls that which our bodies accomplish obscurely."

Phaedrus adds: "In which respect this dancer would, according to you, have something Socratic, teaching us, in the matter of walking, to know ourselves a little better."

These remarks illustrate the constant allusions to the dancers which keep the reader of the dialogue in the presence of the dancers. He hears the voices of the speakers and watches the movements of the dancers at one and the same time, without the least confusion, as he would do in reality; and as his interest in what is being said grows greater as the discussion approaches its resolutions, and as his absorption in the spectacle becomes deeper with his increased understanding of it and because of the momentum toward the ultimate climax, he realizes, for the first time, the excitement of a meaning as it is revealed at once in thought and in act.

The work is regenerative. M. Séchan quoted the words of Plato on the poet: *chose légère, ailée, sacrée.* These words apply equally to Valéry's text. Here again we have what we had in *Eupalinos*, the body as source and the act in relation to the body. Socrates says to Eryximachus:

Do you not see then, Eryximachus, that among all intoxications the noblest, the one most inimical to that great tedium, is the intoxication due to acts? Our acts, and more particularly those of our acts which set our bodies in motion, may bring us into a strange and admirable state. . . .

Still speaking to Eryximachus, he made a gesture in the direction of

. . . that ardent Athikte, who divides and gathers herself together again, who rises and falls, so promptly opening out and closing in, and who appears to belong to constellations other than ours— seems to live, completely at ease, in an element comparable to fire— in a most subtle essence of music and movement, wherein she breathes boundless energy, while she participates with all her being in the pure and immediate violence of extreme felicity.

As he continues, he says what sums up his argument and sums up the whole work:

If we compare our grave and weighty condition with the state of that sparkling salamander, does it not seem to you that our ordinary acts, begotten by our successive needs, and our gestures and incidental movements are like coarse materials, like an impure stuff of duration—whilst that exaltation and that vibration of life, that supremacy of tension, that transport into the highest agility one is capable of, have the virtues and the potencies of flame; and that the shames, the worries, the sillinesses, and the monotonous foods of existence are consumed within it, making what is divine in a mortal woman shine before our eyes?

There is a series of speeches by Socrates in the closing pages of the dialogue which are full of the noble rhetoric of the truth. But they are still rhetoric; and it is the presence of this rhetoric of the truth that makes the work regenerative. It is rhetoric to say: "In a sonorous world, resonant and rebounding, this intense festival of the body in the presence of our souls offers light and joy. . . . All is more solemn, all more light, all more lively, all stronger; all is possible in another way; all can begin again indefinitely. . . ." So, too, it is rhetoric to say: "I hear the clash of all the glittering arms of life! . . . The cymbals crush in our ears any utterance of secret thoughts. They resound like kisses from lips of bronze. . . ." It is, however, this rhetoric, the eloquent expression of that which is precisely true, that gives what it expresses an irresistible compulsion as when Socrates says: "A body, by its simple force, and its act, is powerful enough to alter the nature of things more profoundly than ever the mind in its speculations and dreams was able to do!"

While Socrates is pronouncing his subtle and solemn words, our eyes remain fastened on Athikte, while she tries to make us see that which Socrates is seeking to tell us. She moves through jewels, makes gestures like scintillations, filches impossible attitudes from nature, so that Eryximachus says, "Instant engenders form, and form makes the instant visible." She continues to dance until she falls. When she has fallen and lies, white, on the ground, she says something to herself, the simplest possible thing. Phaedrus asks what it is and Eryximachus replies, "She said: 'How well I feel!' "—a remark immense with everything that Socrates himself had been saying a moment or two before. She has spoken in a rhetoric which achieves the pathetic essential almost without speech. It is obvious that this degree of agitation has been reached in what is, after all, an exegetical work, through the form of the work. Valéry's slim and cadenced French adds its own vitality to the original. It seems enough to present the work in this brief manner. André Levinson said in relation to Dance and the Soul: "To explain a thing is to deform it; to think is to substitute what is arbitrary for the unknowable truth." What Dance and the Soul requires is not so much explanation as—what Valéry called M. Séchan—attentive and fervent critics or, say, readers, willing to experience the transformation which knowing a little about themselves brings about as by miracle or, say, by art.

Man has many ways to attain the divine, and the way of Eupalinos and the way of Athikte and the various ways of Paul Valéry are only a few of them.

◗❁◗

RAOUL DUFY

(A NOTE ON *La Fée Electricité*)

Raoul Dufy's sudden death in March, 1953, was like a rip in the rainbow. His work for the lithographs in the present portfolio had been completed. The collection was far advanced toward its appearance. It was based on his largest and most significant fresco. It had engaged him seriously for a long period of time. He regarded it as a typical and sympathetic undertaking and he looked forward to its publication as a kind of radiant realization. But this realization of the spirit of the artist was destined to be a realization on the part of others after his death. The work reveals Dufy, on a scale beyond comparison with anything else he has done, exploiting, as artist, the world we know and the world of what we know, which are always the same. It is an exploitation of fact by a man of elevation. It is a surface of prose changeable with the luster of poetry and thought.

The lithographs enable us to see how Dufy, for all the documentation that was inevitable, for all the ten supernumeraries from the *Comèdie-Française* who posed for him, for all the cos-

286

tuming, for the full year of study and observation, prevails, in the end, purely as artist; and how all the ideas, documentation, study and observation, of which the original fresco was composed, are subdued, finally, by Dufy's sense; and seeing this clearly, seeing how the artist is enabled to carry lightly the burden imposed on him by a great work, until, when it is finished, we have, not a memorial of work but the happiness of the artist who has achieved what he wanted to achieve as artist (and in this case the peculiar *allegresse* associated with Dufy's name), we experience a confidence that in the many futures of knowledge, the artist will always come through as one of the masters of his particular time.

Dufy was asked to do a mural painting for the electricity pavilion at the International Exposition at Paris in 1937. For this purpose he produced a work about thirty feet high and a little less than two hundred feet wide, in which he traced the history of light and power from pastoral time to the present time. He included figures as large as life of the principal characters who, in the course of history, and this means universal history, contributed by their discoveries or inventions to the coming on of electricity, its uses and the engineering incidental thereto. To overcome the notion of electricity as an abstraction, he symbolized it as *La Fée Electricité*, a fay rather plump and wholesome from the American point of view respecting fays and, perhaps, an improvement on that point of view. Now, what is Dufy's attitude toward all this material? It is the same attitude to which he has accustomed us in his work generally. His personalizing of the scenes that have interested him has always been slight. He has never forged blatant Dufyisms out of what he saw. There was never any melodrama and, although there was poetry, it was pretty much the radiance of exact prose, a gaiety of strokes like a gaiety of words. In consequence, this epic of *La Fée Electricité*, composed, episodically, day by day, over a long period of time, has all the interest and meaning of a simple prose narrative. Yet it is a scroll of poetry in its truth and the implications of its truth. Dufy does not engage in "the dire delight, negative and cantankerous, of men who are lacking in sense." He remains steadfast in his own intelligence delineating and allowing history to crowd its figures upon him. An artist has no being who has no identity. Here in this large work one finds the identity that we recognize as Dufy, engaged in all the delectations that make up his identity, extended and prolonged. He is not speculating about the future of the world, the potentialities of changes inherent in knowledge nor the integrity of the artist. These are glosses. He is not discursive. He knows that everything depends on concentration. He concentrates effortlessly on what is within his focus, so that it is natural for the highest point of his painting to be a collection of electrical machinery in a power plant in Paris, say, instead of some sparkling fantasy acted by his planetary heroine.

The lithographs are original works. To reproduce the original fresco it had to be done over again. When he painted the work for the first time Dufy had to enlarge everything. After the work had been schematized and reduced, Dufy repainted it for this portfolio, in its new scale, making a few changes, as, for example, eliminating figures which in the process of reduction had become too small. The lithographs are the only form in which the work is available, short of the construction of a special building to contain the fresco itself.

Near the figure of Goethe there is a quotation from one of Goethe's letters, as follows:

> I shall turn myself toward the artisans—chemistry—
> The hour of the beautiful has gone by; today, misery and implacable necessity lay claim to our time.

That approach to the modern goes far back, as the lithographs show; but regardless of the degree of remoteness the words of Goethe, or similar words, have always been in the air above the approach. Today more than ever those words are heard on the approach to what is presently modern, since the finality of what is modern is never fully and ultimately attainable. At the moment, the approach is precise, taking nothing for granted. Dufy's *La Fée Electricité* is most definitely a union of drudge and dazzling angel.

The intelligence is part of the comedy of life. It was not only that Dufy tried to dress each of the many figures that appear in his fresco in clothes that were appropriate and which they might have worn; nor that he had a scholar from the Sorbonne tutor him a little in respect to electricity; nor that he visited various central electric stations throughout France; it was not only that he tried to grasp the truth. He tried, also, to express his own intelligence respecting these things, that is: to produce a painting that interests us by its reality and which, in these lithographs, gives us an experience as with a multitude of actualities, an experience intense and yet without extravagance. The lithographs leave us feeling that the dissipations of life inevitably arrange themselves in a final scene, a scene that fills us with optimism and satisfaction as the characters leave the stage with all the lights burning. Is not that, after all, the chief effect of this pageant? Is it not the principal thing that the individuality of Dufy should be the coordinating force and high issue of all these details? And is not this high issue one of those choices of the intelligence of an artist who, by making this choice, goes forward with the train of his characters, of whom he is really one, committed to the same purpose? These great blues of Dufy are a kind of assertion of strength. They create a human self-confidence, as if one had known from the beginning the eventual denouement of knowledge, so long postponed and so incredible.

MARCEL GROMAIRE

(NOTE FOR AN EXHIBITION CATALOGUE)

Catalogues for exhibitions of pictures are the natural habitat of the prose-poem. But in the case of Marcel Gromaire one feels that the need for definition comes first.

Gromaire was born in 1892 in the Département du Nord. This is the Département farthest North East in France beginning at the edge of the North Sea and running, in a narrow strip of farms and factories, half of the whole length of the Belgian border. It is a region in which the relationship with the Belgian of the present and, more particularly, the kinship with the Fleming of the past are strong, so strong, in the case of Gromaire that one's immediate impression of his work is that it is work typical of the mystical realism of a Northerner. One does not usually think of Frenchmen as mystical realists or Northerners.

Yet, for all that, Gromaire is very much of a Frenchman. He lives in Paris and has his atelier there. The paintings shown in the present exhibition are paintings of his maturity. He is now fifty-seven. Some critics have spoken of elements in his work derived from Matisse and Soutine and others have denied these derivations. Certainly, Gromaire is in no way derivative. His principal characteristic is that he is just the opposite. These oddly hallucinatory tableaux (in the English sense) are the pictures of a determined man, somewhat possessed, predestined and, because of these characteristics, also rebellious. Being rebellious is being oneself and being oneself is not being one of the automata of one's time. In consequence of being himself, Gromaire's appearances come to us, one by one, as he experiences them and not as part of the day's great, common flocks and herds and shoals of things alike.

290

One thing that he is determined about is substance. This is one of the truths about Gromaire. He himself speaks of *"la recherche de la substance"*: the pursuit of substance. By substance he means the spiritual fund of the picture, the fund originating in the thought and feeling of the artist and perceptible in the painting. He does not mean the picture as itself a spiritual fund, except in that objective way. He speaks of *"la qualité des œuvres, qui est leur vie même et leur pensée profonde"*: the property of works which is their very life and profound meaning. He speaks of the human spirit seeking its own architecture, its own *"mesure"* that will enable it to be in harmony with the world. It is from the intensity, the passion, of this search that the quality of works is derived, not from the codes and manuals of painting compiled by doctrinaires and conformist pedagogues. And this is the quality sought after by the clairvoyant spectator. These remarks illustrate Gromaire's mystical side.

At the same time he postulates an *"art directement social"* which transmits itself to the spectator without mediation or explanation, as much by reason of its *"chimie intérieure"*: sublimation, say, as by the idea which it materializes; social in the sense of something that affects the march of events, fixes the ephemeral sensation and makes it possible for this sensation *"grâce à cette perennité conquise, d'agir sur le futur et sur le comportement humain,"* makes it possible for the ephemeral sensation, thanks to this acquired characteristic of being perennial, to act on the future and on human behavior. This is not the language of the individual escapist. On the contrary it is that of a painter who visualizes a great epoch for his art, in which painting instead of being *"un jeu désespéré"*: a spiritless game, will be as he says *"un don continu et fraternel, la presence de l'homme et du rhythme universel qui nous régit"* or, paraphrased, a brother's constant giving, a human association and the activity of the universal rhythm that dominates us.

These statements of theory define Gromaire in his own words. They help us to look at his pictures as they are: heterodox, slightly grim (an orthodox element in anything intended to be social comment), dense in color, as becomes a Goth, rugged with realism (what one expects of pictures much thought over and not exclusively sensory or abstract), uncompromising, in the idiom of Verhaeren, endowed with the strength that comes from participation in life's struggle, full of the mesmeric presence of meanings below the surface, things not of the school of Paris, but of some harsher, more fundamental zone—and one need only have in mind, say, much of Europe, much of everywhere, always.

✧◈✧

NOTES ON JEAN LABASQUE

I

It seems that painting based on the man and having a moral axis would be likely to possess a strong literary element. Mr. Labasque agrees. It would also be likely to be allegorical in nature. Since allegory is so conspicuous in moral or architectural painting, it may be that Mr. Labasque is preoccupied with "civic" painting, "civic" art. Thus, his moral and social interests would lead to a role for him, as a "civic" artist. *Preface à une Peinture* read in the light of this comment contains many accents justifying the comment.

II

Mr. Labasque shows a passionate admiration for the work of Rousseau and, by inference, for the work of any primitive deriving from popular art. He works for the people or, at least, finds those that do so congenial. He is interested in communal synthesis. He is hostile to the egocentric. He believes in the human, the simple in art that springs from despair, hope, joy, emotion specified by him.

III

What he does not appear to concede is the interest in painting (from the point of view of Cézanne) on the part of the public, and in poetry. Even though the amateur is ignorant of the technique of painting (for example, the manner in which Cézanne composes), the fact remains that there is a vast amount of art criticism, art history, etc., in circulation and that this has created (or that it fosters) a class of people who "live" in this sort of thing, whether from snobbism or otherwise; and certainly there are many much better reasons than snobbism, and perfectly legitimate ones. Impressionism, in so far as the public was concerned, was a poetic movement. The parasitic developments following it were different. But if the only really great thing in modern art: impressionism, was poetic, the poetic is not to be flipped away because that particular poetic expression is *vieux jeu*.

⊙⊁

A NOTE ON "LES PLUS BELLES PAGES"

Apparently the poem means that the conjunction of milkman and moonlight is the equivalent of the conjunction of logician and saint. What it really means is that the inter-relation between things is what makes them fecund. Interaction is the source of poetry. Sex is an illustration. But the principle is not confined to the illustration. The milkman and the moonlight are an illustration. The two people, the three horses, etc., are illustrations. The principle finds its best illustration in the inter-action of our faculties or of our thoughts and emotions. Aquinas is a classic example: a figure of great modern interest, whose special force seems to come from the interaction of his prodigious love of God. The idea that his theology, as such, is involved is dismissed in the last line. That the example is not of scholarly choice is indicated by the title. But the title also means that les plus belles pages are those in which things do not stand alone, but are operative as the result of interaction, inter-relation. This is an idea of some consequence, not a casual improvisation. The inter-relation between reality and the imagination is the basis of the character of literature. The inter-relation between reality and the emotions is the basis of the vitality of literature, between reality and thought, the basis of its power.

◇◇

CONNECTICUT

The thrift and frugality of the Connecticut Yankee were necessary to life in the Colony, and still are. They were imposed on him by the character of the natural world in which he came to live, which has not changed. And now, after three centuries or more of this tradition, the people of the state are proud of it. They are proud of the kind of strength of character which they have derived from this necessity, proud of the intelligent ingenuity with which they faced their many hardships—and with which they rose to the high general level of intelligence and dignified style of living that is now so characteristic of them.

Early in April, when the weather was still bleak and everything still had the look of winter, I went on the railroad from my city of Hartford to Boston, in Massachusetts. Everything seemed gray, bleached and derelict, and the word *derelict* kept repeating itself as part of the activity of the train. But this was a precious ride through the character of the state. The soil everywhere seemed thin and difficult, and every cutting and open pit disclosed gravel and rocks in which only the young pine trees seemed to do well. There were chicken farms and there were cowbarns. There were orchards of apples and peaches. Yet in the sparse landscape with its old houses of gray and white there were other houses, smaller, fresher, more fastidious.

And spring was coming on. It was as if the people whose houses I was seeing shared the strength that was beginning to assert itself. The man who loves New England, and particularly the spare region of Connecticut, loves it precisely because of the spare colors, the thin light, the delicacy and slightness and beauty of the place. The dry grass on the thin surfaces would soon change to a lime-like green and later to an emerald brilliance in a sunlight never too full. When the spring was at its height we should have a water-color, not an oil, and we should all feel that we had had a hand in the painting of it, if only in choosing to live there where it existed. Now, when all the primitive difficulties of getting started have been overcome, we live in the tradition which is the true mythology of the region and we breathe in with every breath the joy of having ourselves been created by what has been endured and mastered in the past.

There are only some two million people living in the state, which is the third smallest in the country. Of those a quarter of a million are foreign born. Of those who were born in the state, many are the children of parents who were themselves foreign born, or of parents whose parents, generation back of generation, were foreign born. All of us together constitute the existing community. There are no foreigners in Connecticut. Once you are here, you are—or you are on your way to become—a Yankee. I was not myself born in the state. It is not that I am a native, but that I feel like one.

There is nothing that gives the feel of Connecticut like coming home to it. Truly Connecticut is much like a single metropolis, highly industrial, with factories and mills and shops and schools and homes spread out everywhere, with a few major concentrations in Bridgeport, New Haven, Hartford, New London. One could say in a few words simply that Connecticut is an industrial and business center.

That would leave out the salt water of Noank and Stonington, the hills in which the various Cornwalls are situated, the sense of being on high land, of being on a rich plateau, at Pomfret, the rare rich fields over East, the heights and depths of our Western and part of our Northern borders, the special river countries of the Housatonic and the Thames. Yet to return to these places would not be quite what I had in mind when I spoke of the coming home that gives one the feel of Connecticut. What I have in mind was something deeper that nothing can ever change or remove. It is a question of coming home to the American self in the sort of place in which it was formed. Going back to Connecticut is a return to an origin. And, as it happens, it is an origin which many men all over the world, both those who have been part of us and those who have not, share in common: an origin of hardihood, good faith and good will.

A NOTE ON THE DATES

The dates assigned to the material included in this book are either dates of publication or, insofar as can be determined, dates of composition.

With the poems, I have combined the date of publication and the date of composition as accurately as possible. For the most part the date of publication may be assumed to follow fairly closely the date of composition, always making allowances for an adequate lapse of time between the actual date of composition and the appearance of a given poem or group of poems in print. Of the previously unpublished poems, some have been dated on internal evidences of style; a few, such as the stanzas for "Le Monocle de Mon Oncle" and "This Vast Inelegance," could be placed by other means. In any case, all dates not in italics, for poetry, plays, and prose, indicate dates of publication. I alone am responsible for the dates assigned to previously unpublished work.

Chronological order, which was favored by Stevens himself in his later books, seemed the best plan to follow with the poems. The essays, however, I have grouped together more or less by subject. A long poem, such as "Owl's Clover," occupied most of the author's attention during the period of its composition; it seemed unnecessary, therefore, to indicate that "The Old Woman and the Statue" originally appeared in *The Southern Review* in 1935, and that "Mr. Burnshaw and the Statue" appeared in 1936, three days before the appearance of *Owl's Clover* in book form. In the revised version of "Owl's Clover," published in 1937 with "The Man with the Blue Guitar," "Mr. Burnshaw and the Statue" appears as "The Statue at the World's End," and has been considerably shortened. This is a point of some interest to the student of Stevens, but hardly important enough to call to the attention of the reader in the text. Much the same may be said of the group called "Five Grotesque Pieces," although the text of the two poems published separately in 1934 is the text that appears in the group in which they appeared in 1942. It may be that all five poems belong to the period of *Ideas of Order* (1930–5), but it is difficult to be sure.

S.F.M.

Poems from "Phases," I–VI	(I–IV, *Poetry*, November 1914)
The Silver Plough-Boy	(*Others*, August 1915)
Blanche McCarthy	(*ca. 1915–16*)
Bowl	(*Others*, March 1916)
Poems from "Primordia," 1–7	(*Soil*, January 1917)
Poems from "Lettres d'un Soldat," I–IX	(II–V and VII, *Poetry*, May 1918)
Architecture	(*The Little Review*, December 1918)
Stanzas for "Le Monocle de Mon Oncle"	(*1918*)
Peter Parasol	(*Poetry*, October 1919)
Exposition of the Contents of a Cab	(*Poetry*, October 1919)
Piano Practice at the Academy of the Holy Angels	(*1919*)
The Indigo Glass in the Grass	(*Poetry*, October 1919)
Romance for a Demoiselle Lying in the Grass	(*ca. 1919–20*)
Anecdote of the Abnormal	(*ca. 1919–20*)
Infernale	(*ca. 1920*)
This Vast Inelegance	(*1921*)
Lulu Gay	(*Contact*, 1921)
Lulu Morose	(*Contact*, 1921)
Saturday Night at the Chiropodist's	(*1922*)
Mandolin and Liqueurs	(*The Chapbook*, April 1923)
The Shape of the Coroner	(*The Measure*, May 1923)
Red Loves Kit	(*The Measure*, August. 1924)
Metropolitan Melancholy	(*June 19, 1928*)
Annual Gaiety	(*Modern American Poetry*, 1930)

Good Man, Bad Woman	(*Poetry*, October 1932)
The Woman Who Blamed Life on a Spaniard	(*Contempo*, December 15, 1932)
Secret Man	(*Modern Things*, 1934)
The Drum-Majors in the Labor Day Parade	(*Smoke*, Autumn 1934)
Polo Ponies Practicing	(*Westminster Magazine*, Autumn 1934)
Lytton Strachey, Also, Enters into Heaven	(*Rocking Horse*, Spring, 1935)
Table Talk	(*ca. 1935*)
A Room on a Garden	(*ca. 1935*)
Agenda	(*Smoke*, Summer 1935)
Owl's Clover	(Alcestis Press, 1936)
Stanzas for "The Man with the Blue Guitar"	(*1935–6*)
Five Grotesque Pieces	(*Trend*, March 1942)
I. One of Those Hibiscuses of Damozels	(*ca. 1934*)
II. Hieroglyphica	(*Direction*, October 1934)
III. Communications of Meaning	(*1934*)
IV. What They Call Red Cherry Pie	(*Alcestis*, October 1934)
V. Outside of Wedlock	(*ca. 1934?*)
Life on a Battleship	(*Partisan Review*, Spring 1939)
The Woman That Had More Babies Than That	(*Partisan Review*, Spring 1939)
Stanzas for "Examination of the Hero in a Time of War"	(*1941*)
Desire & the Object	(*Accent*, Summer 1942)
Recitation after Dinner	(*The Saint Nicholas Society*, 1945)
This as Including That	(*ca. 1944–5*)
Memorandum	(*Poetry Quarterly*, Winter 1947)
First Warmth	(*1947*)
The Sick Man	(*Accent*, Spring 1950)

As at a Theatre (*Wake,* Summer 1950)

The Desire to Make Love in a
    Pagoda (*Wake,* Summer 1950)

Nuns Painting Water-Lilies (*Wake,* Summer 1950)

The Role of the Idea in Poetry (*Wake,* Summer 1950)

Americana (*Wake,* Summer 1950)

The Souls of Women at Night (*Wake,* Summer 1950)

A Discovery of Thought (*Imagi,* Summer 1950)

The Course of a Particular (*The Hudson Review,* Spring
    1951)

How Now, O, Brightener . . . (*Shenandoah,* Spring 1952)

The Dove in Spring (*Seven Arts No.* 2, 1954)

Farewell without a Guitar (*New World Writing No.* 5,
    1954)

The Sail of Ulysses (1953–4)

Presence of an External Master
    of Knowledge (*Times Literary Supplement,*
    September 17, 1954)

A Child Asleep in Its Own Life (*Times Literary Supplement,*
    September 17, 1954)

Two Letters (*Vogue,* October 1, 1954)

Conversation with Three Wo-
    men of New England (*Accent,* Autumn 1954)

Dinner Bell in the Woods (*Perspective,* Autumn 1954)

Reality Is an Activity of the Most
    August Imagination (*Perspective,* Autumn 1954)

Solitaire under the Oaks (*Sewanee Review,* Winter 1955)

Local Objects (*Sewanee Review,* Winter 1955)

Artificial Populations (*Sewanee Review,* Winter 1955)

A Clear Day and No Memories (*Sewanee Review,* Winter 1955)

Banjo Boomer (*Atlantic Monthly,* March 1955)

July Mountain (*Atlantic Monthly,* April 1955)

The Region November (*Zero,* Spring 1956)

On the Way to the Bus (1954)

As You Leave the Room (1947–55?)

Of Mere Being (1955?)

A Mythology Reflects Its Region (1955?)

Moment of Light	(*The Modern School*, October 1918)
Three Paraphrases from Léon-Paul Fargue	(1951)
Three Travelers Watch a Sunrise	(*Poetry*, July 1916)
Carlos among the Candles	(*Poetry*, December 1917)
A Ceremony	(1944)
Adagia	(1930?–55)
A Collect of Philosophy	(1951)
Two or Three Ideas	(*CEA Chapbook*, October 1951)
The Irrational Element in Poetry	(1937?)
The Whole Man: Perspectives, Horizons	(*The Yale Review*, Winter 1955)
On Poetic Truth	(1954?)
Honors and Acts	(individually dated in text)
A Poet That Matters	(*Life and Letters Today*, December 1935)
Williams	(*Collected Poems, 1921–1931*, by William Carlos Williams, 1934)
Rubbings of Reality	(*Briarcliff Quarterly*, October 1946)
John Crowe Ransom: Tennessean	(*Sewanee Review*, Summer 1948)
The Shaper	(*Paul Rosenfeld, Voyager in the Arts*, 1948)
A Note on Martha Champion	(*Trial Balances*, 1935)
A Note on Samuel French Morse	(*Time of Year*, 1944)
Two Prefaces	(*Dialogues*, by Paul Valéry, 1956)
Raoul Dufy	(1953)
Marcel Gromaire	(1949)
Notes on Jean Labasque	(1940–1?)
A Note on "Les Plus Belles Pages"	(1952)
Connecticut	(1955)